Game Backend Development

With Microsoft Azure and PlayFab

Balint Bors

Apress®

Game Backend Development: With Microsoft Azure and PlayFab

Balint Bors
Munich, Germany

ISBN-13 (pbk): 978-1-4842-8909-9   ISBN-13 (electronic): 978-1-4842-8910-5
https://doi.org/10.1007/978-1-4842-8910-5

Managing Director, Apress Media LLC: Welmoed Spahr
Acquisitions Editor: Joan Murray
Development Editor: Laura Berendson
Coordinating Editor: Jill Balzano
Copy Editor: Kezia Endsley

Cover designed by eStudioCalamar

Cover image by Wrongtog on Unsplash (www.unsplash.com)

Distributed to the book trade worldwide by Apress Media, LLC, 1 New York Plaza, New York, NY 10004, U.S.A. Phone 1-800-SPRINGER, fax (201) 348-4505, e-mail orders-ny@springer-sbm.com, or visit www.springeronline.com. Apress Media, LLC is a California LLC and the sole member (owner) is Springer Science + Business Media Finance Inc (SSBM Finance Inc). SSBM Finance Inc is a **Delaware** corporation.

For information on translations, please e-mail booktranslations@springernature.com; for reprint, paperback, or audio rights, please e-mail bookpermissions@springernature.com.

Apress titles may be purchased in bulk for academic, corporate, or promotional use. eBook versions and licenses are also available for most titles. For more information, reference our Print and eBook Bulk Sales web page at http://www.apress.com/bulk-sales.

Any source code or other supplementary material referenced by the author in this book is available to readers on GitHub (https://github.com/Apress). For more detailed information, please visit http://www.apress.com/source-code.

Printed on acid-free paper

To my wife and our three sons, for all the love, joy, and fun.

Table of Contents

About the Author

Balint Bors is a cloud solutions architect based in Munich, Germany. He has over 15 years of experience developing software and building IT infrastructures for many companies and industries. Balint also consults with and advises technical teams on applying cloud technologies. He is a Microsoft Certified Azure Solutions Architect Expert.

About the Technical Reviewer

Doug Holland is a software engineer and architect at Microsoft. He holds a master's degree in software engineering from the University of Oxford. Before joining Microsoft, he was honored with the Microsoft MVP and Intel Black Belt Developer awards.

Introduction

In recent years, with advances to networks and the cloud, massive backend support has become essential to all successful games. Having backend features enriches players' game experiences and gives your games a competitive advantage.

A typical example is support for multiplayer mode, which allows people to play with each other in the same game session at the same time. Even from far away, the network infrastructure makes this possible. A game stands out from the crowd immediately when it supports multiplayer mode.

Another classic question that game makers face is how to motivate players to play their game longer. One answer is by utilizing backend services. For example, you can implement a leaderboard for players to compete for the best place. Or, you can let players buy game items from a catalog. These are popular ways to engage players to stay with your game. And by the way, they also allow game creators to earn real money.

Further, many people publish their games, yet know nothing about how people experience them. Is there some level in the game that is impossible to accomplish? When do most players give up on your game? Insight into your players' behaviors helps you improve your game immensely.

For all of this, you need a backend infrastructure. You need servers to synchronize the world state among players in multiplayer mode. You need advanced analytics to gather, store, and evaluate game data and get insights into the players' behavior. You need to store catalogs, items, and statistics. You need networks, databases, storage, servers, and the cloud. These are all typical topics you have to deal with as a game developer.

How Does This Book Help?

The cloud and the backend infrastructure is a very complex topic. It's hard to find a good place to start. This book breaks this topic down and focuses only on the aspects relevant to gaming. Games have specific requirements, which differ from web applications, for example.

Through easy and practical examples, this book gives you a comprehensive guide on how to implement the most important backend features for your game.

You learn two ways to implement the backend. One is when you choose a traditional cloud provider; the other is when you are less interested in the backend and want a quick solution, using a Game Backend-as-a-Service (GBaaS) provider. Regardless of the method you choose, this book helps you understand the concepts and gives you step-by-step instructions.

You will learn about backend features, for example, what a virtual economy is and how game analytics help elucidate player behavior. You can use the provided source code to experiment and see how the concepts work in reality.

When you finish this book, you will be able to implement backend features into your game. For example, you'll be able to enable multiplayer mode or create an economy to monetize your game. There are also many other exciting features covered here that can bring your game to another level.

During the last 15 years, I developed infrastructures for many applications. I started my cloud journey with IBM Cloud, then Amazon WebServices (AWS) and Azure. I consulted clients, technical teams, and management, helping them to achieve their goals.

Years ago, when I started developing games, I realized that the game developer community did not have enough guides to incorporate backend services for games. So I decided to support the community and, using my background as an Azure architect, I helped game developers get started with backend. I also started blogging (https://www.gamebackend.dev/) and engaged with the community.

I learned that game development is not easy. You need to learn a lot. This book aims to be part of this learning process by teaching you about implementing backend features, which are essential elements of modern games.

What Are the Benefits of Reading This Book?

- You will learn new and worthy skills. Tutorials and step-by-step instructions will guide you so you can implement sophisticated backend features.

- It will save you time and money. It is a comprehensive guide covering all of the most relevant information and will help you quick-start implementing game backends.

- It resolves uncertainty. It shows you where to start with certain backend topics and guide you through complex subjects in a simple way.

- It is practical. You can execute the source code in your environment and see right away how each feature works and contributes to your game.

- It is to the point. The product documentation is often overwhelming. The book focuses only on the main properties of each feature and describes practical steps.

- You can stand out from the crowd. A lot of games do not use backend features. Your game has a competitive advantage over others when you incorporate backend services.

- You learn that implementing the backend can be fun. It's enjoyable to create a game that uses advanced features.

What Does This Book Cover?

This book aims to describe the key game backend services. The following diagram shows the structure of this book and how each chapter is built on each other. In order to implement a specific topic, the underlying building blocks are prerequisites.

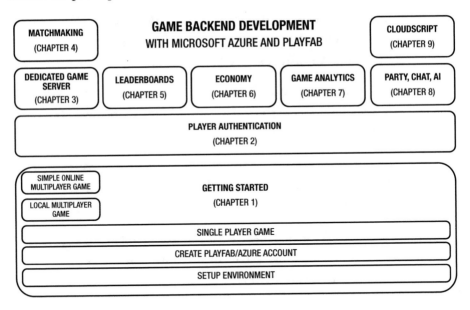

Each chapter deals with one backend topic, describing the concept, and then the implementation by Microsoft PlayFab and Azure cloud services.

- **Chapter 1, Getting Started.** You start by setting up the environment and creating a simple game in Unity. Then, you'll extend this to a local multiplayer game. You will also enable online multiplayer game mode, which requires backend support.

- **Chapter 2, Player Authentication.** In this chapter, you learn how to determine the player's identity and implement player authentication in different ways. This is a key feature, as only authenticated players can use other backend functions.

- **Chapter 3, Dedicated Game Servers.** You will build and use scalable backend infrastructures to run online multiplayer game servers.

- **Chapter 4, Matchmaking.** You will use and implement an automated process to bring players together in one multiplayer game session.

- **Chapter 5, Leaderboards.** In this chapter, you build leaderboards to store information like the highest scores achieved. This contributes to the competition among players and encourages player engagement.

- **Chapter 6, Economy.** You will build a virtual economy that allows players to purchase items using real or virtual currencies.

- **Chapter 7, Game Analytics.** In this chapter, you will investigate and implement ways to get insights into players' behavior and gather specific events so that you can optimize your games.

- **Chapter 8, Party, Chat, AI.** You will implement in-game player communication and use cognitive services to process the messages in order to improve your players' experience.

- **Chapter 9, CloudScript and Azure Functions.** You will investigate how to develop server-side logic so that you can implement all kinds of custom backend features.

Future-Proof Technology

This book uses the GBaaS provider Microsoft's Azure PlayFab and pure Azure services. These products are mature enough for implementing a game backend for games of any size.

PlayFab claims to host over 2.5 billion player accounts in over 5,000 games. Azure is the second largest cloud provider in the world. Microsoft heavily invests in the game industry, so you can assume the ecosystem will grow even more.

However, you can use other GBaaS and cloud providers as well. Cloud services are very similar and conceptually there should not be any difference. The book uses reference architectures and considers best practices.

Who Is This Book For?

This book is primarily for game developers who may be skilled in game development, but possess little to no skills in GBaaS and cloud computing. This book is also for professionals working in the cloud solutions space who want to learn about the specific challenges in the gaming domain.

Where Can You Find the Source Code?

All of the source code from this book is available on GitHub at:

```
https://github.com/apress/game-backend-development
```

What's Next?

After reading this book, you will understand the most important game backend functionalities—player authentication, enabling multiplayer games, matchmaking, buying items and creating virtual economies, leaderboards, chatrooms, and game analytics, as well as any other custom features you want to implement with the help of cloud scripts.

You will know their basic building blocks, how to implement them, and how to integrate them into your game. With those, you will learn a worthy skill and be able to bring your future games to the next level.

Every day, hundreds and thousands of new games are published. The best ones have integrated backends. Yours should not be left behind.

Let's get started. Read, learn, and implement. Have fun!

CHAPTER 1

Getting Started

Game engines such as Unity and the Unreal Engine simplify the development process and allow you to start developing quickly. In this chapter, you will create a simple game in Unity, which will help you see the backend features discussed in the following chapters in action.

First, however, you learn about and set up some key technologies that you will use throughout this book—Unity, PlayFab, Terraform, and Azure, to name the most important ones.

Then, you will set up Mirror Networking (or Mirror), which enables the basic networking functionality for this game. With the help of Mirror, you can turn this simple game into a local multiplayer one.

Thereafter, you will build a minimum infrastructure in the cloud to host your game server and enable an online multiplayer game.

By the time you complete this chapter, you will have a good foundation for building backend game features. Let's get started.

Game Frontend and Backend

To begin, it is important to define the game's *backend* and *frontend,* at least within the scope of this book.

When implementing a client-server topology for networked games, the software that runs on the clients is called the game's frontend. The server contains all the services (which can be a dedicated multiplayer server as well), and this is the game's backend. See Figure 1-1.

© Balint Bors 2023
B. Bors, *Game Backend Development*, https://doi.org/10.1007/978-1-4842-8910-5_1

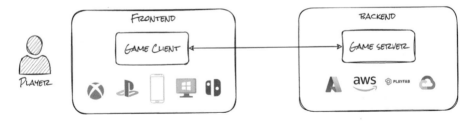

Figure 1-1. *Game frontend and backend*

This is analogous to a web application architecture, where the frontend is what you see in your browser (developed in Angular, React, etc.), and their backends (developed in PHP or Java) are running on a server in the cloud.

Game Frontend

A frontend developer of a game has to deal with many more graphical components and effects than a developer of a web application. The frontend includes your game running on your device. This device can be a PC, mobile phone, or console (Xbox, PlayStation, Nintendo Switch, etc.).

You'll use Unity in this book to implement the game's frontend. Unity is a cross-platform game engine that enables everyone to start creating games, even with limited resources. It provides out-of-the-box 2D and 3D graphics, animation, physics, virtual reality, and a lot more. You can start using it for free and pay only when your game gets traction. It is very popular among individual game developers.

Game Backend

All the servers and services are in the backend, and they are not directly visible to the clients (or players). Still, without them, the game can only operate in a very limited capacity. For example, backends allow buying items or playing with other players.

These backends are hosted in a central location, by a *cloud* or *GBaaS* (*Game Backend-as-a-Service*) providers, and the clients connect to them. Next, you'll review what a cloud is and the added value of GBaaS compared to pure cloud services.

Cloud Computing

Hosting dedicated servers was a difficult task in the early days. You had to invest in expensive IT server infrastructure, which then served the potential clients. In the worst case, the servers stood there without being used. It was hard to buy the exact necessary resources.

Cloud computing, among others, solved this problem. It allows you to reserve resources based on your actual needs. You can scale the servers up and down accordingly and pay as much as you use. A cloud gives you a flexible way to host your servers and provides a couple of important backend services that you can use for your game.

There are a lot of cloud providers nowadays. The three most prominent ones are Amazon Web Services (AWS), Microsoft Azure, and Google Cloud. The competition is fierce, and they keep on improving their services. They are always cheaper, and they give you a free tier where you can try their offerings for free or with discounts.

In this book, you'll implement the backend features on a Microsoft Azure cloud. You can use these ideas and concepts with any other cloud providers, as they are very similar.

Game Backend-as-a-Service (GBaaS)

The rising popularity of GBaaS providers enables game developers to achieve faster time-to-market and deal with the backend infrastructure more easily. Developers do not need to worry about building an infrastructure. With the help of APIs, game developers can easily access and utilize sophisticated backend features.

GBaaS is also backed by a cloud service, but it provides an additional layer on top, which implements specific services for games. In this book, you'll use PlayFab, which is backed by Azure.

Choosing GBaaS vs. a Cloud

Both have advantages and drawbacks, so it depends on your situation and requirements. Generally, building your own custom backend on the cloud is better for bigger projects and teams, while GBaaS is a great fit for smaller or individual developers. See Table 1-1.

Table 1-1. *Comparing Cloud and GBaaS (the More +, the Better)*

	Cloud	GBaaS	Comparison
Difficulty	+	+++	Learning the cloud takes more effort.
Flexibility	+++	+	Cloud's biggest advantage is that it is much more customizable
Implementation efforts	+	+++	With the cloud, you build your own infrastructure and develop the logic.
Maintenance	++	+++	GBaaS provides a fully managed backend infrastructure.
Price	++	+	The cloud provides more options to optimize cost and fit resources to your needs.
Quality	+++	++	Highly depends on providers. But big cloud providers can invest more in availability, security, etc.

In this book, you will find an implementation of each feature with both pure cloud and GBaaS providers. Sometimes you can integrate these two worlds; for example, in the case of CloudScripts, you can call Azure functions through the PlayFab API.

You can also create a hybrid solution, where you implement some of the features on the cloud and some of them with GBaaS. This book aims to help you choose the right situation for your needs and gives you a comprehensive view of both options.

Setting Up the Development Tools

Now you can move on to the practical part. First, you will learn how to set up your development environment and install the required tools.

Unity Editor

You'll start with the frontend. To experiment and learn about the features discussed in this book, you need to have Unity (at least version 2021.3.6f1). You can download it from:

```
https://unity3d.com/get-unity/download
```

Because this book focuses on the backend part, we do not discuss Unity any further here. The Unity game example is very simple, and the goal here is to learn how to use backend features. You can also use your own game as a frontend.

Visual Studio Code

Next, you'll get ready for the backend. You will develop the backend infrastructure with code, much in the same way you do for an application.

I suggest developing your infrastructure code in a separate place from your game code, which is in the sovereignty of the Unity Editor.

Basically, you can use any text editor to develop your infrastructure code. I use Visual Studio Code, as it is free, and it provides a convenient integrated development environment with its extensions.

```
https://code.visualstudio.com/
```

Note   Install the HashiCorp Terraform extension for syntax highlighting, which will help you develop your code.

Terraforming Your Infrastructure

In this book, you use Terraform to provision the servers and accompanied services in the cloud. Terraform allows you to define your infrastructure as source code. It is also called Infrastructure-as-Code (IaC).

Terraform declares every resource (servers, networks, etc.) with all of their attributes in files. It supports multiple cloud providers.

Generally, learning the working mechanisms of Terraform is an extremely worthy skill. You can use it to easily build infrastructures, also on other clouds. It comes with the HashiCorp Configuration Language (HCL), which is easy to learn and use.

You just define the infrastructure components you need in one or more files. Then, you build it in the cloud with one command. With another command, you can destroy the whole thing. You can be sure that nothing is left behind. The next time, you can rebuild the same exact infrastructure. To achieve this manually through the portal or the command-line interface (CLI) is almost impossible. The more your infrastructure grows, the more you will need an IaC.

You can also use Azure Resource Manager (ARM) templates or other third-party tools (such as Ansible) to automate your infrastructure. ARM has better support for the latest Azure changes, but Terraform stands out with its cloud independence and simplicity.

Terraform comes with a single executable file. You can download and execute it:

```
www.terraform.io/downloads.html
```

Note   Put Terraform into your PATH environment variable so that
you can reach it from your project folder.

Creating a Single Player Game

After you install the development tools, you can start by creating your
game. The intention here is to keep the game frontend as simple as
possible. I used a freely downloadable Unity Asset, which includes some
3D characters. I use the Unity Asset called RPG Monster Dui PBR Polyart
for the demonstration, because I found the characters hilarious. You
can, of course, use your own game and apply the concepts described in
this book.

First Steps to Building Your Game

If you choose to use the Unity Asset, here are the detailed steps to follow:

1. Create a new 3D Core project, called MyGame, with
    the help of the Unity Hub, as shown in Figure 1-2.

Figure 1-2. *Creating a new Unity project*

2. Go to the Unity Asset Store (choose Unity Editor
   ➤ Window ➤ Asset Store) and search for Unity
   Asset RPG Monster Duo PBR Polyart from this link:
   `https://assetstore.unity.com/packages/3d/`
   `characters/creatures/rpg-monster-duo-pbr-`
   `polyart-157762`.

3. Choose Add to My Assets ➤ Open in Unity ➤
   Package Manager ➤ Import.

4. After you import the game into Unity, go to the
   sample scene (choose Project Panel ➤ Assets ➤
   Scenes) and double-click it.

You can add a *plane* to the scene (right-click to choose Hierarchy
Window ➤ 3D Object ➤ Plane) to be the floor where the players will move.

Go to a character prefab (choose Project Panel ➤ Assets ➤ RPG Monster Duo PBR Polyart ➤ Prefabs ➤ Slime) and select it. In the Inspector window, add a Rigidbody and a Box Collider component to it. You should make sure the collider fits with the character (0.5 on the Y value should be fine for this character).

Control and Animation of the Character

Create a new folder of scripts and add a new C# script called Controller. cs. You will put all the required logic to move and animate the character in this script. Copy the following code into it:

```
using UnityEngine;

public class Controller : MonoBehaviour
{
    private float speed = 0.01f;
    Animator animator;
    void Start()
    {
        animator = GetComponent<Animator>();
    }
    void Update()
    {
        Vector3 movement = new Vector3(Input.
        GetAxis("Horizontal") * speed, 0, Input.
        GetAxis("Vertical") * speed);
        transform.position = transform.position + movement;

        if ((movement.x != 0) || (movement.y !=0) ||
        (movement.z !=0))
        {
```

```
        transform.rotation = Quaternion.
        RotateTowards(transform.rotation, Quaternion.
        LookRotation(movement), 10000 * Time.deltaTime);
        animator.SetBool("moving", true);
    } else
    {
        animator.SetBool("moving", false);
    }
  }
}
```

Add this script to your Slime prefab as a new component.

The Controller script simply moves the character by reading the changes of the input and turns it in the right direction. It sets the moving parameter if the character moves.

To use this, create new transitions between Idle Normal and RunFWD in the Animator panel (choose Window ➤ Animation ➤ Animator) of the prefab. Right-click IdleNormal, click Make Transition, and choose RunFWD. Now click the transition arrow.

Then, go to the Parameters tab of the Animator and add the moving parameter as bool. After that, you can add the condition for the state transition. If the moving parameter is true, the character should start to run. You can see this configuration in Figure 1-3, after you drag-and-drop your character prefab into the Hierarchy window. See if you can control it.

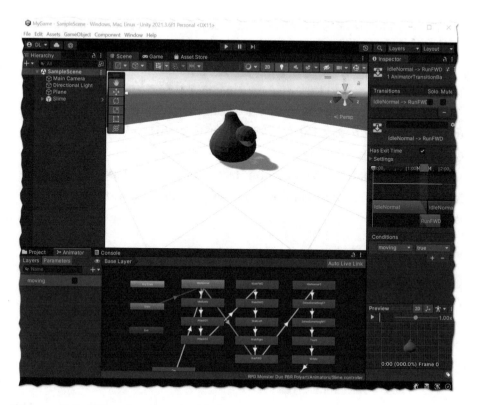

Figure 1-3. *Simple game in Unity*

You have now a very simple single player game, which you will extend in the following sections of this book.

Creating a Menu for Your Game

Now you'll create a very simple menu, so your players can choose what they want to do. In this book, you implement everything twice, once in PlayFab and once with Azure, and the menu should trigger both implementations.

Use the GUILayout class to implement a minimalistic menu. Of course, you should build a fancier menu for your game.

First, create two new game objects, PlayFab and Azure. We add all the scripts under the related game objects in this book.

Create another game object, called ControlPanel, and a script called ControlPanel.cs. Add this script to the ControlPanel game object.

The following code shows one possible structure. You can download the complete code from GitHub. We also extend this code in the following chapters with more features.

This allows you to start functions by clicking the buttons. It also makes it possible to open a new window and assign multiple buttons or other input elements.

```
using UnityEngine;

public class ControlPanel : MonoBehaviour
{
    public const int ROOTMENU = 0;
    public const int PLAYFAB_LOGIN = 1;
    public const int AZURE_LOGIN = 2;
    // TBD: Additional features

    int selection;

    GameObject playFab;
    GameObject azure;

    private void Start()
    {
        playFab = GameObject.Find("PlayFab");
        azure = GameObject.Find("Azure");
    }

    void OnGUI()
    {
        if (selection == ROOTMENU)
```

```
    GUILayout.Window(0, new Rect(0, 0, 300, 0),
    OptionsWindow, "Options");

  if (selection == PLAYFAB_LOGIN)
      GUILayout.Window(0, new Rect(0, 0, 300, 0),
      LoginWithPlayFabWindow, "Login with PlayFab");

  // TBD: Additional features
}

void OptionsWindow(int windowID)
{
    if (GUILayout.Button("Login with PlayFab"))
        // TBD: Implement actions to buttons

    if (GUILayout.Button("Login with Azure"))
        selection = AZURE_LOGIN;

    GUILayout.Space(10);

    // TBD: Additional buttons
}

void LoginWithPlayFabWindow(int windowID)
{
    GUILayout.Label("Display name:");
    // TBD: Implement each sub-window
}

void LoginWithAzureWindow(int windowID)
{

    if (GUILayout.Button("Login with Azure"))
        // TBD: Implement actions to buttons, such as
        // azure.GetComponent<AzureAuth>().
            LoginWithAzure();
```

```
        if (GUILayout.Button("Cancel"))
            selection = ROOTMENU;
    }
}
```

Now you have a simple single player game with a menu that allows you to invoke different backend functionalities. You can move on to the backend.

Creating a Local Multiplayer Game

Before you learn how to implement an online multiplayer game, we investigate how to implement a local multiplayer game. You will see it is much easier, because the server is one of the local machines. Later, you will extend this solution to a dedicated game server in the cloud, so understanding these basic components is important for the following chapters.

What Is a Local Multiplayer Game?

In this context, "local" means all the players connect to the same local network, for example, all are on your home network. These machines are not accessible from outside of your home, through the Internet.

Figure 1-4 shows four players with their clients. All the clients are connecting to a local network. Player 1 hosts the game. Under the hood, on Player 1's machine, besides the client, there is also a server.

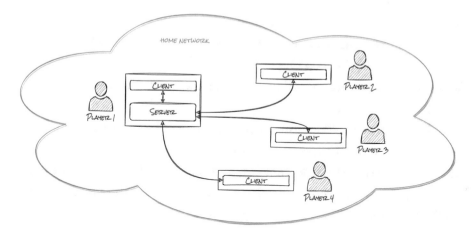

Figure 1-4. *Local multiplayer game*

Getting Started with Mirror Networking

Mirror is an open source networking library for Unity. It ran originally as the own networking API for Unity under the name of UNET, but after Unity deprecated it, the community developed it further under the name Mirror Networking. It is free, which is an advantage over its opponents.

You can get Mirror from the Asset Store (choose Unity Editor ➤ Window ➤ Asset Store, and search for "Mirror"). Then choose Add to My Assets ➤ Open in Unity ➤ Import. You can uncheck the Examples folder, as you will use your own game.

If having trouble finding Mirror, try this link: `https://assetstore. unity.com/packages/tools/network/mirror-129321`.

Be aware that Mirror keeps on developing quickly, so you might find deprecated or nonexistent functions. You may need to make some changes in your code if you use later versions of Mirror. This book uses version 66.0.9.

After you import Mirror into Unity, add its key components to your game. With that, you have enabled networking functionality in your game. You will need at least Mirror's core components—the `NetworkManager` and the NetworkIdentity assigned to objects to be synced on the network. Mirror contains some additional components as well, such as NetworkDiscovery, which helps to find servers on the local network. In this book, we focus on the key components that you will need to implement the backend features.

Figure 1-5 summarizes the mirror components for the local multiplayer game. Be aware that certain components, such as the NetworkAnimator, NetworkIdentity, and the NetworkTransform, have to be assigned to your game object that you want to sync with other players on the network.

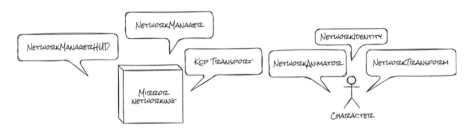

Figure 1-5. *Mirror components*

The Core Components: NetworkManager and NetworkIdentity

Add a new game object called NetworkManager to your hierarchy in Unity Editor. Then add the NetworkManager component to it. This is a core component of your multiplayer game. It is responsible, for example, for spawning (creating) new game objects. For example, putting a new player on the scene when the player joins to the game.

When you add the NetworkManager, Mirror will also add the KcpTransport component to your game object. You can change this to other transport protocols like TCP or UDP. Mirror uses KCP by default and claims that it is faster and reliable than the others.

Make sure that you remove the `Smile` game object from the hierarchy. We will work with the prefab (choose Assets ➤ RPG Monster Duo PBR Polyart ➤ Prefabs ➤ Slime).

Add a `NetworkIdentity` component to it. Mirror will only know game objects that have the `NetworkIdentity` component assigned to them.

Drag-and-drop your character prefab to the `NetworkManager` component's `Player` prefab. From now on, Mirror will spawn the player automatically when a client starts.

Synchronize Moving and Animation

You also need to add the `NetworkTransform` component to the character, as you want to synchronize the transform parameters (position, rotation, scale) over the network, so that other players can also see the changes in their local machine.

Check the Client Authority checkbox in the `NetworkTransform` component. By default, the server has authority over all game objects, but if you give authority to the client on a certain game object, the client itself will send the movement information to other clients. Be aware that you should always add these networking components to the prefab and not to the game object in the hierarchy.

Mirror does not synchronize the animation between the two clients by default. The characters belonging to remote clients are just sliding without animation on the scene.

To resolve this issue, go to the prefab and add a `NetworkAnimator` component to it. Check the Client Authority checkbox. You also have to assign the animator that will sync the animation over the network. To achieve this, drag-and-drop the prefab to the `NetworkAnimator`'s `Animator` property.

Network Manager Heads-up Display

I advise you to add the NetworkManagerHUD (heads-up display) to the NetworkManager. You can disable the ControlPanel game object for now, as it can overlap the heads-up display.

The NetworkManagerHUD will generate UI buttons that allow you to become the host (both server and client at the same time), only the server, or be the client and join a server IP.

After you finish adding and configuring Mirror, you can start the game. Notice that your character is not visible anymore. You can choose to be the host on the NetworkManagerHUD, whereby you would start the server and client, and Mirror will spawn the character to the scene. In this case, your client joins the local server on your own machine.

Setting Up Unity for Multiplayer Games

To develop games that are used by multiple players, you need to have multiple Unity instances running locally. Unfortunately, you cannot simply run multiple Unity Editor on one project.

As a workaround, you can use some tools (such as SyncToy) or Unity add-ons to clone your project folder to another folder regularly, after every change.

Alternatively, you can apply *symbolic links,* which are pointers to the original files and folders, for the second Unity Editor instance.

To configure symbolic links, follow these steps:

1. In Windows, start the Command Prompt as Administrator (search for cmd, right-click it, and choose Run as Administrator). In MacOS, start a Terminal window.

2. Create a clone folder:

   mkdir MyGame-Clone

3. In Windows, create the symbolic links by using the
    mklink command on the Assets, Packages, and
    ProjectSettings folders (in macOS, use the ln -s
    command instead):

```
mklink /J C:\Unity\Games\MyGame-Clone\Assets
C:\Unity\Games\MyGame\Assets
mklink /J C:\Unity\Games\MyGame-Clone\
Packages C:\Unity\Games\MyGame\Packages
mklink /J C:\Unity\Games\MyGame-Clone\
ProjectSettings C:\Unity\Games\MyGame\
ProjectSettings
```

Note   After you clone your project, you will want to avoid making changes to the clone project instance. Only work on the original project.

In the Unity hub, add the new cloned folder, select the same Unity version as the original one, and load the project. For the cloned version, you have to open the scene in Unity Editor.

Starting Your First Multiplayer Game

In the cloned Unity Editor, you can reload the project (a popup window will always inform you about changes in the original project) and start it. If you click client with localhost IP (since your server is also on the same machine), it will join the server and you should see the two players in one game. Congratulations, you made your first multiplayer game! You still have a major issue to fix.

Controlling Only Your Character

If you try to move your character, you notice the inputs apply to all players. This is because, with each new joining player, Mirror clones the character prefab where the same controller scripts will run. You need to somehow restrict the application of the keys to the local player.

You can achieve this by using the hasAuthority variable in the NetworkBehaviour class. This class is inherited from MonoBehaviour, so you can change MonoBehaviour to NetworkBehaviour in your Controller class.

Change the Controller.cs script using the hasAuthority condition. This will cause Unity to only consider the input for the game objects on which the player has authority:

```
using Mirror;

public class Controller : NetworkBehaviour
{
    ...
    void Update()
    {
        if (!hasAuthority) return;
...
```

Now you have a simple local multiplayer game. You will learn how to extend this to an online multiplayer game in the coming chapters. You can experiment further with Mirror Networking and its features. It is important to optimize the parameters of Mirror to your current game requirements in order to deliver a great game experience to your players.

Getting Started with PlayFab

Before creating your first online multiplayer game, you need to access the cloud. If you don't have a Microsoft account, you need to create one. You will use it throughout this book:

`https://signup.live.com/`

You can use this account to:

- **Sign in to PlayFab.** You can use up to ten titles in development mode, with up to 100,000 users per title for free.

- **Sign in to Azure.** If you are a first-time Azure user, you will get 12 months free usage of a couple of services. This includes 750 hours of B1s virtual machines, or 750 hours of a PostgreSQL database.

Create your PlayFab account now. Simply go to `https://playfab.com/` and use your Microsoft account to create a PlayFab account. (Choose Sign in with Microsoft.)

In PlayFab, enter your contact information and set your studio name. By default, it is "My Studio Name, and you will get a default title called "My Game." You can change this name later and add studios and titles to your account.

Note   PlayFab currently does not support deleting studios. So if you create one, it will be always there.

Import PlayFab SDK in Unity

The next step is to download the PlayFab Software Development Kit (SDK) and import it into Unity:

`https://aka.ms/playfabunitysdkdownload`

Note   This link does not go to a download page, but directly downloads the `unitypackage` file. If you have trouble importing the package into Unity, visit this site for information: `https://docs.unity3d.com/Manual/AssetPackagesImport.html`

You will find a new folder in your Project window called `PlayFabSDK`. You can use the PlayFab Unity Editor extension, download it, and import it into Unity. However, this is optional. It helps you download and upgrade the SDK and configure your title automatically. It brings you some convenience, but you can integrate Unity with PlayFab without the extension, so you will not use it in the next steps. You can find the extension here:

`https://aka.ms/PlayFabUnityEdEx`

Configure PlayFab in Unity

Now that you have both PlayFab and Unity set up, let them "know" each other. You need to add your actual title and the developer secret key to the PlayFab configuration in Unity.

For that, go to Assets ➤ PlayFabSDK ➤ Shared ➤ Public ➤ Resources and double-click `PlayFabSharedSettings.asset` in the Project window. In the Inspector window, set the following configurations:

- **Title ID:** Go to the Game Manager in PlayFab and click the gearwheel next to your title's name. Then select My Studios and Titles. You can see the ID of your game (don't mix it with the Title name).

- **Developer Secret Key:** You can find this in the Game Manager. Choose the gearwheel next to your title's name then choose Title Settings ➤ Secret Keys. Copy and paste the secret key into the respective field in the Inspector.

You can leave the other settings at their defaults. You should now be able to communicate with PlayFab from Unity.

Signing Up for Azure

You can use a Microsoft account to sign up for Azure:
https://azure.microsoft.com/

If this is the first time you've used Azure, you will get services free for 12 months and an additional $200 credit to consume any services in the first month. Still, always be careful when using services and check their prices. Always remove unused resources, and if possible, use free tier resources for development and only pay for productive resources.

Once you have signed up, you can look around in the Azure Portal.
https://portal.azure.com/

Note   You can check your expenses in the Azure Portal (https://portal.azure.com), under Cost Management + Billing. Azure gives you also a forecast about your spending. You can set up cost alerts, so that Azure informs you when you reach a certain threshold.

After you have access to the Azure Portal, download and install the Azure Command-Line Interface (CLI):
https://docs.microsoft.com/en-us/cli/azure/install-azure-cli
Then, try it from the command prompt:

```
az login
```

Later on, you will use Azure Kubernetes Service (AKS). For that, you should also install the CLI, as follows:

```
az aks install-cli
```

Creating Your First Online Multiplayer Server

In this section, you further extend the earlier local multiplayer game. As shown in Figure 1-6, you will put the server in the cloud, allowing players to play together even when they are not in the same location.

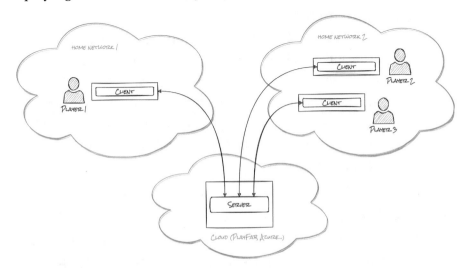

Figure 1-6. *Multiplayer server in the cloud*

Practically, you have to deploy a virtual machine in Azure and install a server version of the game on it. This server will listen on a port, waiting for clients to connect.

Building Your Infrastructure

Create a file (such as `provider.tf`) where you define the provider. Terraform officially supports multiple cloud providers; in this case, let's add Azure:

```
terraform {
  required_providers {
    azurerm = {
      source  = "hashicorp/azurerm"
      version = "=3.13.0"
    }
  }
}

provider "azurerm" {
  features {}
}
```

First create a resource group in Azure that allows the logical grouping of resources. The resource blocks are the core elements in Terraform. You define each resource that Terraform deploys in the cloud. Create a new file called resourcegroup.tf and add the following code to it:

```
resource "azurerm_resource_group" "this" {
  name     = "mygame-rg"
  location = "West Europe"
}
```

The resource block declares the following:

- **Resource type:** In this case azurerm_resource_group refers to a resource group in Azure.

- **Resource name:** In this case this is a naming convention of Terraform. If no other resource exists with this type, use this. The name allows you to refer to this resource within the module.

- **Arguments:** Within the { } block, you can define the parameters of the resource. Here, it's the name and the location of the resource group.

Note   The location of the resource group does not imply the location of the contained resources in that resource group. It is only an indicator that resources in this resource group are in that specific region.

Now you'll define the network-related resources in another file. Create a file called `network.tf` and add the code that describes a virtual network. We refer back to the name and location of the resource group that we described earlier:

```
resource "azurerm_virtual_network" "this" {
  name                = "mygame-vnet"
  address_space       = ["10.0.0.0/16"]
  location            = azurerm_resource_group.this.location
  resource_group_name = azurerm_resource_group.this.name
}
```

Within that virtual network, add a subnet:

```
resource "azurerm_subnet" "internal" {
  name                 = "internal"
  resource_group_name  = azurerm_resource_group.this.name
  virtual_network_name = azurerm_virtual_network.this.name
  address_prefixes     = ["10.0.2.0/24"]
}
```

You also need a public IP to access the server through the Internet. Create a network interface and assign it to this public IP:

```
resource "azurerm_public_ip" "this" {
  name                = "mygame-pip"
  resource_group_name = azurerm_resource_group.this.name
```

```
  location              = azurerm_resource_group.this.location
  allocation_method     = "Dynamic"
}

resource "azurerm_network_interface" "this" {
  name                = "mygametitle-nic"
  location            = azurerm_resource_group.this.location
  resource_group_name = azurerm_resource_group.this.name

  ip_configuration {
    name                          = "mygame-publicip"
    subnet_id                     = azurerm_subnet.this.id
    public_ip_address_id          = azurerm_public_ip.this.id
    private_ip_address_allocation = "Dynamic"
  }
}
```

And finally, the virtual machine. You definitely don't want to have the admin password directly in your Terraform code, but to demonstrate the workings, leave it like that for now. Note that the B1s virtual machine instance is free for the first 12 months, so it is optimal for experimentation. Create a new file called vm.tf and copy the following code:

```
resource "azurerm_linux_virtual_machine" "this" {
  name                = "mygame-vm"
  resource_group_name = azurerm_resource_group.this.name
  location            = azurerm_resource_group.this.location
  size                = "Standard_B1s"
  admin_username      = "mygamevmuser"
  admin_password      = "njkwer43GFBS@#"
  disable_password_authentication = false
```

```
network_interface_ids = [
  azurerm_network_interface.this.id,
]

os_disk {
  caching                = "ReadWrite"
  storage_account_type = "Standard_LRS"
}

source_image_reference {
  publisher = "Canonical"
  offer     = "UbuntuServer"
  sku       = "16.04-LTS"
  version   = "latest"
}
}
```

These Terraform codes will deploy the defined infrastructure components. By default, the state file is on the local machine. If you work in teams on the Terraform code, it is better to store this state file in the cloud, in this case, in Azure Storage. It is also a safe way to store the state file of your infrastructure, even if it has some cost.

The state file always contains the actual resources and their parameters in the cloud. If you delete the virtual machine manually through the Azure Portal, the next "Terraform apply" will deploy it again, exactly the same way it was earlier. If you remove the virtual machine resource from the Terraform script, the next "Terraform apply" will remove the virtual machine from Azure.

When you finish your script and start Terraform, initialize the Terraform configuration in the current working directory:

```
terraform init
```

Then run your script with the following command and make sure it executes without any error messages:

```
terraform apply
```

You may notice that Terraform hangs and never finishes the execution. You can enable logging for troubleshooting with the following commands:

```
set TF_LOG_PATH=terraform.log
set TF_LOG=TRACE
```

Note   On macOS, use the EXPORT command to set environment variables.

Later, if you want to remove the virtual machine and all other related resources you created with Terraform, simply execute the following:

```
terraform destroy
```

Creating the Game Server Instance

In Unity, go to File ➤ Build Settings... Select Linux as the target platform and then select the Server Build checkbox. Click the Build button, create a folder, and let Unity generate the server code for you.

Retrieve the public IP address of your virtual machine:

```
az network public-ip show -g singlevm-resources -n
mygame-pip --query "ipAddress"
```

Upload the server files to the virtual machine:

```
scp -r <server-build-folder> mygamevmuser@<publicIP>:/home/
mygamevmuser
```

Execute the server:

```
ssh mygamevmuser@<publicIP>
chmod 755 mygame-server.x86_64
./mygame-server.x86_64
```

Testing and Next Steps

Going back to Unity, start the game and, on the heads-up display, change the IP address from the localhost to the public IP of your virtual machine in the cloud. Your client should connect to the server, and Mirror should spawn the character on the screen. You can try starting your second Unity Editor with the cloned project and see if both can join the server. All should work fine.

With that, you have created the simplest online multiplayer game. It uses a dedicated server hosted in the cloud. This single virtual machine is quite limited and not really usable in a real environment. It does not scale at all, so after more players join, the server will run out of resources. Also, it does not support multiple sessions. We address these issues in the following chapters.

Summary

In this chapter, you learned about the tools and technologies you will use in this book. You created a simple game to showcase the backend features. You learned about the basic functionality of Mirror Networking to create local multiplayer games. With the help of a dedicated server deployed in the cloud, you learned the basic idea of how to implement an online multiplayer game that allows players to play together from any distance. The next chapters extend this concept further and show you how to build a more robust and scalable solution.

Review Questions

1. How do you implement and test a multiplayer game with the help of Unity?

2. What is Infrastructure-as-Code (IaC) and which tools can you use?

3. How do you configure PlayFab in Unity?

4. What is the difference between a local and an online (non-local) multiplayer game?

5. How does Mirror Networking extend the Unity Engine?

6. What are the main components of Mirror and what are their functions?

7. How do you distinguish between local and remote players in Mirror? Why is this necessary?

8. Which resources are required to have a virtual machine in Azure?

9. Which command do you use to execute your Terraform scripts?

10. How do you make a server build of a game in Unity?

CHAPTER 2

Player Authentication

This chapter shows how to implement mechanisms to authenticate your players. Each player needs an identity. This is an essential step that allows you to distinguish between them, store their attributes, scores, achievements, and enable multiplayer games.

This chapter first implements authentication by PlayFab. It is an important feature, as it is a prerequisite for features discussed in the next chapters.

Azure also provides powerful identity management. You will see how to implement and explore different methods of authentication, such as authentication with a single ID, authentication with username and password, and authentication using a third-party provider.

Authentication Levels

Every game is different. You should consider your authentication strategy based on your specific requirements. This section reviews some of the options you have.

Player authentication can happen at multiple levels. PlayFab supports many features, and Azure does as well. You need to balance cost, efforts, requirements, and usability. The following list can help you consider your options:

- You do not implement player authentication at all. This is very convenient for your users, as they don't have to trouble with a login process. On the other hand, you cannot identify them.

- Identification is only based on the same device or custom ID. This can be a simple list of IDs stored centrally in a configuration file or database. This is still convenient for players, as they can have access to backend services, but they cannot keep their identity and related information if they leave the game.

- Identification with a username and password; users are stored centrally in a database; encryption is possible. At this level, the players need some interaction with your game to authenticate themselves, but the backend part is very simple and restricted only to a centrally stored list of users.

- Identification, including management functions, such as password policies, user, and group management. You will need an identity provider or an authentication supporting GBaaS provider to authenticate and manage your users.

- Advanced level authentication, including, for example, multifactor authentication, third-party providers, or biometric recognition. At this level, you reach maximum security to identify your players and manage their credentials. On the other hand, this can require the most effort from your players.

Regardless of the authentication method you choose, the result of the authentication process should be a token that the player uses to prove their identity to the backend services.

The following sections go through some examples and show different authentications with the help of PlayFab and Azure.

PlayFab

This section implements two different ways of authentication using PlayFab. Basically, there are two levels of authentication:

- **Anonymous.** Without player interaction, the client software authenticates itself in the background so that an ID represents the client. The player cannot refer to this ID, so it cannot recover anything that happened in earlier game rounds.

- **Recoverable.** Using some interactive method, the player identifies themselves, so any data related to their account on the server side will be recoverable when they log back in again.

As a best practice, use the anonymous authentication and then recommend to players that they switch to a recoverable method.

PlayFab supports several methods for implementing authentication for your game. The easiest ways to implement it are the custom ID and the username, password-based authentication. If you want to use external identity providers, you may need to use third-party SDKs and configure an external service. Table 2-1 contains a summary of the supported authentication methods.

Table 2-1. *PlayFab Supported Authentication Methods*

	(A)nonymous/ (R)ecoverable	Your Target Platform or Distribution Method	Player Interaction Required	Third-party (SDK Required)
LoginWithCustomID	A	Any	No	No
LoginWithAndroidDeviceID	A	Android	No	No
LoginWithIOSDeviceID	A	IOS	No	No
LoginWithPlayFab	R	Any	Yes	No
LoginWithKongregate	R	Kongregate	Yes	Yes (No)
LoginWithSteam	R	Steam	Yes	Yes (No)
LoginWithTwitch	R	Twitch	yes	Yes (No)
LoginWithGameCenter	R	IOS	yes	Yes (No)
LoginWithFacebook	R	Facebook	yes	Yes (Yes)
LoginWithGoogleAccount	R	Google Play	yes	Yes (Yes)
LoginWithWindowsHello	R	Windows	yes	Yes (Yes)
LoginWithXBox	R	Xbox	yes	Yes (Yes)
LoginWithPSN	R	PlayStation	yes	Yes (Yes)
LoginWithNintendoSwitch DeviceId	R	Nintendo Switch	yes	Yes (Yes)
LoginWithApple	R	Apple	yes	Yes (Yes)

Login with CustomID

Let's begin with the implementation. Create a `PlayFabSettings.cs` script and add it to the PlayFab game object (if you haven't created that yet, just right-click Hierarchy and select Create Empty).

You will store some important PlayFab IDs in the PlayFabSettings:

```
using UnityEngine;

public class PlayFabSettings : MonoBehaviour
{
    public string buildId;
    public string sessionId;
    public string entityId;
    public string displayName;
    public string networkId;
}
```

Logging in with the CustomID is the most basic way to authenticate a player. With no user dialog box, you send a generated ID to PlayFab. Add the `PlayFabAuth.cs` script to the PlayFab game object. Then, add the following code to it:

```
using UnityEngine;
using PlayFab;
using PlayFab.ClientModels;
using System;

public class PlayFabAuth : MonoBehaviour
{
    public void PlayFabLoginWithCustomID(string displayName)
    {
        var guid = Guid.NewGuid().ToString();
```

```
PlayFabClientAPI.LoginWithCustomID(new
LoginWithCustomIDRequest
{
    CustomId = guid,
    CreateAccount = true
},
result =>
{
    Debug.Log("Login with CustomID succeeded.");
    GetComponent<PlayFabSettings>().entityId = result.
    EntityToken.Entity.Id;
    UpdateDisplayName(displayName);
    GetComponent<PlayFabSettings>().displayName =
    displayName;
},
error =>
{
    Debug.Log("Login with CustomID failed. " + error.
    ErrorMessage);
});
}

private void UpdateDisplayName(string displayName)
{
    PlayFabClientAPI.UpdateUserTitleDisplayName(
        new UpdateUserTitleDisplayNameRequest
        {
            DisplayName = displayName
        },
        (UpdateUserTitleDisplayNameResult result) =>
        {
            Debug.Log("Display name updated.");
```

```
            },
            (PlayFabError error) =>
            {
                Debug.LogError(error.GenerateErrorReport());
            });
    }
}
```

Note that you must start an additional request to set the DisplayName. This differs from the username. It will be visible to the players. For example, on the leaderboards or during the chat.

Implementing the Control Panel

Before this section goes into the details, you need to implement the control panel, which allows you to invoke different authentication methods. Add the following code to your ControlPanel.cs script and add it to the ControlPanel game object:

```
using UnityEngine;

public class ControlPanel : MonoBehaviour
{
    public const int ROOTMENU = 0;
    public const int PLAYFAB_LOGIN = 1;
    public const int PLAYFAB_LOGINWITHUSERPASS = 2;

    int selection;

    string username = "";
    string password = "";
    string displayName = "";
```

```csharp
GameObject playFab;

private void Start()
{
    playFab = GameObject.Find("PlayFab");
}

void OnGUI()
{
    if (selection == ROOTMENU)
        GUILayout.Window(0, new Rect(0, 0, 300, 0),
        OptionsWindow, "Options");

    if (selection == PLAYFAB_LOGIN)
        GUILayout.Window(0, new Rect(0, 0, 300, 0),
        LoginWithPlayFabWindow, "Login with PlayFab");

    if (selection == PLAYFAB_LOGINWITHUSERPASS)
        GUILayout.Window(0, new Rect(0, 0, 300, 0),
        LoginWithPlayFabUserPass, "Login with username/
        password");
}

void OptionsWindow(int windowID)
{
    if (GUILayout.Button("Login with PlayFab"))
        selection = PLAYFAB_LOGIN;
}

void LoginWithPlayFabWindow(int windowID)
{
    GUILayout.Label("Display name:");
    displayName = GUILayout.TextField(displayName, 20);
```

```
    if (!displayName.Equals(""))
    {
        if (GUILayout.Button("Login as Guest"))
        {
            playFab.GetComponent<PlayFabAuth>().PlayFabLogi
            nWithCustomID(displayName);
            selection = ROOTMENU;
        }

        if (GUILayout.Button("Login with username/password"))
        {
            selection = PLAYFAB_LOGINWITHUSERPASS;
        }
    }

    if (GUILayout.Button("Cancel"))
        selection = ROOTMENU;
}

void LoginWithPlayFabUserPass(int windowID)
{
    GUILayout.Label("User name:");
    username = GUILayout.TextField(username, 10);
    GUILayout.Label("Password:");
    password = GUILayout.PasswordField(password, '*', 10);

    if (GUILayout.Button("Register and/or Login"))
        playFab.GetComponent<PlayFabAuth>().PlayFabLogin
        WithUsernameAndPassword(username, password,
        displayName);

    if (GUILayout.Button("Cancel"))
    {
```

```
            displayName = playFab.
            GetComponent<PlayFabSettings>().displayName;
            selection = ROOTMENU;
        }
    }
}
```

Testing and Verification

Now you should run the game in Unity to test it. If you still have the NetworkManagerHUD active, remove it from the NetworkManager.

Note   Don't forget to do the steps described in Chapter 1's section entitled "Configure PlayFab in Unity."

After starting the game, use the menu to choose PlayFab as the backend. Regardless of the login you choose, you have to provide a DisplayName.

Click Login as Guest. You should see on the console `"Login with CustomID succeeded."`

Always save the entity ID, which will be important for the matchmaking process. Now put it into the PlayFabSettings.

In PlayFab's Game Manager, you can verify the new player. Go to Players and click the Search button to see the list of players.

If your game is going to run on Android or iOS devices, you can choose to log in with Android or iOS IDs. That user account will be related to the player's device, and as long as the player uses the same device, your game will recognize then as the same recurring player.

Login with Username and Password

The login with username and password method is recoverable. The player with the credentials can log in again and can continue to use the account. With a custom ID, this is not possible.

Note   The name and password must both be at least six characters long, otherwise PlayFab will not accept them.

Let's implement the login with username and password. Add the following methods to your existing PlayFabAuth class:

```
public void PlayFabLoginWithUsernameAndPassword(string
name, string password, string displayName)
{
    PlayFabClientAPI.LoginWithPlayFab(new
    LoginWithPlayFabRequest
    {
        Username = name,
        Password = password,
        InfoRequestParameters = new
        GetPlayerCombinedInfoRequestParams
        {
            GetPlayerProfile = true
        }
    },
    result =>
    {
        Debug.Log("Login with PlayFab succeeded.");
        GetComponent<PlayFabSettings>().entityId = result.
        EntityToken.Entity.Id;
```

43

```
        GetComponent<PlayFabSettings>().displayName =
        result.InfoResultPayload.PlayerProfile.DisplayName;

    },
    error =>
    {
        Debug.Log("Login with PlayFab failed. " + error.
        ErrorMessage);
        if (error.Error == PlayFab.PlayFabErrorCode.
        AccountNotFound)
            RegisterPlayFabUser(name, password,
            displayName);
    });
}

private void RegisterPlayFabUser(string name, string
password, string displayName)
{
    PlayFabClientAPI.RegisterPlayFabUser(new
    RegisterPlayFabUserRequest()
    {
        Username = name,
        Password = password,
        RequireBothUsernameAndEmail = false

    },
    result =>
    {
        Debug.Log("PlayFab user is registered.");
        GetComponent<PlayFabSettings>().entityId = result.
        EntityToken.Entity.Id;
        UpdateDisplayName(displayName);
```

```
        GetComponent<PlayFabSettings>().displayName =
        displayName;

    },
    error =>
    {

        Debug.Log("PlayFab user registration failed. " +
        error.ErrorMessage);
    });
}
```

Start by logging in with the username and password. If it fails with an "Account not found" message, you can carry on and register the player with the credentials.

You can check the players in PlayFab. PlayFab stores hashed passwords, and you should not store them locally to remain compliant.

With that, you have implemented different authentication methods using PlayFab. This is important, as only authenticated users can participate in matchmaking, virtual economy, and so on, so this is a prerequisite for implementing other backend features provided by PlayFab. The next section explains how to implement authentication using Azure.

Azure

In this section, you use Azure Active Directory B2C to authenticate and store your users. It provides identity and access management for customer-facing applications (B2C refers to business-to-consumer). It has also a free tier version (up to 50,000 active users per month), which is optimal for development and testing purposes.

You will see how to implement two scenarios: one is the traditional username (email) and password-based authentication, and the other is using an account of a third-party identity provider.

45

In this example, we invoke Google, which is one of the most popular providers. Using this process, you can easily integrate other providers (such as Microsoft or Facebook) as well. We use the open standard OpenID Connect (OIDC) to authenticate users. Let's get started.

Authentication Flow

Figure 2-1 shows the high-level flow of how to authenticate a player. You will implement the following steps:

1. The game provides a button or link for the user for authentication. This leads to the Azure AD B2C service, which opens a consent screen in the player's browser. The appearing window is different for each identity provider. The player provides an email and password and submits them to the authentication server.

2. The Azure AD B2C service checks the local account or gathers the response from the third-party identity provider. If it verifies the user, it sends an authentication code to the client.

3. The client starts a new request to the Azure AD B2C service. With the help of the authentication code, the client requests the access code and the ID token.

4. The client receives the ID token, which proves its identity to the backend services.

5. The client accesses the APIs with the help of the ID token.

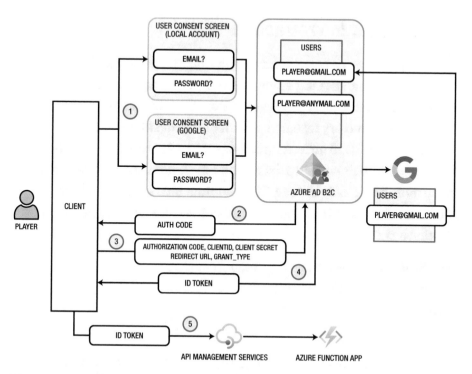

Figure 2-1. *Player authentication flow*

To implement this, you have to work on two sides: you need to build the backend, which authenticates the user, and you need to develop the client, which enables players to log in by invoking the backend.

Creating the Backend

You have to build and configure your infrastructure in Azure and integrate it with the third-party provider. We use Terraform and Azure Portal as well as Google's Developer Console.

47

Building Your Infrastructure

Azure requires resource provider registration for your subscription. By default, you cannot use any resources, only the ones that are registered to conform with the least privileges principle. Make sure that you register Azure Active Directory resource provider for your subscription.

It is a new feature in Terraform to create an Azure AD B2C tenant, so keep your Azure provider up to date with the latest version. The domain name must be globally unique. The Premium SKU should not frighten you, as the free tier with 50,000 active users is still available. Let's start by creating a resourcegroup.tf file:

```
resource "azurerm_resource_group" "auth" {
    name     = "auth-resources"
    location = "West Europe"
}
```

Then create a aadb2c.tf file and copy the following code into it:

```
resource "azurerm_resource_provider_registration" "auth" {
    name = "Microsoft.AzureActiveDirectory"
}

resource "azurerm_aadb2c_directory" "auth" {
    country_code            = "DE"
    data_residency_location = "Europe"
    display_name            = "gamebackend"
    domain_name             = "gamebackend2022.onmicrosoft.com"
    resource_group_name     = azurerm_resource_group.auth.name
    sku_name                = "PremiumP1"
}
```

You must explicitly register the Azure Active Directory as a resource provider.

Execute Terraform (`terraform apply`) to generate the Azure AD B2C tenant. Unfortunately, further configuration is not possible by Terraform, or pretty inconvenient. The same applies to Azure CLI. To make it simple, I suggest configuring Azure AD B2C on the Azure Portal.

Configure Azure AD B2C

Start by switching to your new directory. Figure 2-2 illustrates how to switch between directories. Be aware that after you switch, you will not find the resources deployed in your default directory.

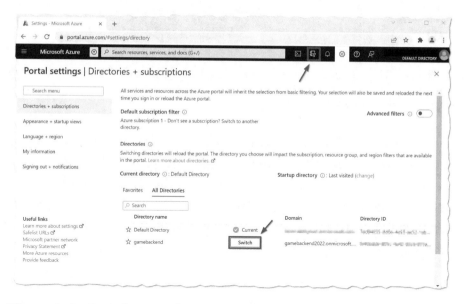

Figure 2-2. *Switching to the new Azure AD B2C directory*

After arriving at the new portal, search for Azure AD B2C and select it, then register a new application, as illustrated in Figure 2-3.

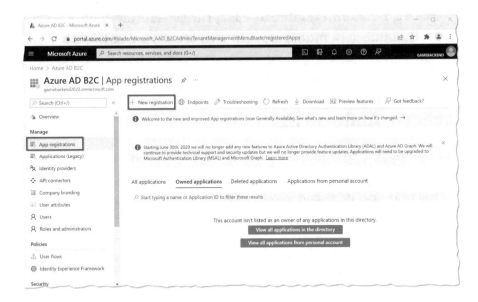

Figure 2-3. *Register a new application*

For the redirect URI, use `https://jwt.ms/`. This is a simple page, and it shows the token received after the authentication process. You will change later this to localhost when you want to receive the token in your local machine. This redirect URI value determines where you are awaiting the answer to the authentication request, to where the client should receive the token.

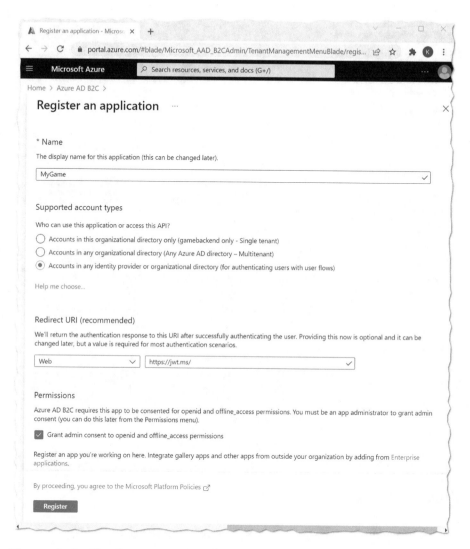

Figure 2-4. *Configure your application*

When you finish registering your application, go into the portal and under Authentication, select Access Token, as in Figure 2-5. Pick the token that you want to receive from the authentication endpoint. If you do not check this, the endpoint will not send a token to the client.

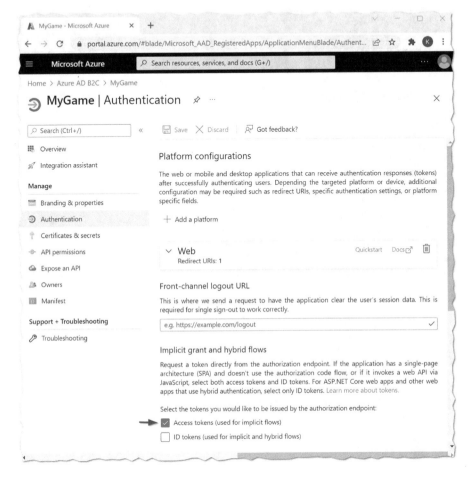

Figure 2-5. *Select access token*

To move on from here, you need to configure the Google API so that you can get its client ID and its secret, which allows you to access it through Azure AD B2C.

Configure Google API

To configure Google as an identity provider, you first need to configure it. As a prerequisite, you need to have a Google account. Go to `https://console.developers.google.com/`, log in, and create a project for your game.

Select API & Services from the navigation menu of the Google Cloud Platform. This will now be the only product that you will use from Google, so you can also pin it in the navigation menu so that you can find it easier later.

Select External for the User Type, as shown in Figure 2-6. Internal users apply only to users in your organization, and you want to authenticate unknown players. After you click Create, provide the mandatory fields with your email address and leave the other fields empty for now.

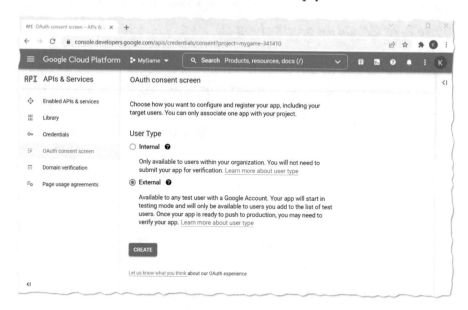

Figure 2-6. *Select the External user type from the OAuth consent screen*

Under the Credentials menu, navigate to Create Credentials and select OAuth Client ID, as shown in Figure 2-7.

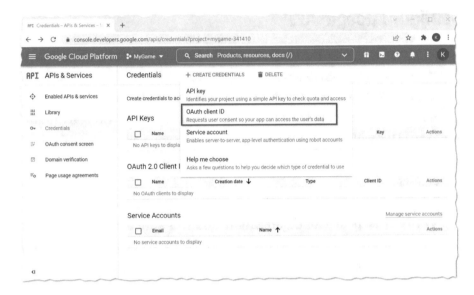

Figure 2-7. *Create an oAuth client ID*

To fill the Create OAuth client ID form, you need your tenant's name. You can find this in the Azure Portal at your Azure AD B2C resource. The domain name looks like `<your-tenant-name>.onmicrosoft.com`.

If you have your tenant name, you can fill in the form of Google (as in Figure 2-8) with the following values:

- Application type: Web application

- Name: `<your-application-name>`

- Authorized JavaScript Origin: `https://<your-tenant-name>.b2clogin.com`

- Authorized Redirect URIs: `https://<your-tenant-name>.b2clogin.com/gamebackend2022.onmicrosoft.com/oauth2/authresp`

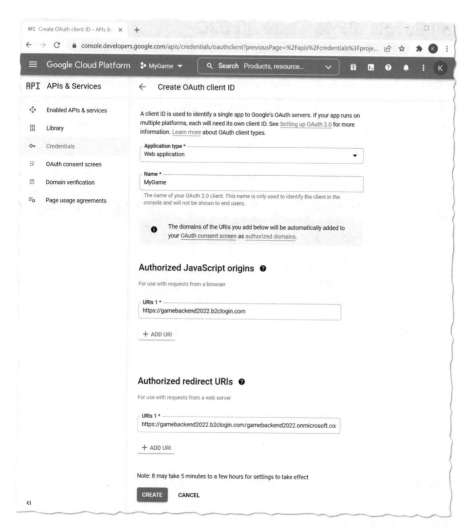

Figure 2-8. *Configure an OAuth client ID*

Save the client ID and client secret for the next step.

Add Google IDP to Azure AD B2C

In this step, you add Google as an identity provider to Azure AD B2C. In the Azure Portal, navigate to the identity providers shown in Figure 2-9 and fill in the form about Google. Note that the origin and callback URLs must be the same as you configured in the previous step. Add the client ID and secret and then save the configuration.

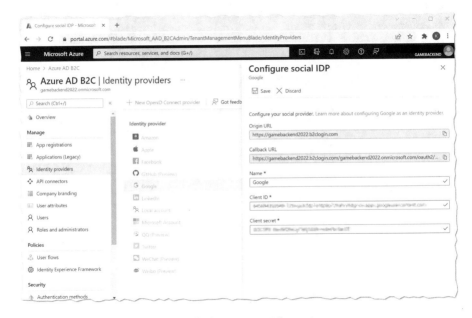

Figure 2-9. *Configure the identity provider*

Configure User Flow

Now you'll add a new user flow by navigating to User Flows under Policies, as shown in Figure 2-10. Here, you define the interaction page for users with the application during the authentication process. These are the most common actions—signing up, signing in, changing profile information, and resetting the password.

Figure 2-10. *New user flow*

Select sign up and sign in user flow type with the recommended version. Select both the Email sign-up and the Google identity provider. Later, you can set multifactor authentication or gather other attributes from your users. For now, let's do the basic settings. See Figure 2-11.

Figure 2-11. *Configure user flow*

Test the Backend

Finally, you need to verify that the authentication works with both a custom email address and with your Google account. Run your user flow, as shown in Figure 2-12.

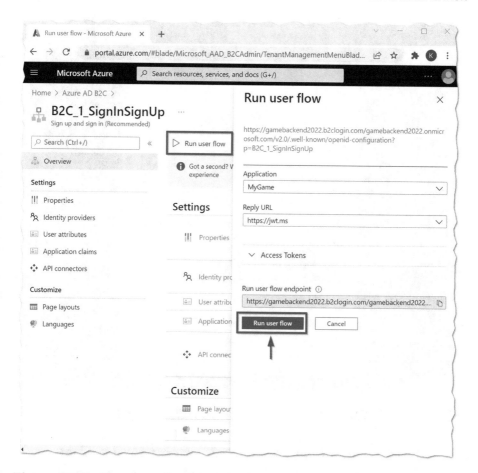

Figure 2-12. *Run user flow*

If you did everything correctly, you see a new window, as shown in Figure 2-13. Users can sign in as well as sign up here with their email or their Google account. After a successful authentication, the client gets a token to `https://jwt.ms/` with which the client can prove that it is authenticated.

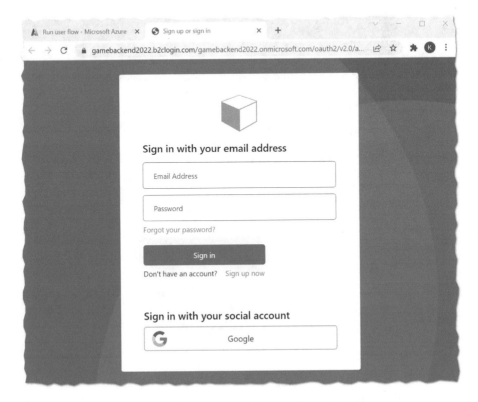

Figure 2-13. *Sign in and sign up with email or Google*

At the user menu of your Azure AD B2C, you can see that all the users went through this authentication process. You can also review their profiles or sign-in logs. In this way, you can fill your directory with identified users, which is key for implementing any other backend services for your game.

Developing the Client

In this section, you will learn to develop the client-side logic to reach the same goal as in the previous chapter. You need to implement the following requirements:

- A GUI component that players can use to start the authentication process. As the current solution will bring up a web page that contains all the required GUI elements, this client code will only contain a simple button to start the authentication.

- A listener on a specific port that's waiting for the incoming token. This will be instead of the `https://jwt.ms/` page. As soon as the authorization token arrives, the client can read and use it to prove its identity.

- Start an authorization request by opening a browser window with the authorization endpoint.

- Start a request to the token endpoint to exchange the authorization token to an access token. This will require a client secret.

Note that you implement the most simplistic scenario here. You should align and structure the code according to your actual architecture. For actual usage, also consider strengthening security, for example, by using PKCE (Proof Key for Code Exchange).

Create a Client Secret in Azure

You will communicate with Azure AD B2C from the client, so you have to generate a client secret. Note that you could access Google directly, and in that case, you would use the client ID and secret from Google. In this case, you'll access Google indirectly through Azure.

Under your application, create a new client secret, as shown in Figure 2-14. Jot down the value field.

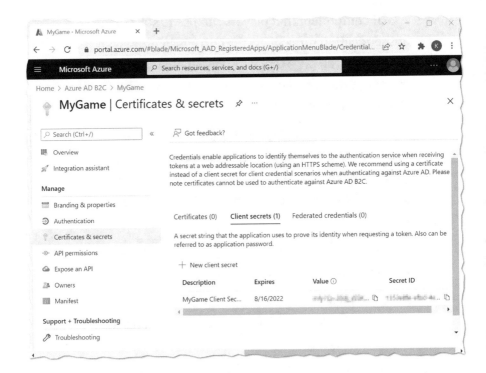

Figure 2-14. *Creating a new client secret*

Get Authorization and Token Endpoints

The client needs to know the authorization and token endpoints. OpenID
Connect provides a discovery document for clients to get these values.
You can go to your user flow, and under Run User Flow, you can find your
actual discovery document link. From the discovery document, you can
retrieve the the authorization and token endpoints.

Configure Redirect URI

Reconfigure your application, as shown in Figure 2-15, and set `http://
localhost:56789/` (instead of `https://jws.ms/`) as the redirect URI
with whatever port available on your local machine. Make sure you use

http with localhost only for development. On this port, the clients will listen and wait for the authorization token.

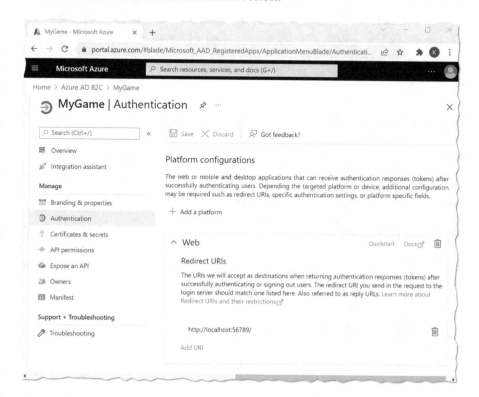

Figure 2-15. *Setting the redirect URI*

Install NuGet for Unity

Coming back to the Unity Editor, you need to get some preparation work done before you start implementing the client. You want to read the content of the Jwt security token, so you need a special library that helps you.

NuGet is the package manager for .NET. Fortunately, there is a also a NuGet client built for Unity. With its help, you can add packages to your project. You can import this client into Unity from here:

https://github.com/GlitchEnzo/NuGetForUnity/releases/
download/v3.0.5/NugetForUnity.3.0.5.unitypackage

After that, restart Unity and you will see a new menu item called
NuGet. Click Manage NuGet Packages. Search for System.IdentityModel.
Tokens.Jwt and install it. From now on, you can use this namespace in
your project.

Implement the Authorization Request

Now you can start creating your client in Unity. You need a place where
you will store the result of the authentication process. Create a new script
called AzureSettings.cs and add it to the Azure game object:

```
using UnityEngine;

public class AzureSettings : MonoBehaviour
{
    public string token;
    public string displayName;
    public string playerID;
}
```

Create the AzureAuth.cs file. This will contain all the logic required
on the client to do the authentication. Let's add this script to the earlier
created Azure game object.

Start by adding specific configuration to AzureAuth.cs. It should look
similar to the following:

```
using UnityEngine;
using System.Text;
using System.Threading.Tasks;
using System.IO;
using System.Net;
```

```csharp
using Newtonsoft.Json;
using System.IdentityModel.Tokens.Jwt;
using System.Linq;

public class AzureAuth : MonoBehaviour
{
    private string authorizationEndpoint = "https://
gamebackend2022.b2clogin.com/gamebackend2022.onmicrosoft.
com/oauth2/v2.0/authorize?p=b2c_1_signinsignup";
    private string tokenEndpoint = "https://gamebackend2022.
b2clogin.com/gamebackend2022.onmicrosoft.com/oauth2/v2.0/
token?p=b2c_1_signinsignup";
    private string clientID = "xxxxxxxx-xxxx-xxxx-xxxx-
xxxxxxxxxxxx";
    private string clientSecret = "xxxxxxxxxxxxxx";
    private string redirectURI = "http://localhost:56789/";
}
```

You can start the authentication process by configuring an HTTP listener on your local machine. Then you'll generate an URL with the standard OpenID Connect parameters and open it in a new browser window. Add a new method called GetToken to the AzureAuth class to implement it:

```csharp
private async Task<string> GetToken()
{
    var httpListener = new HttpListener();
    httpListener.Prefixes.Add(redirectURI);
    httpListener.Start();

    string authURL = string.Format("{0}&client_
id={1}&redirect_uri={2}&scope=openid%20
profile&response_type=code",
```

```
authorizationEndpoint,
clientID,
redirectURI);

Application.OpenURL(authURL);

HttpListenerContext context = await httpListener.
GetContextAsync();
```

...

After the player authenticates itself, the authorization code will arrive at your listening port. You'll then want to close the browser window. With a simple trick, you can solve this. Send back to the browser a JavaScript command. Let's continue the GetToken method with the following:

```
string authorizationCode = context.Request.QueryString.
Get("code");

byte[] buffer = Encoding.UTF8.GetBytes("<html><body><sc
ript>window.close();</script></body></html>");
await context.Response.OutputStream.WriteAsync(buffer,
0, buffer.Length);

context.Response.OutputStream.Close();
httpListener.Stop();
```

...

Implement the Token Request

Now that you have the authorization code, you can create a new token request to your token request endpoint. You have to fill the request body with the required OpenID Connect parameters and send a POST request to the endpoint. Again, continue the GetToken method with the following code:

```
string tokenRequestData = string.Format("code={0}&client_
id={1}&client_secret={2}&redirect_uri={3}&grant_
type=authorization_code",
            authorizationCode,
            clientID,
            clientSecret,
            redirectURI);

    HttpWebRequest request = (HttpWebRequest)WebRequest.
    Create(tokenEndpoint);
    request.Method = "POST";

    byte[] data = Encoding.ASCII.
    GetBytes(tokenRequestData);
    request.ContentType = "application/x-www-form-
    urlencoded";
    request.ContentLength = data.Length;

    Stream requestStream = request.GetRequestStream();
    requestStream.Write(data, 0, data.Length);
    requestStream.Close();

    HttpWebResponse response = (HttpWebResponse)request.
    GetResponse();
    StreamReader reader = new StreamReader(response.
    GetResponseStream());
    string result = reader.ReadToEnd();
...
```

The response is in JSON format. You only need to extract the id_token information from the response. For that, create a new class with the required field and deserialize the JSON response for getting the token:

```
public class TokenEndpointResponse
{
    public string id_token;
}
```

Then finish the GetToken method:

```
TokenEndpointResponse tokenEndpointResponse =
JsonConvert.DeserializeObject<TokenEndpointResponse>
(result);
return tokenEndpointResponse.id_token;
```

By this token, the player is authenticated. You can configure the backend services to only work with authenticated players, if they provide a token with their requests.

Extract the DisplayName

One final step is missing: you want the token to contain the DisplayName attribute. Go to the Azure Portal and select both the Display Name user attribute and the application claim under your User Flow, as shown in Figure 2-16. As a result, this value will be returned to the application in the token.

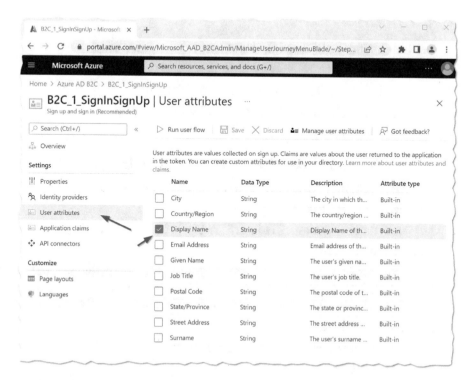

Figure 2-16. *Selecting the Display Name user attribute*

Let's implement the extraction in your AzureAuth function. At first, you request the token by using the earlier implemented GetToken method. Then, with the help of the System.IdentityModel.Tokens.Jwt package, you can decode the token and read out the name and ID attributes. Store these values in the AzureSettings for later:

```
public class AzureAuth : MonoBehaviour
{
    GameObject azure;

    private void Start()
    {
        azure = GameObject.Find("Azure");
```

```
}
public async void LoginWithAzure()
{
    string encodedToken = await GetToken();
    azure.GetComponent<AzureSettings>().token =
    encodedToken;

    var handler = new JwtSecurityTokenHandler();
    var token = handler.ReadToken(encodedToken) as
    JwtSecurityToken;
    var name = token.Claims.First(claim => claim.Type ==
    "name").Value;
    azure.GetComponent<AzureSettings>().displayName = name;

    var playerID = token.Claims.First(claim => claim.Type
    == "sub").Value;
    azure.GetComponent<AzureSettings>().playerID =
    playerID;

}
```

With that, you have implemented the backend and the client side. Make sure that it runs without any compilation errors and move on to testing.

Testing If All This Works

First, let's extend the control panel and add a button to invoke Azure-based authentication. You just need a button to invoke the LoginWithAzure function. Add the following code to ControlPanel.cs:

```
public class ControlPanel : MonoBehaviour
{
    public const int AZURE_LOGIN = 3;
```

```
GameObject azure;

    private void Start()
    {
        azure = GameObject.Find("Azure");
    }

    void OnGUI()
    {
        if (selection == AZURE_LOGIN)
            GUILayout.Window(0, new Rect(0, 0, 300, 0),
            LoginWithAzureWindow, "Login with Azure");
    }

    void OptionsWindow(int windowID)
    {
        if (GUILayout.Button("Login with Azure"))
            selection = AZURE_LOGIN;
    }

    void LoginWithAzureWindow(int windowID)
    {
        if (GUILayout.Button("Login with Azure"))
            azure.GetComponent<AzureAuth>().LoginWithAzure();

        if (GUILayout.Button("Cancel"))
            selection = ROOTMENU;
    }
}
```

A new window should appear in your browser asking for credentials. This is the same as what you saw in Figure 2-13, but this time it's called from your game client. If you successfully authenticate your user, the token, display name, and player ID should appear in your AzureSettings.

Summary

In this chapter, you implemented different player logins and registrations. The chapter introduced different levels of authentication that you can consider according to your specific game requirements.

PlayFab and Azure both provide several techniques and methods. To implement with PlayFab, the custom ID and PlayFab-based authentication are very simple. However, adding an identity provider to PlayFab can be considerable effort. The same is true if you directly use Azure's identity provider. Your decision should depend on the backend provider you're going to use, to implement other backend features.

Review Questions

1. What are the levels of authentication you can implement for your game?

2. What are anonymous and recoverable authentication? Give examples.

3. List some supported authentication methods in PlayFab.

4. Explain the difference between authentication with custom ID and authentication with username and password in PlayFab.

5. What is the role of OpenID Connect in authentication?

6. Which Azure service provide identity and access management?

7. What is a Redirect URI used for?

8. What is the user consent screen?

9. What is the role of the authorization code in the authentication process?

10. What should the player receive as the result of the authentication flow?

CHAPTER 3

Dedicated Game Servers

In Chapter 1, you implemented a very simple way of server hosting. In this chapter, you go further and implement a more advanced solution with the help of PlayFab, as well as in Azure with Kubernetes and Agones. You will explore and learn what you need to create online multiplayer games.

First, you will review different server hosting alternatives. Then, using PlayFab's multiplayer server hosting feature and the provided SDK, you will enable online multiplayer mode for your game.

In the second part of this chapter, you move on and build a server hosting environment in the cloud. Agones, on top of Kubernetes, will manage and allocate the servers for each online game session. You will learn how to build your own backend infrastructure.

Server Hosting Alternatives

Dedicated game server hosting means basically that you want your server to run somewhere in the cloud and your clients to have access to it, even if the clients are located all over the world. Cloud-hosted game servers allows players to play together, without being in the same location or on the same network.

© Balint Bors 2023
B. Bors, *Game Backend Development*, https://doi.org/10.1007/978-1-4842-8910-5_3

Technically, these two capabilities must be in place:

- **Server hosting.** The server must run on a machine somewhere on the Internet and be reachable by all clients.

- **Server management.** Some logic must manage the lifecycle of game servers. For example, you want to allocate servers for specific players or shut down servers if the players finish the game. If you consider it in broader terms, scaling up or down the servers can also belong here. This implies that a single virtual machine will not be sufficient.

Figure 3-1 shows three ways to host your server.

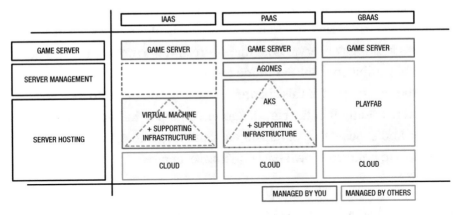

Figure 3-1. *Dedicated game server hosting in the cloud*

- The most basic and traditional way is when you have a (virtual) machine with public Internet access or pay for a hosting provider to host your server. You can also buy virtual machines from a cloud provider, then you decide on the Infrastructure as Service (IaaS) model. Here, you only have a machine with no capability to manage your game servers or even scale on demand. You need to write your custom logic to solve these problems, which can take considerable effort. You can see an example of this solution in Chapter 1.

- The most convenient way is to let a Game Backend-as-a-Service (GBaaS) provider do everything. You use their API to access their services and you only need to worry about making your game. In this chapter, we implement this approach with the help of PlayFab.

- In between, you find the Platform as a Service (PaaS) model. Azure Kuberentes Service (AKS) is a fully managed PaaS offering from Microsoft. Still, you have to configure it, which can be a daunting task. But it implements a lot of useful functionalities, for example, it scales automatically when demand grows. On top of this, you need the game server management functionality. You can use an existing production-proof solution, such as Agones. In this chapter, you implement this approach in Azure with the help of Kubernetes.

Now that you have understanding the various server hosting options, let's start by exploring the GBaaS way.

PlayFab

PlayFab provides a convenient way for server hosting. You only need to configure PlayFab and use the PlayFab Game Server SDK (GSDK) to access the servers. PlayFab arranges all the management tasks. It scales the servers according to your need.

Configuring PlayFab

By default, PlayFab disables the multiplayer server feature. After you log in to PlayFab, you should enable it from the Multiplayer menu. If you have not yet added your credit card information, choose Add Credit Card.

PlayFab will not charge you until you reach the limit. Currently, it is 750 free core hours and 10GB of egress (outgoing) traffic. It is good enough to experiment with PlayFab.

Caution   Be aware that this means core hours. If you choose, for example, a two core virtual machine, which is the minimum, you only have 375 core hours. You can run out of the free tier limit easily and then PlayFab will charge you.

On this page, you can see the current pricing of PlayFab services: `https://playfab.com/pricing/`

After you submit your credit card information, you can enable the multiplayer server feature of PlayFab.

A *game server* is basically a process that runs on an operating system, which runs on a machine. Nowadays, we use the more flexible *virtual machines* (VMs) instead of real hardware. So you need a *provider*, which hosts the virtual machine and the server process on it. But what happens if thousands of players suddenly want to use your game?

You then need more virtual machines to serve the increasing demands, and an automatism which spins up additional VMs. You cannot know how many VMs you need in advance. Instead of saying you need a specific amount of VMs, you define how and when PlayFab should create VMs.

You define this in PlayFab with the help of game server build. A *build* contains the following properties:

- **Virtual machine size.** PlayFab currently provides Dasv4 (2-16 cores) VMs. This type comes from Azure's virtual machines instances. The D-type is for running general-purpose workloads.

- **Servers per machine/server type.** If you choose the Containers server type, PlayFab will generate as many containers on each virtual machine as many servers per machine you choose. Each container will have a different port number, but they will all map to the game port you define for Mirror in Unity (the default value is 7777).

- **Assets.** These are files you upload to the server in compressed (ZIP) format. This should contain your server process, which will automatically run on the VM (as defined under the Start command).

- **Network.** The port and protocol for incoming network traffic. If you choose the default Mirror settings, the port is 7777 and the protocol is UDP (KCP counts as UDP).

- **Region.** Currently the options are EastUS or NorthEurope. You define two important parameters here. These are the only parameters that you can also change later for your build:

  - **StandingBy server.** This is the number of servers in StandingBy state waiting to become active. These are running servers flagged as StandingBy because currently no player is using it. Starting up a server can take time, so PlayFab starts up these servers before players actually allocate them. You can also set the Dynamic Standby option later, which will provision additional StandingBy servers dynamically with the growing demand.

- **Max servers.** The maximum number of servers in the chosen region. Obviously, the number of StandingBy servers must be smaller than or equal to the configured max servers.

Caution   Except for the number of StandingBy and Max servers, you cannot change any parameters of your build later.

To each build, you will get a BuildID. Figure 3-2 illustrates the key components of the multiplayer server hosting implementation in PlayFab. You can have multiple builds, and within each build, you have multiple regions. Each region can have multiple servers (virtual machines), and each server has containers where the server process runs.

To join to a specific server, clients should only provide the BuildID, the PreferredLocation, and the SessionID.

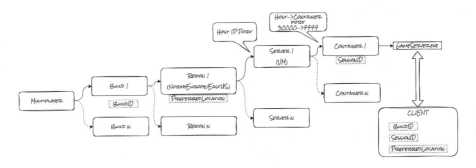

Figure 3-2. *Multiplayer server hosting implementation*

When first creating a new build, it will turn into the Initialized state. You need to increase the number of StandingBy servers, so that the build goes into the Deployed state. First, it goes through the Deploying state, checking if the server you created in Unity can turn into the StandingBy state. This happens only if you implemented the ReadyForPlayers method and call it periodically.

Configuring Unity

First, you need to download the PlayFab Game Server SDK (GSDK) for the Unity game engine. The simplest way to download the Unity package is from the following URL. Then import all the assets into your project:

https://github.com/PlayFab/gsdk/raw/main/UnityGsdk/MpsGsdk.unitypackage

In order to use it, you need to enable the ENABLE_PLAYFABSERVER_ API directive in the Unity Editor. Go to File ➤ Build Settings...and select Dedicated Server and Switch Platform. Now go to Player Settings... ➤ Player ➤ Dedicated Server Settings ➤ Other Settings ➤ Scripting Define Symbols. Then add the directive to it and click Apply.

Without this directive, you cannot compile, because of the #if ENABLE_PLAYFABSERVER_API directive in the GSDK code.

Create two game objects, called PlayFabServer and PlayFabClient, and add them to your scene as a child of the PlayFab game object. Also create two scripts (such as PlayFabServer.cs and PlayFabClient.cs) which will contain the code. You should add these scripts to the respective game objects, so that Unity can run them.

Inherit the server and the client scripts from Mirror's NetworkManager. Make sure that you have only one NetworkManager at one time on the scene.

> **Note** You can put the client and server in separate projects if you want. This can be useful, especially if it is a bigger project. For this tutorial, we keep them in one project.

Implementing the Server

You can now create the server. From the GDSK, you need to start PlayFabMultiplayerAgentAPI and call the ReadyForPlayers() method every five seconds. Put all the server code into the PlayFabServer.cs script.

```
using System.Collections;
using UnityEngine;
using Mirror;
using PlayFab;
public class PlayFabServer : NetworkManager
{
    void StartPlayFabAPI()
    {
        PlayFabMultiplayerAgentAPI.Start();
        StartCoroutine(ReadyForPlayers());

    }

    IEnumerator ReadyForPlayers()
    {
        yield return new WaitForSeconds(.5f);
        PlayFabMultiplayerAgentAPI.ReadyForPlayers();
    }
}
```

You have to start the Mirror server as well. You inherited the PlayFabServer class from the NetworkManager, so that you can call the StartServer method of Mirror right away by initializing PlayFab. Add the Start method to the PlayFabServer class:

```
void Start()
{
    StartPlayFabAPI();
    this.StartServer();
}
```

The server will then listen to a port for incoming remote client connections.

Note   Here, you merely start a server and not a host. In case of a host, you would also start a client on the same machine.

In Unity's Inspector, you can see the following server parameters:

- **Transport.** By default, Mirror currently uses KCP transport, which claims to be the fastest and best suited protocol for game-related traffic. You can choose from many, but basically use TCP if reliability is important, and UDP if speed has precedence over losing data.

- **Network address.** For servers, it is always the localhost.

- **Max. connections.** The maximum number of allowed concurrent connections.

- **Disconnect inactive connections.** When you want to remove players whose clients are not responding to the given Disconnect Inactive Timeout time period.

Although the `Transport` and the `NetworkManager` cannot live without each other, they have a separate component by design. Mirror wanted to separate the way of transport, so that you can change it any time and use the most suitable one.

Check your PlayFabServer in the Inspector. If your Transport field is None, drag-and-drop the Kcp Transport component into it.

You can change the transport parameters in Unity Inspector. For now, the most important parameter is the port number. It is the port your game server is listening on. By default, Mirror uses 7777. Be sure to avoid port conflicts; in most cases, the default value just works fine. Other parameters help optimize the performance of data transfer between the clients and the server.

Shutting Down the Server

It is important to implement server shutdown procedures to avoid running servers that no one uses. You can simply count the number of newly joining players. When a player leaves the session, you decrease this counter. As soon as the counter reaches zero, that means you can stop the server process and have PlayFab free up the container for new sessions. To achieve this, add the following code to your `PlayFabServer` class:

```
private int numberOfConnectedPlayers = 0;
public override void OnServerConnect(NetworkConnectionToCl
ient conn)
{
    base.OnServerConnect(conn);
    Debug.Log("Connected client to server, ConnectionId: "
    + conn.connectionId);
    numberOfConnectedPlayers++;

}
```

```
public override void OnServerDisconnect(NetworkConnection
ToClient conn)
{
    base.OnServerDisconnect(conn);
    Debug.Log("Client disconnected from server,
    ConnectionId: " + conn.connectionId);
    numberOfConnectedPlayers--;

    if (numberOfConnectedPlayers == 0)
    {
        StartCoroutine(Shutdown());
    }
}
private IEnumerator Shutdown()
{
    yield return new WaitForSeconds(5f);
    Application.Quit();
}
```

Building the Server

Make sure you disable the NetworkManager and the PlayFabClient
game objects. Drag-and-drop the PlayFabServer.cs script to the
PlayFabServer game object. Add the player prefab (Slime) to it just as in
case of the NetworkManager. Then, go to File ➤ Build Settings... and select
Dedicated Server.

Note   In Unity Hub, the Linux Dedicated Server Build Support must
be installed.

Select a folder and generate your game server.

Testing Your Server

You can choose to test your server on your local machine before uploading it to PlayFab. It's useful to debug if you have an issue integrating the GSDK. You have these options:

- **LocalMultiplayerAgent.** Previously called MockVMAgent, which emulates the PlayFab environment on your local machine. With the VmAgent, the game server can go through the states you will also have in your real PlayFab deployment (https://github.com/PlayFab/MpsAgent).

- **Thundernetes.** A newer initiative to debug your server locally, where you deploy your server to a customized Kubernetes cluster. The PlayFab team implemented custom resources for Kubernetes to manage the state transitions of your server (https://github.com/PlayFab/thundernetes).

Both solutions are available only for testing and debugging your solution and not for using in real situations. You also have a third option for debugging:

- **PlayFab Connect.** You can connect to your virtual machine directly through your PlayFab Game Manager. Here you use a remote desktop or SSL and go to your virtual machine directly. You can inspect each server and log with the help of simple command-line tools.

Unfortunately, PlayFab does not give you too much information when there is an issue with your server. For example, when it is hanging at deployment. It is a good idea to test it locally first. You will see how to use Thundernetes for local testing.

Thundernetes

You can create a Docker image, which includes an operating system and the game server files. Then, you'll create running containers from this image when a new session starts. Now you just need something that automates this process. Kubernetes is a production-proof container orchestration system, which is exactly what you need.

Thundernetes runs on top of Kubernetes. This is an extra layer that implements the behavior you need for running game servers.

You'll now install a local Kuberentes cluster with Thundernetes and deploy your game server on it. Start by installing the prerequisites for this scenario:

- Docker Engine for containerizing:

  `https://docs.docker.com/engine/install/`

- Chocolately (on Windows) as package manager:

  `https://docs.chocolatey.org/`

- Kubernetes CLI to run commands against the cluster:

  `choco install kubernetes-cli`

- Minikube as a local Kubernetes implementation:

  `choco install minikube`

Start Minikube and verify that it creates a Kubernetes cluster and pods in the `kube-system` namespace:

```
minikube start
kubectl config current-context
kubectl get pods -A
```

Install Thundernetes on the cluster.

Tip   You can find more information about the installation steps of Thundernetes at `https://playfab.github.io/thundernetes/quickstart/installing-thundernetes.html`.

Start by installing the certificate manager for Kubernetes:

```
kubectl apply -f https://github.com/cert-manager/cert-manager/
releases/download/v1.8.0/cert-manager.yaml
```

Verify that the installation was successful:

```
kubectl get pods -n cert-manager
```

Install the Thundernetes core logic:

```
kubectl apply -f https://raw.githubusercontent.com/PlayFab/
thundernetes/main/installfiles/operator.yaml
```

Remove the DaemonSet for Windows, because you will use Linux servers in this example:

```
kubectl delete -n thundernetes-system daemonset thundernetes-
nodeagent-win
```

Verify that the pods are up and running:

```
kubectl get pods -n thundernetes-system
```

Next, you have to create your Linux-based image, which will include your game server. Go to your game server's folder and create a file called Dockerfile. Copy the following into it:

```
FROM ubuntu:18.04
WORKDIR /game
ADD . .
CMD ["/game/mygameserver.x86_64", "-nographics", "-batchmode",
"-logfile"]
```

Execute the following command in your Dockerfile's folder. Make sure you provide a tag for your image:

```
docker build -t mygameserver-image:0.1 .
```

Verify that the image was built:

```
docker image ls mygameserver-image
```

Now load this into Minikube:

```
minikube image load mygameserver-image
```

And verify that the image is loaded:

```
minikube image ls
```

Create a new file called GameServerBuild.yaml. You can read about each parameter of a game server build in this documentation: https://playfab.github.io/thundernetes/gameserverbuild.html

```
apiVersion: mps.playfab.com/v1alpha1
kind: GameServerBuild
metadata:
  name: mygameserver-build
spec:
  titleID: "ABCD"
  buildID: "85ffe8da-c82f-4035-86c5-9d2b5f42d6f5"
  standingBy: 3
  max: 3
  crashesToMarkUnhealthy: 5
  portsToExpose:
    - 7777
  template:
    spec:
      containers:
```

```
- image: docker.io/library/mygameserver-image:0.1
  name: mygameserver
  ports:
  - containerPort: 7777
    name: gameport
```

Apply this configuration to the Kubernetes cluster:

```
kubectl apply -f GameServerBuild.yaml
```

This creates a new kind of Kubernetes resource called GameServerBuild. It will instruct the earlier deployed Thundernetes resources how to deal with game servers. Verify that everything is working fine:

```
kubectl get gsb
NAME                        STANDBY ACTIVE    CRASHES     HEALTH
mygameserver-build          3/3                           Healthy
kubectl get pods
NAME                        READY   STATUS    RESTARTS    AGE
mygameserver-build-ehusv    1/1     Running   0           9m20s
mygameserver-build-tuvhm    1/1     Running   0           9m20s
mygameserver-build-zkewy    1/1     Running   0           9m20s
```

If the pods are not in the Running state, you can troubleshoot with the help of these commands:

```
kubectl describe pod mygameserver-build-ehusv
kubectl logs mygameserver-build-ehusv --follow
```

The logs should show a StandingBy state. Let's allocate a server to see if the transition to the active state happens, and if the client receives a server IP of the allocated server.

Tunnel the Thundernetes controller's external IP to your localhost with the help of Minikube. This is important, because otherwise you cannot reach the API:

```
minikube tunnel
```

Now verify that the external IP became your localhost:

```
kubectl get svc thundernetes-controller-manager -n
thundernetes-system
NAME                              TYPE
CLUSTER-IP       EXTERNAL-IP    PORT(S)            AGE
thundernetes-controller-manager    LoadBalancer
10.105.20.188    127.0.0.1     5000:31270/TCP    3h29m
```

You can now allocate a server with a POST request, and Thundernetes provides the appropriate IP and port where your clients can connect:

```
curl -X POST "http://localhost:5000/api/v1/allocate" -H
"Content-Type: application/json" --data-raw "{\"buildID\":
\"<your build Id>\",\"sessionID\": \"<your session Id>\"}"
{"IPV4Address":"192.168.58.2","Ports":"7777:10006","SessionID":
"ac1b7082-d811-47a7-89ae-fe1a9c48a6da"}
```

Finally, verify that you have one active server:

```
kubectl get gsb
NAME                  STANDBY   ACTIVE   CRASHES   HEALTH
mygameserver-build    2/3       1                  Healthy
```

If the server works on the local Thundernetes cluster, it should also work on PlayFab. You can now move on to deploy it to PlayFab.

Creating a Build in PlayFab

Now you have everything to create a build in PlayFab. Choose Multiplayer ➤ Builds ➤ New Build. Upload the earlier created docker image to the provided registry.

Check with Docker that the image is available:

```
docker image ls mygameserver-image
```

In PlayFab's New Build form, select the Upload to Container Registry link. Then, click the Copy Docker Login command. This will allow you to log in to the container registry. Execute it on your command line:

```
docker login -u <username> -p <password> <registryId>.
azurecr.io
```

Create the image using the registry:

```
docker build -t <registryId>.azurecr.io/mygameserver-
image:0.1 .
```

Upload it to the registry:

```
docker push <registryId>.azurecr.io/mygameserver-image:0.1
```

After you have uploaded the image, fill in the form as shown in Figure 3-3. Because this image contains the game server files, you don't need to ZIP it and upload it again.

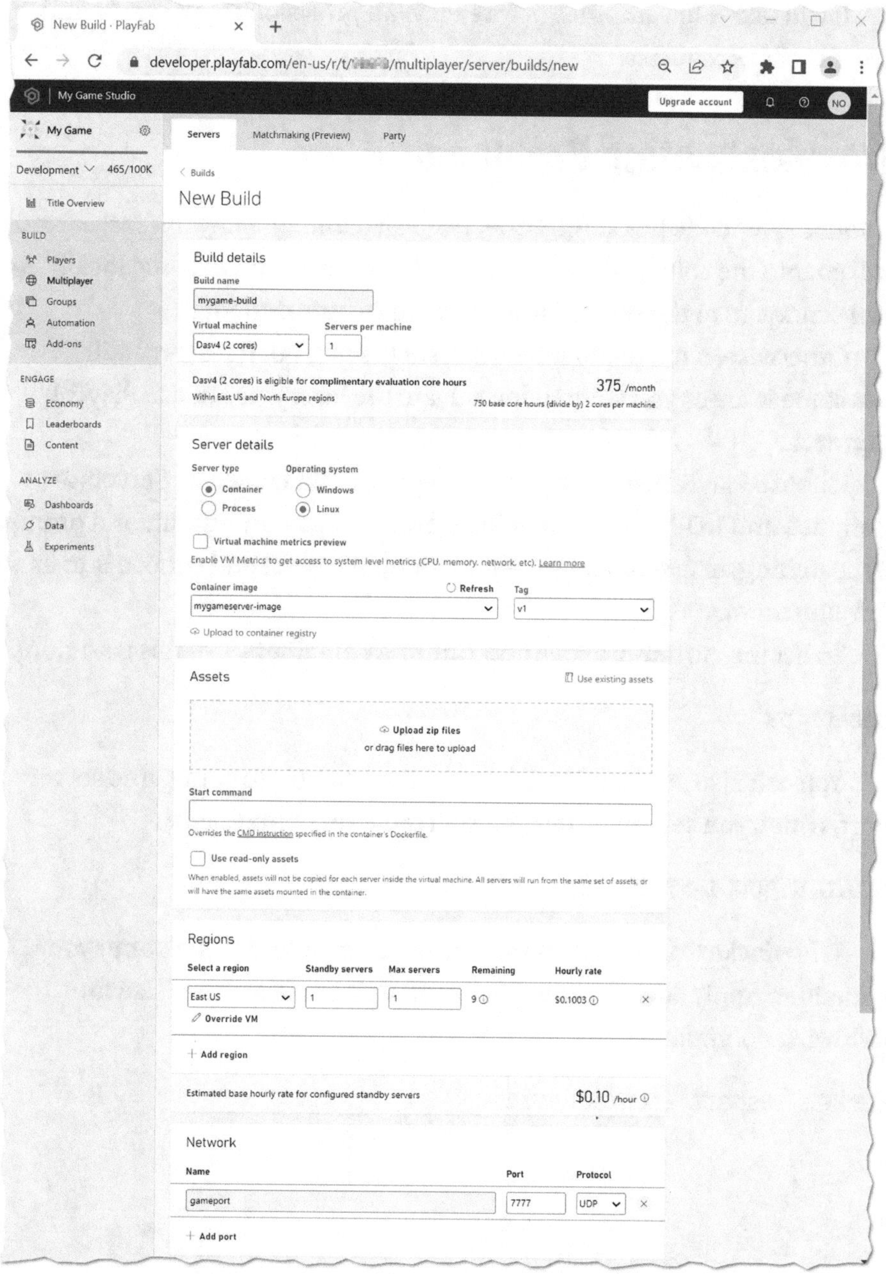

Figure 3-3. *Creating a new build in PlayFab*

It will take a few minutes before PlayFab provisions your server and accepts client requests.

Troubleshooting Problems

If your server code has some issue, PlayFab cannot deploy the server, and it will go into the Unhealthy state. Here, you can only try to debug locally, as you cannot go to the server directly with a remote desktop.

Otherwise, if the deployment was successful, but the server still has some issue or you want to investigate the logs, you can use PlayFab Connect.

Choose PlayFab ➤ Multiplayer ➤ <your build name> ➤ Servers ➤ Connect, and RDP onto the machine. You should start a command prompt by searching for cmd on the server. Then right-click it and choose Run as Administrator.

To list the currently active and running containers, use this command:

```
docker ps
```

You can also see how Docker maps the VM port to your game server port, which you set up in Unity at the Transport component:

```
0.0.0.0:30001->7777/udp
```

With docker inspect, you can get runtime information about your container. Apply docker ps to get the container ID and then use the following command:

```
docker inspect <containerid>
```

You can also inspect the logs coming from each server. You can see the actual state of your server and follow the changes with the following command:

```
docker logs <containerid> --follow
```

```
state: PlayFab.MultiplayerAgent.Model.HeartbeatRequest, payload:
{"CurrentGameState":"StandingBy","CurrentGameHealth":null,
"CurrentPlayers":[]}
```

```
Operation: Continue, Maintenance:, State: StandingBy
```

Another possibility is to go directly onto the container and investigate problems from there (on Linux start sh instead of cmd):

```
docker exec -it <containerid> cmd
```

Creating the Client in Unity

On the client side, you have to call the RequestMultiplayerServer method and pass the following information to PlayFab:

- **BuildId.** This is the ID you get after creating the build in PlayFab's Game Manager. You can find the ID under your build's name (choose Multiplayer ➤ Server ➤ Builds).

- **PreferredRegions.** This must fit to the region configured for your build (currently either EastUS or NorthEurope). You can have multiple regions configured for one build. With this parameter, you can route the player to the closest region to reduce latency.

- **SessionId.** This can be an existing ID, which means
  the player joins an active game session. Or this can be
  a new ID, which means the player starts a new game
  where other players can join.

It is simple to implement, and you can let PlayFab do the heavy work
for you. With these three parameters, you can navigate your clients to the
proper server. Create a new script file PlayFabClient.cs and add it to the
PlayFabClient game object.

```
using System.Collections.Generic;
using UnityEngine;
using Mirror;
using PlayFab.MultiplayerModels;
using PlayFab;
using kcp2k;

public class PlayFabClient : NetworkManager
{
    GameObject playFab;
    public void StartPlayFabClient()
    {
        playFab = GameObject.Find("PlayFab");

        RequestMultiplayerServerRequest requestData = new
        RequestMultiplayerServerRequest();

        requestData.BuildId = playFab.
        GetComponent<PlayFabSettings>().buildId;
        requestData.PreferredRegions = new List<string>() {
        "EastUs" };
        requestData.SessionId = playFab.
        GetComponent<PlayFabSettings>().sessionId;
        if (requestData.SessionId.Equals(""))
```

```
    {
        requestData.SessionId = System.Guid.NewGuid().
        ToString();
        playFab.GetComponent<PlayFabSettings>().sessionId =
        requestData.SessionId;
    }

    PlayFabMultiplayerAPI.RequestMultiplayerServer
    (requestData, OnRequestMultiplayerServer,
    OnRequestMultiplayerServerError);
}

private void OnRequestMultiplayerServer(RequestMultiplayer
ServerResponse response)
{
    this.networkAddress = response.IPV4Address;
    this.GetComponent<KcpTransport>().Port = (ushort)
    response.Ports[0].Num;
    Debug.Log("Server found. IP " + this.networkAddress +
    ":" + this.GetComponent<KcpTransport>().Port);
    Debug.Log("SessionId: " + response.SessionId);
    this.StartClient();
}
private void OnRequestMultiplayerServerError(PlayFab
Error error)
{
    Debug.Log(error.ErrorMessage);
}

}
```

If the request was successful, the OnRequestMultiplayerServer method provides RequestMultiplayerServerResponse, which contains the IP address and port number of the server assigned to this session. You pass this information to the Mirror client, so that it can connect to the listening server.

Extending the ControlPanel

To simulate the client starting a new game, give a button to the Control Panel. Go to the ControlPanel.cs script and simply add a button that allows you to start a PlayFab client:

```
GameObject playFabClient;

private void Start()
    {
        playFabClient = GameObject.Find("PlayFabClient");
    }
void OptionsWindow(int windowID)
    {
        if (GUILayout.Button("Start PlayFab Client"))
        playFabClient.GetComponent<PlayFabClient>().
        StartPlayFabClient();
}
```

Testing

You can start your client from a Unity Editor instance and see if it joins the server automatically. Disable PlayFabServer and enable the PlayFabClient game object. Drag-and-drop your player prefab (Slime) to the Player Prefab field of PlayFabClient. When you start your game, don't forget to authenticate the player first.

If you want to join to the same session, open the cloned project in another Unity Editor. Copy the session ID from `PlayFabSettings` in the original project so a second player can join to the same session. With matchmaking, you can simplify this step. The matchmaker will decide if you can join to an existing session or start a new one.

You can observe how the server changes from `StandingBy` to `Active` in PlayFab's Game Manager, and also back to `StandingBy` when all the players leave.

Now that you have learned how to build and use multiplayer game servers in the backend in PlayFab, the next section shows you how to build the same functionally with Azure.

Azure

It is time to build your server in Azure and compare it to the GBaaS solution. You need a basic understanding of containerization, Docker, Kubernetes, and a general understanding of cloud computing and Azure, as well as Terraform. The earlier chapters help with in this, explaining the main concepts and commands to move forward.

The Problems

Basically, you want your Mirror server to run on a machine, listening on a port, to which you can connect with your clients. The clients only need an IP and a port number for the connection. In theory, you could simply put the Mirror server to a virtual machine in Azure and connect to it to the clients.

However, this solution is too simplistic. You would notice its limitations quickly:

- Every time a new player starts a new game, a new session will start. For additional game sessions, you need additional servers. Thus, you need an automatism to create new servers generated when the players start new game sessions. On the other hand, you need an automatism to deallocate the game server when the game finishes and the players leave the session. You need a mechanism to handle the transition of game server states, i.e. some kind of logic that manages your servers.

- Your player base will increase (hopefully) with time. At the beginning, you might have only ten players, but that can go up to millions of players. The backend should automatically increase the number of servers, or even decrease when fewer player want to use it. This scaling up and down of the infrastructure should happen automatically.

If you go with pure Azure services, you would quickly encounter these problems. You can decide to implement game server management and scaling on your own. That's a lot of work, and I would not suggest it for individuals or small development teams. Here is where Agones, on top of Kubernetes, can be a valid option.

Kubernetes and Agones

Agones is a free, open-source library to host, run, and scale dedicated game servers on top of Kubernetes. Kubernetes is the de facto standard for container orchestration used by many companies around the world. The problem with Kubernetes is that Google originally invented it to manage web-based workloads.

A web session is usually stateless, so a client's request can go once to one server, the next time to another, and it will not disturb the user. In case of games, however, your client needs to communicate with the same server. Also, if the server goes down, the game session is over.

For a stateless web application, this would not be a problem. So Kubernetes could solve the scaling problem, but you need something specific for the game. That is where Agones helps. Agones will manage the state of your game servers throughout the complete lifecycle, from their creation to shutting them down.

With that, you can conclude that the combination of Kubernetes and Agones provides a powerful foundation to host your game servers. If you got to know Thundernetes earlier, you will notice the similarity between them.

Be aware that building a Kubernetes cluster with Agones is relatively easy, but more challenging than building it with a GBaaS solution, such as PlayFab. This chapter goes through each step, explaining what happens and why. For this solution, the developer should understand not only the game code but also the infrastructure code.

Building Agones

Nothing is easier than installing Agones on a Kubernetes (AKS) cluster. Download the following Terraform script:

```
https://github.com/googleforgames/agones/blob/
release-1.24.0/examples/terraform-submodules/aks/module.tf
```

Copy it into an empty folder and execute the following commands:

```
terraform init
terraform apply
```

After the Terraform script finishes, you receive a readily built AKS cluster with Agones on top. You could deploy the game. In reality, you will face the following problems:

- The Terraform script will not run through completely at first. You can start debugging to determine why.

- You don't know what exactly you have deployed with the Terraform script. That can cost a lot of money. Using resources in the cloud costs money, so you have to be careful as to which services you use.

- You want to understand the infrastructure (code) as much as you want to understand the application code. Otherwise, you cannot fix, extend, or operate it.

- You should only deploy the minimum required infrastructure resources to minimize costs.

The solution is to build and learn your infrastructure step-by-step.

Three Steps to Build the Infrastructure

I suggest using Visual Studio Code with the related plugins and terminal window for developing the Terraform scripts and executing CLI commands.

To have some structure, you can put each resource in its own file (such as aks.tf, acr.tf, and so on). When you execute `terraform apply`, Terraform will go through all the files in the current folder.

Later, if you want to extend the infrastructure with additional resources, you can also distribute the Terraform code in multiple folders and modularize it.

Figure 3-4 shows the steps needed to build the infrastructure for the game servers on Azure. You can divide the steps into three major blocks:

1. Provisioning the Azure infrastructure resources (such as the AKS cluster, public IP, or the container registry).

2. Deploying Agones and the game server image on top of the infrastructure you created in the earlier step.

3. Creating Agones resources (such as fleets) for running game servers, automatically scaled, and providing the server IP and port of ready servers for clients.

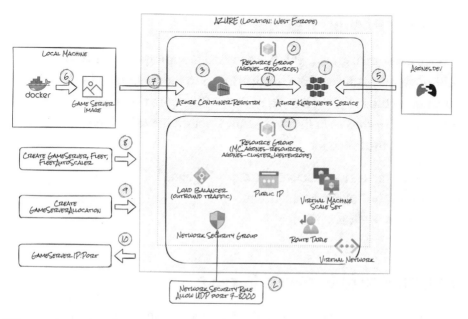

Figure 3-4. *Implementing Agones on Azure*

To summarize what you need to build: first, you will provision a couple of resources with the help of Terraform in Azure. This starts with an AKS cluster, which comes with a lot of additional resources such as load balancer, network security group, and public IP. After the Kubernetes cluster is running, you will deploy and configure Agones on top of it.

You will also need to create a container registry to store the server image. From this registry, Kubernetes deploys the game servers as needed. Agones will manage the game servers by organizing them in fleets and allocate according to the needs of your clients.

The next sections go through these steps in detail.

Provisioning Azure Resources

You take the Terraform code from the previous chapters and extend it with the resources built in this chapter.

Create a Resource Group

Create a resource group, which is a logical grouping of Azure resources. Although the resource group itself is location independent, it shows the location of the included resources. You will refer to this location's value from other resources in the next steps. Create a file called resourcegroup.tf and add the following content:

```
resource "azurerm_resource_group" "agones" {
    name     = "agones-resources"
    location = "West Europe"
}
```

Build Azure Kubernetes Service

You create the core component, the Azure Kubernetes (AKS) cluster, next. Note that even though the Terraform code looks short, Azure will generate several additional resources as well in the subscription.

Here you refer to the location you set in the previous step on the resource group and to the resource group (agones-resources) itself, so you should add the AKS cluster to that group.

A node on Kubernetes means a virtual machine, a virtual machine is a scale set in Azure. At the default_node_pool you define the type of the virtual machine you want to use under the AKS cluster. The Standard_B2 is one of the cheapest (if not the cheapest) virtual machine, so for experimenting and building the infrastructure, it is the most cost effective. You can also choose to have only one node (one VM) for the same reason. In production, you can increase this based on the number of players.

It is important to set the enable_node_public_ip to get public IPs on nodes. Otherwise, it will not be possible to access the servers from the outside world. Create a file called aks.tf with the following content:

```
resource "azurerm_kubernetes_cluster" "agones" {
    name                  = "agones-cluster"
    location              = azurerm_resource_group.agones.location
    resource_group_name   = azurerm_resource_group.agones.name
    dns_prefix            = "agones"

    default_node_pool {
    name                  = "default"
    node_count            = 1
    vm_size               = "Standard_B2s"
    enable_node_public_ip = true
    }

    identity {
      type = "SystemAssigned"
    }
}
```

When creating a Kubernetes cluster in Azure, Azure will automatically create multiple AKS supporting infrastructure components. For those it will create a new resource group (which starts with MC_). If you observe the content of this resource group, you will find the following components generated:

- **Network security group**: This is a kind of firewall to control which inbound and outbound traffic Azure allows. It is associated with the AKS subnet. You can extend this with your own network security rule.

- **Route table:** This determines where to route the traffic; what the next hop IP address is.

- **Virtual machine scale set**: This includes the VM instances; the nodes under the Kubernetes cluster.

- **Load balancer**: This is only for outbound traffic. The VMs under AKS sometimes have to reach the Internet, for example, to download updates.

- **Public IP**: This is attached to the Load Balancer for outbound traffic.

- **Virtual network**: All the components are in a virtual network, which you can further divide into subnets. This determines the internal address space and IPs for the servers.

Verifying the Cluster

After you have all the terraform scripts done, run them with the following:

```
terraform apply
```

If Terraform finishes without any problem, you have the Kubernetes cluster in Azure. You can check this in the Azure Portal or through the command line.

Kubectl is the command you use to manage Kuberentes resources. Before using it, you should configure the kubeconfig file. With the help of Azure's CLI, you can get the cluster's credentials easily. With the following command, you put cluster administrator credentials in a file:

```
az aks get-credentials --name agones-cluster --resource-group
agones-resources --file agones-kubernetes-config --admin
```

Without giving a filename, the credentials will go into the default $HOME/.kube/config file. You need to set the KUBECONFIG environment variable to your own configuration file, otherwise kubectl will look for the default kubeconfig file:

```
set KUBECONFIG=C:\Agones\agones-kubernetes-config
```

You have to make sure that you are in the right context. You can have multiple clusters, for example, the one you created with Minikube locally. Make sure that kubectl works with is context you created in Azure.

```
kubectl config get-contexts
```

```
CURRENT    NAME                  CLUSTER
AUTHINFO                         NAMESPACE
*          agones-cluster-admin  agones-cluster
clusterAdmin_agones-resources_agones-cluster
```

Add a Network Security Rule

Agones will generate the port numbers for the servers between 7000 and 8000. With the AKS cluster, you have already received a network security group. However, you need to add a new rule to allow inbound UDP traffic for the ports between 7000 and 8000.

You need to apply a small trick to get the name of the network security group. Terraform provides the opportunity to read resources, which were not directly created by Terraform itself. In this case, you only created the Kubernetes cluster by Terraform, which then created the corresponding network security group, so in Terraform it is not directly defined. To resolve this, you need to search for a network security group type in the node resource group and pass it as a parameter to the network security rule. Create a new file called nsg.tf and add the network security group to it:

```
data "azurerm_resources" "agones" {
  resource_group_name = azurerm_kubernetes_cluster.agones.node_
  resource_group
  type = "Microsoft.Network/networkSecurityGroups"
}
```

```
resource "azurerm_network_security_rule" "gameserver" {
    name                         = "gameserver"
    priority                     = 100
    direction                    = "Inbound"
    access                       = "Allow"
    protocol                     = "Udp"
    source_port_range            = "*"
    destination_port_range       = "7000-8000"
    source_address_prefix        = "*"
    destination_address_prefix   = "*"
    resource_group_name          = azurerm_kubernetes_cluster.
                                   agones.node_resource_group
    network_security_group_name = data.azurerm_resources.agones.
                                   resources.0.name
}
```

Be aware that this may not give you the network security group name upon the first Terraform apply. This is an API issue. In this case you need to run Terraform later again or copy the network security group's name directly into the Terraform code. Fortunately, it is generated from the DNS prefix of the nodes. If it is agones, then the name of the network security group will always be aks-agentpool-55978144-nsg.

Build Azure Container Registry

You also need an Azure internal container registry, where you store the server images. Kubernetes will pull this image and create a container when Agones requires a new server. By enabling the admin user, you can later push the game server image to ACR with the provided username and password. Create a new file called acr.tf and add the following resource:

```
resource "azurerm_container_registry" "agones" {
  name                 = "agonesacr"
  resource_group_name  = "agones-resources"
  location             = azurerm_resource_group.agones.location
  sku                  = "Basic"
  admin_enabled        = true
}
```

Accessing ACR from AKS

It is important to attach the Azure Container Registry to AKS, otherwise AKS cannot pull images from there. You will store the images in ACR and AKS should be able to pull images anytime it needs. Note that you can also do this step through CLI, after you have AKS and ACR. This is also valid for all the terraform code, but in this case, you may find it more convenient to do it with the CLI.

```
az aks update -n agones-cluster -g agones-resources --attach-acr agonesacr
```

However, you want that all the infrastructure code is in Terraform. Let's attach the ACR to the AKS. Here you will use the Azure Active Directory provider (azuread). First, register an application in Azure AD. Let's extend the acr.tf with the following:

```
resource "azuread_application" "agones" {
  display_name = "agones"
}
```

Then create a service principal and associate it with the registered application:

```
resource "azuread_service_principal" "agones" {
  application_id = azuread_application.agones.application_id
}
```

Add a password to the service principal. Azure will automatically generate it and Terraform will export the value of it:

```
resource "azuread_service_principal_password" "agones" {
  service_principal_id = azuread_service_principal.agones.id
}
```

In the scope of ACR, you need to assign the AcrPull role to the service principal:

```
resource "azurerm_role_assignment" "agones" {
  scope                = azurerm_container_registry.agones.id
  role_definition_name = "AcrPull"
  principal_id         = azuread_service_principal.agones.
                         object_id
}
```

Finally, change the system assigned identity of the AKS cluster to this newly created service principal. Make sure that the service principal is newer than the AKS cluster with the depends_on meta argument.

```
resource "azurerm_kubernetes_cluster" "agones" {
...
  # identity {
  #  type = "SystemAssigned"
  # }

  service_principal {
    client_id     = azuread_application.agones.application_id
    client_secret = azuread_service_principal_password.
                    agones.value

  }
```

```
depends_on = [
    azuread_application.agones,
    azuread_service_principal.agones,
    azuread_service_principal_password.agones
  ]
}
```

With this method, you have allowed AKS to pull images from ACR.

Install Agones Using Helm

Now that you have created the Azure infrastructure, it is time to deploy
Agones. With the help of Helm CLI, it is really easy. Helm will use your
kubeconfig. Make sure you are in the right context.

```
helm repo add agones https://agones.dev/chart/stable
helm repo update
helm install my-release --namespace agones-system --create-
namespace agones/agones
```

Creating and Deploying the Server

After you have deployed the Agones infrastructure, you have to develop the
server code in Unity that will receive the client requests. After building the
code, create an image from it and push it to the container registry in Azure.

Implementing the Server

You have to add Agones Unity SDK to Unity first. Go to Unity ➤ Window ➤
Package Manager ➤ + ➤ Add Package from GIT URL..., and copy the
following URL to the text box:

```
https://github.com/googleforgames/agones.git?path=/sdks/
unity#v1.22.0
```

In Unity Editor, create two new game objects, AzureServer and AzureClient, and add them as child objects of the Azure game object. You should also add the two core Mirror components, NetworkManager and KcpTransport, to them. Drag-and-drop the player prefab to the Player prefab field.

Create a new script called AzureServer.cs and fill it with the following:

```
using UnityEngine;
using Agones;

public class AzureServer : MonoBehaviour
{
    private AgonesSdk agones = null;

    async void Start()
    {
        agones = GetComponent<AgonesSdk>();
        bool ok = await agones.Connect();
        if (ok)
        {
            Debug.Log("Server is connected.");
        }
        else
        {
            Debug.Log("Server failed to connect.");
            Application.Quit();
        }
        ok = await agones.Ready();
        if (ok)
        {
            Debug.Log("Server is ready.");
        }
        else
```

```
{
        Debug.Log("Server ready failed.");
        Application.Quit();
    }
  }
}
```

Without these calls, the game server will be stuck in Unhealthy state. You have to add the AgonesSDK component to the AzureServer game object.

Now leave only the AzureServer game object enabled and create a server build. Go to Unity Editor, File ➤ Build Settings..., select Dedicated Server as Platform, and set the Target Platform to Linux. Click Build and select a new folder for the server files.

Create Your Game Server Image

In this step, you create the game server image. Go to the folder where you created your server build. Create a file named Dockerfile and copy it into the game server folder. This describes your image. When a container is created, your server will start automatically. Also, you have to wait for some time until the sidecar container starts up.

```
FROM ubuntu:18.04
WORKDIR /game
ADD . .
CMD sleep 2 && ./mygameserver.x86_64
```

In the same folder, execute Docker to build the image. It is important to set the tag of the registry to the target ACR. You can also set the images with the actual version numbers:

```
docker build -t agonesacr.azurecr.io/mygame-server:0.1 .
```

As a result, the image is stored locally, and you can check it with the following command:

```
docker images agonesacr.azurecr.io/mygame-server:0.1
```

Push the Image to ACR

Now you just want to push the image to ACR. You need to log in to ACR with Docker. Let's use Azure's CLI to get the credentials for the docker login.

```
az acr credential show --name agonesacr
docker login agonesacr.azurecr.io
```

If the login was successful, you can push the game server image to ACR:

```
docker push agonesacr.azurecr.io/mygame-server:0.1
```

Now AKS will be able to pull the image from ACR as soon as Agones requests it.

Agones Configuration

You have configure in the Terraform script that you have public IPs reachable for the clients on the nodes. Agones will create the game servers on demand and assign a unique port to them. This IP:port pair will tell the clients exactly which server they should use for their session. See Figure 3-5.

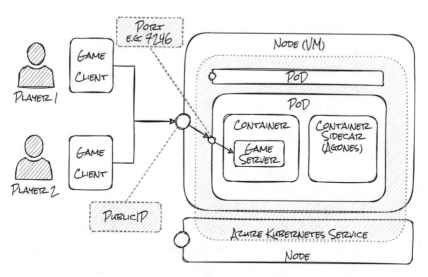

Figure 3-5. *Access of game servers in Agones*

Agones works with custom resource definitions. There are built-in resources in Kubernetes, such as pods, services, deployments, and so on. Agones defines new ones, for example, the gameserver resource. Let's create one game server. Create a yaml file (called gameserver.yaml) and add the following content to it:

```
apiVersion: "agones.dev/v1"
kind: GameServer
metadata:
  generateName: "mygame-server-"
spec:
  ports:
  - name: default
    portPolicy: Dynamic
    containerPort: 7777
  template:
    spec:
      containers:
```

```
- name: mygame-server
  image: agonesacr.azurecr.io/mygame-server:0.1
  resources:
    requests:
      memory: "128Mi"
      cpu: "128m"
    limits:
      memory: "128Mi"
      cpu: "128m"
```

In this file, you describe the parameters of a GameServer, such as its name, the container's port, the image used, the requested CPU, and the container memory. It is important to give it enough resources or the pod will simply crash and never run.

Now create this resource on the AKS cluster:

```
kubectl create -f gameserver.yaml
```

With the following command, you can check if the game server is in the ready state:

```
kubectl get gs
NAME                    STATE       ADDRESS         PORT
NODE                                AGE
mygame-server-rfb6j     Scheduled   40.118.53.172   7833
aks-default-29929622-vmss000000     3m42s
```

You can also check if the pods are running:

```
kubectl get pods
NAME                    READY   STATUS    RESTARTS   AGE
mygame-server-8hdln     2/2     Running   0          36s
```

You can test if your game client can connect to the address and port. To do so, you have to temporarily disable the Azure game object and enable NetworkManager. Use a NetworkManagerHUD component to provide the server IP and add the port number to the KcpTransport in the inspector.

Note that the IP is the public IP address of the node, and the port is generated and assigned to the game server by Agones.

Create a Fleet

Having one game server is not enough, because then you can only start one game session. You need a fleet of servers, and Agones helps with this. Fleet is a custom resource in Kubernetes implemented by Agones, which generates multiple servers according to your definitions.

Create a file (called fleet.yaml) and fill it with the following content:

```
apiVersion: "agones.dev/v1"
kind: Fleet
metadata:
  name: mygame-server
spec:
  replicas: 5
  template:
    spec:
      ports:
      - name: default
        containerPort: 7777
      template:
        spec:
          containers:
          - name: mygame-server
            image: agonesacr.azurecr.io/mygame-server:0.1
            resources:
              requests:
```

```
      memory: "128Mi"
      cpu: "128m"
    limits:
      memory: "128Mi"
      cpu: "128m"
```

It is similar to the GameServer resource. The only difference is the replicas parameter, which will determine the number of game servers generated automatically. If you remove a game server, the fleet will generate a new one. Practically, if players exit a session, the game server goes into shutdown state, and it will be removed from Kubernetes.

Create the fleet resource and check on the number of game servers:

```
kubectl create -f fleet.yaml
kubectl get gs
```

Tip   If you want to start over again without any game servers deployed, use the following command to remove all the game servers and their pods:

```
kubectl delete gs,fleet,pod --all
```

Fleet Autoscaler

The fleet autoscaler allows you to create and remove game servers dynamically according to the current demand. Also, you don't want to reserve CPU and memory in advance.

Create a new file (called fleetautoscaler.yaml) and fill it with the following content:

```
apiVersion: "autoscaling.agones.dev/v1"
kind: FleetAutoscaler
metadata:
  name: mygame-server-autoscaler
```

```
spec:
  fleetName: mygame-server
  policy:
    type: Buffer
    buffer:
      bufferSize: 2
      minReplicas: 2
      maxReplicas: 10
```

The fleetName must match the name of the earlier defined fleet. Using min and maxReplicas, you can set the limits of scaling. The bufferSize shows the number of game servers that are always ready. Note that the replicas setting of the fleet resource will be overwritten by the fleet autoscaler. In this example, by default there will be only two game servers ready. If one becomes allocated, a new one will be added as ready. That way, there are always two servers in the ready state.

Game Server Allocation

The Game Server Allocation chooses a ready server and provides its IP and port to the calling client. Create a gameserverallocator.yaml file:

```
apiVersion: "allocation.agones.dev/v1"
kind: GameServerAllocation
spec:
  required:
    matchLabels:
      agones.dev/fleet: mygame-server
```

Execute this yaml from the command line:

```
kubectl create -f gameserverallocation.yaml -o yaml
```

The output should contain the allocated server's IP and port. You can check that one of the servers is allocated, and the fleet autoscaler keeps two servers ready for new allocations:

```
kubectl get gs
NAME                         STATE       ADDRESS
PORT    NODE                             AGE
mygame-server-r9ghp-7chqq    Ready       40.118.53.172
7094    aks-default-29929622-vmss000000  115s
mygame-server-r9ghp-8dfs4    Ready       40.118.53.172
7368    aks-default-29929622-vmss000000  49s
mygame-server-r9ghp-fn9jn    Allocated   40.118.53.172
7701    aks-default-29929622-vmss000000  115s
```

Extending the Control Panel

Now you can allow players to join these servers. You need a simple way to manually provide the server IP and port to the client. For that, you have to extend the control panel with the following code:

```
using Mirror;
using kcp2k;

public class ControlPanel : MonoBehaviour
{
    public const int AZURE_STARTCLIENT = 4;

    string serverIP = "";
    string serverPort = "";

    GameObject azureClient;
```

```
private void Start()
{
    azureClient = GameObject.Find("AzureClient");
}

void OnGUI()
{
    if (selection == AZURE_STARTCLIENT)
        GUILayout.Window(0, new Rect(0, 0, 300, 0),
        StartAzureClient, "Start Azure Client");
}

void OptionsWindow(int windowID)
{
    if (GUILayout.Button("Start Azure Client"))
        selection = AZURE_STARTCLIENT;
}

void StartAzureClient(int windowID)
{
    GUILayout.Label("Server IP:");
    serverIP = GUILayout.TextField(serverIP, 20);
    GUILayout.Label("Server Port:");
    serverPort = GUILayout.TextField(serverPort, 10);

    if (GUILayout.Button("Start Azure Client"))
    {
        azureClient.GetComponent<NetworkManager>().
        networkAddress = serverIP;
        azureClient.GetComponent<KcpTransport>().Port =
        (ushort)int.Parse(serverPort);
        azureClient.GetComponent<NetworkManager>().
        StartClient();
    }
```

```
    if (GUILayout.Button("Cancel"))
        selection = ROOTMENU;
  }
}
```

Copy any running server's IP and port into the text fields of the control panel, click Start Azure Client, and verify that the client can connect to the server and the character appears on the screen.

The next chapter extends this with an automatic matchmaker, so that players will be automatically connected to ready servers without having to type in the server IP and port.

Summary

In this chapter, you implemented the PlayFab and Azure dedicated servers, which allow online multiplayer gaming from any distance between players. You learned that you need much more effort to implement it in Azure. On the other hand, you have endless possibilities to customize the solution to your needs. But you may think that PlayFab costs much more. Let's do a quick comparison.

PlayFab provides a generous 750 hours (for one core) free evaluation time. If you compare the price after the evaluation period, it aligns closely to Azure VM costs. Table 3-1 compares the cost of the PlayFab and Azure virtual machines.

Table 3-1. *Prices of PlayFab and Azure Virtual Machines*

Instance	vCPU	RAM	Storage	PlayFab	Azure	Difference
D2asv4	2	8 GiB	16 GiB	$0.208/hour	$0.199/hour	**$0.009/hour**
D4asv4	4	16 GiB	32 GiB	$0.4159/hour	$0.398/hour	**$0.0178/ hour**
D8asv4	8	32 GiB	64 GiB	$0.8318/hour	$0.796/hour	**$0.0358/ hour**
D16asv4	16	64 GiB	128 GiB	$1.6636/hour	$1.592/hour	**$0.0716/ hour**

As you can see, there is almost no difference between the price of the PlayFab and Azure pay-as-you-go instances. However, the difference becomes considerable if you are ready to buy reserved instances on Azure, as shown in Table 3-2.

Table 3-2. *Prices of PlayFab and Reserved Virtual Machines in Azure*

Instance	PlayFab	Azure 1Y	Azure 3Y	Difference
D2asv4	$0.208/hour	$0.1549/hour	$0.1323/hour	**$0.0757/hour**
D4asv4	$0.4159/hour	$0.3098/hour	$0.2645/hour	**$0.1514/hour**
D8asv4	$0.8318/hour	$0.6198/hour	$0.5290/hour	**$0.3028/hour**
D16asv4	$1.6636/hour	$1.2394/hour	$1.0579/hour	**$0.6057/hour**

If you decide to host your server purely on Azure VMs, you will pay around the same price. But if you are ready to reserve VMs for up to three years, you can save 30-40 percent, compared to PlayFab hosting. Be aware that on Azure you will have additional costs (such as load balancers, firewalls, and monitoring), while in PlayFab you only have to pay for the VMs.

Review Questions

1. Why do you need dedicated game servers hosted in the cloud?

2. What are the possible ways to host game servers? How do they compare?

3. What is a build in PlayFab?

4. What are the options to troubleshoot issues with the PlayFab server?

5. What are the problems with a single virtual machine when implementing server hosting for multiplayer games?

6. Which features of Kubernetes and Agones support multiplayer games?

7. What is the role of containerization when using Kubernetes?

8. How do you access game servers in Agones?

9. What is the purpose of fleets in Agones?

10. Compare the realization of multiplayer game servers regarding cost and complexity.

CHAPTER 4

Matchmaking

Matchmaking is a key feature when developing online multiplayer games. It helps players find opponents based on their attributes, such as rank, skill level, or location.

A well-implemented matchmaking feature can highly improve player engagement. A beginner player doesn't want to play with an advanced one. The matchmaker feature also finds players close to each other to minimize latency.

Players can find each other in a lobby, or in a more automatic way by matchmaking. This chapter explains how to implement matchmaking with the help of PlayFab and Azure.

First, the chapter reviews the ways that players can find each other to start an online game session. It then goes through the matchmaking process in PlayFab and implements it. Finally, the matched players start the game on an automatically allocated server.

In Azure, you have to implement your own matchmaking logic. For that, you'll use Azure Functions and a PostgreSQL database. The game clients will reach the matchmaker backend through Azure API Management using REST calls.

Ultimately, you will integrate the server allocation mechanism from the previous chapter using the matchmaking process. This allows matched players to automatically start online game sessions.

© Balint Bors 2023
B. Bors, *Game Backend Development*, https://doi.org/10.1007/978-1-4842-8910-5_4

Bringing Players Together

Figure 4-1 shows a typical process that players need to follow before starting a game session with others. This process can vary and you should align it to your actual game's needs.

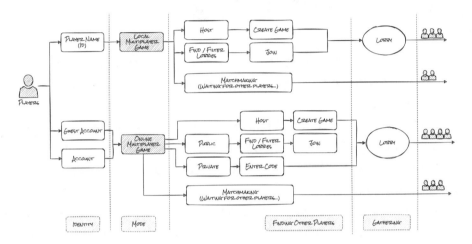

Figure 4-1. *Player's journey from login to a game session*

Let's review the phases of this process. Each player who wants to play in a multiplayer game session needs an unique *identity*. In single player mode, this is not necessary.

For a local multiplayer game, the authentication is more simple than for an online multiplayer game, because you don't need a globally unique identity. With online multiplayer mode, you can authenticate the players by third-party authentication providers to get a unique identity and create an *account*.

If you don't want to bother the players with a tedious authentication process, you at least have to generate an ID in the background and let them play using a *guest account*.

After players have an identity, they can choose between *local* and *online multiplayer mode*. In the case of a local multiplayer game, the players connect to the local network and enjoy low-latency connections with their friends in the same location. The advantage of this local mode is that you don't need to pay for expensive cloud server hosting. An online multiplayer game allows playing from different networks.

After players decide between local and online mode, the next step is to find other players. Modern games provide two ways for players to get into a game session and play with or against each other. Either they find each other manually, or the game matches them automatically based on certain criteria, such as skill level or location. Let's discuss both of these options:

With the manual way, you implement a *lobby system*, which allows players to wait in virtual rooms for each other and then start the game from there at the same time. They can even communicate and enjoy the time during this stay in the lobby.

Each player can either host a game or join someone else's. Either way, the players end up in a lobby, where they proceed to the game session.

The advantage of this manual way is that the owner of this room determines the parameters for the upcoming game, such as the map type, speed of the game, or difficulty, and others can decide if they want to play with those circumstances.

The automatic way is when your game hands over the players directly to the *matchmaker* without waiting in a lobby. The matchmaker will then find the right match and forward them to a game server. The matchmaker tries to match the best players together as quickly as possible, as long waiting times can annoy players.

A nice feature to add here is to allow players to decide whom they want to play with, instead of matching random players together. In such a scenario, the players agree using a *shared code,* which they use to join their common lobby and game session.

At the end of the process, the player is grouped with other players, and the backend (or some of the clients in the case of a local game) assigns a server to host the game session. The players get the address of this server and they can join and start the game.

The next sections explain how to implement the matchmaking functionality with the help of PlayFab and Azure.

PlayFab

PlayFab provides a convenient way to match players, by using the PlayFab API. It implements the whole matchmaking logic for you, and you just have to set the conditions based on your players. PlayFab also makes it possible to allocate servers and provides the server IP and port to the players.

Configuring PlayFab

In PlayFab, only players who are logged in can take part in the matchmaking process. The method of authentication does not matter, only that the player has an ID, which PlayFab can match to another one.

The *queue* is a core element in PlayFab. It stores tickets submitted by clients. The matchmaking engine will match certain tickets from a specific queue.

In PlayFab's Game Manager, under the title, go to BUILD ➤ Multiplayer ➤ Matchmaking and create a new queue, as shown in Figure 4-2.

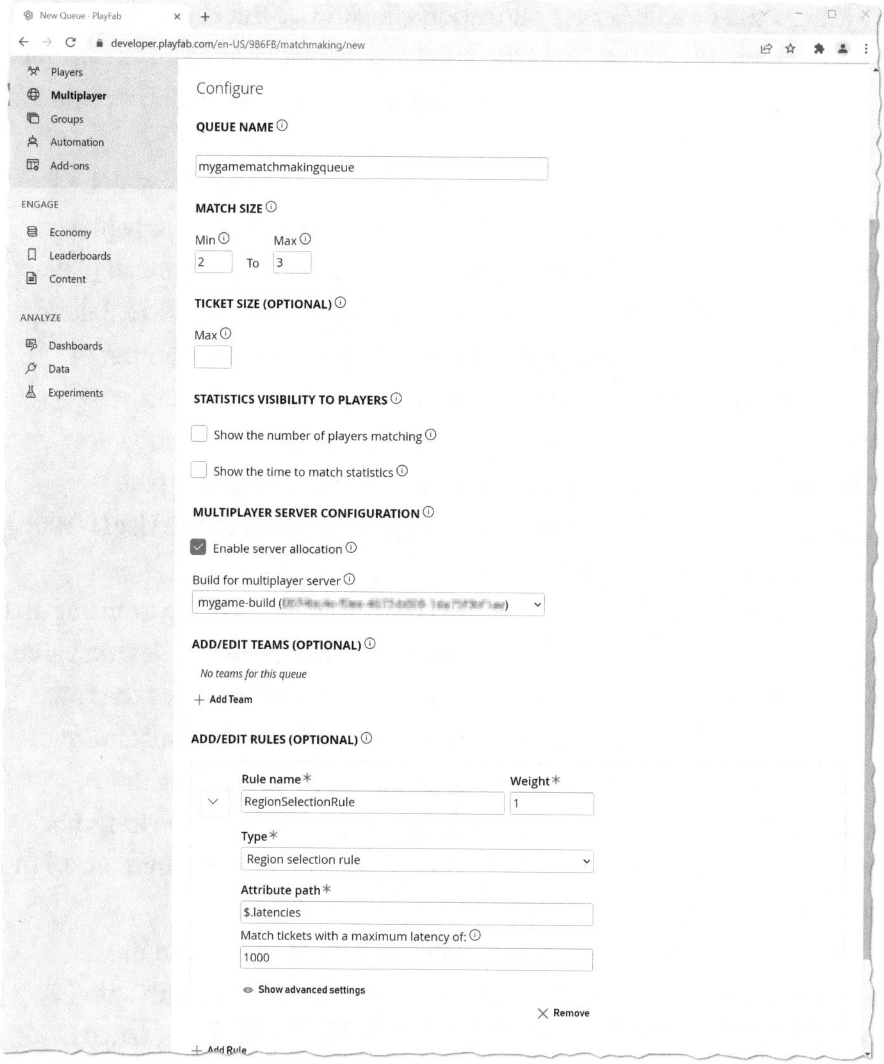

Figure 4-2. New matchmaking queue

First, you must provide a unique Queue Name in your queue. You can also have multiple queues per title. The Match Size determines the number of players in a match. Obviously, it must be at least two.

Check the Enable Server Allocation checkbox. After the matchmaker finds a match, PlayFab assigns the most appropriate server for the players to play on. You also have to select the appropriate build, which was defined in the previous chapter.

Click Add Rule. You can optionally define rules to specify which players PlayFab should match. For example, say you want to match only players with the same skill level, and not match beginners with advanced players.

From the Type field, you can, for example, set the Team Size Balance Rule, which ensures that the playing teams have a similar number of players. Or, the String Equality Rule ensures that a specific attribute is the same in the matching tickets. Using Attribute Source, you can determine how to submit player attributes—either by calling the CreateMatchmakingTicket (in this case, you should pick the User option) or by using the Player Entity object.

The Behavior When the Attribute Is Not Specified setting indicates that, when the player doesn't specify an attribute, PlayFab uses a default value. Another option, If the Attribute Is Missing, lets PlayFab ignore the rule.

Under the advanced settings, you'll find the Seconds Until Optional settings. You can optionally define that the rules become inactive after a certain period of time. This prevents players from waiting too long, just because there is no perfect match. This happens typically when one of the rules is too strict.

For this scenario, select Region Selection Rule as Type. In the Attribute Path field, use JSON path to navigate to the right attribute ($. latencies). Set 1000 for the Match Tickets with Maximum Latency field. This is the maximum allowed latency between the client and the server in milliseconds.

Click Create Queue to continue the matchmaking process.

Matchmaking Process

Figure 4-3 shows the matchmaking process in PlayFab. It contains the followings steps:

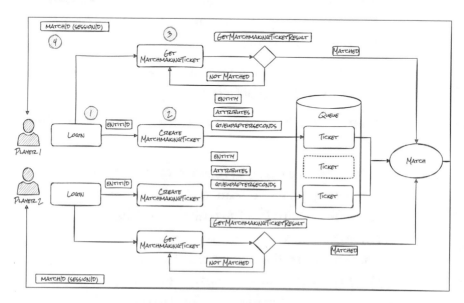

Figure 4-3. *Matchmaking process in PlayFab*

1. The players log in with their accounts or play as guests. If the login process is successful, they get an `entityId`.

2. Each player calls the `CreateMatchmakingTicket` method to create and submit a ticket to the predefined queue, including the following information:

   a. **EntityKey.** This includes the entity ID and type. It can be an individual player (the type is then `title_player_account`) or a group of players.

b. **Attributes.** You can assign any attributes to the actual entity, such as the skill level of the player, progress in the game, or owned items. This is key to the matchmaking process, as the matchmaking rules will decide based on these attributes whether two tickets match. You configure these rules in the PlayFab's Game Manager.

c. **Give up after seconds.** The time to wait before canceling the search for matching players.

d. **Queue name.** The target queue on which the player submits the ticket.

3. After submitting a ticket, the players poll the matchmaking queue. You can implement this using a coroutine in Unity. PlayFab limits the number of requests, but if you poll every six seconds, you are still within the allowed request count. Unfortunately, PlayFab does not currently support any other push mechanism to inform the clients when it finds a match. Keep on polling the queue until you have a match. Then, stop polling. As a result, all the matched clients will get a `matchId`.

4. The `matchId` is actually the `sessionId`. All the matched players receive the same `sessionId`, so they can request a server in the same way as they would without the matchmaking process.

Now that you know the steps, let's continue developing the client in Unity.

Developing the Client

Now create a new script file, called PlayFabMatchmaking.cs. Add it to the existing PlayFab game object, so that you can easily access the entityId from the authentication process. With the following method, you will create a matchmaking ticket in PlayFab:

```
using System.Collections;
using UnityEngine;
using PlayFab;
using PlayFab.MultiplayerModels;
using kcp2k;
public class PlayFabMatchmaking : MonoBehaviour
{
    string ticketId;
    private IEnumerator coroutine;
    GameObject playFabClient;
    string myQueueName = "mygamematchmakingqueue";
    public void StartPlayFabMatchmaking()
    {
        CreateMatchMakingTicket(GetComponent<PlayFabSettings>
        ().entityId);
        playFabClient = GameObject.Find("PlayFabClient");
    }
    public void CreateMatchMakingTicket(string entityId)
    {
        PlayFabMultiplayerAPI.CreateMatchmakingTicket(
        new CreateMatchmakingTicketRequest
        {
            Creator = new MatchmakingPlayer
            {
                Entity = new EntityKey
```

```
        {
            Id = entityId,
            Type = "title_player_account",
        },

        Attributes = new MatchmakingPlayerAttributes
        {
            DataObject = new
            {
                latencies = new object[]
                    {
                        new {
                            region = "NorthEurope",
                            latency = 100
                        },
                        new {
                            region = "EastUs",
                            latency = 150
                        }
                    }
            },
        },
    },

    QueueName = myQueueName,
},

this.OnMatchmakingTicketCreated,
this.OnMatchmakingError);
    }

}
```

If everything went fine (OnMatchmakingTicketCreated), call your polling coroutine every six seconds to check if PlayFab found a match:

```
private void OnMatchmakingTicketCreated(CreateMatchmaking
TicketResult obj)
{
    Debug.Log("Matchmaking Ticket Created: " + obj.
    TicketId);
    ticketId = obj.TicketId;
    coroutine = WaitAndGetMatchingTicket(6.0f);
    StartCoroutine(coroutine);
}
private void OnMatchmakingError(PlayFabError obj)
{
    Debug.Log("Matchmaking Error: " + obj.Error);
}

private IEnumerator WaitAndGetMatchingTicket(float
waitTime)
{
    while (true)
    {
        GetMatchingTicket();
        yield return new WaitForSeconds(waitTime);
    }
}
public void GetMatchingTicket()
{

    PlayFabMultiplayerAPI.GetMatchmakingTicket(
    new GetMatchmakingTicketRequest
    {
        TicketId = ticketId,
```

```
        QueueName = "mygamematchmakingqueue",
    },
    this.OnGetMatchmakingTicket,
    this.OnMatchmakingError);
}
```

If PlayFab finds a match, the client stops polling. With the GetMatch method, you request the server IP and port of the allocated server. With this information, you can now start the Mirror client:

```
private void OnGetMatchmakingTicket(GetMatchmakingTicket
Result obj)
{
    Debug.Log("GetMatchmakingTicket: " + obj.Status);

    if (obj.Status.Equals("Matched"))
    {
        StopCoroutine(coroutine);
        PlayFabMultiplayerAPI.GetMatch(new GetMatchRequest
        {
            QueueName = myQueueName,
            MatchId = obj.MatchId

        },
        this.OnGetMatchResult,
        this.OnMatchmakingError);
    }
}

private void OnGetMatchResult(GetMatchResult result)
{
    playFabClient.GetComponent<PlayFabClient>().
    networkAddress = result.ServerDetails.IPV4Address;
```

```
    playFabClient.GetComponent<KcpTransport>().Port =
    (ushort)result.ServerDetails.Ports[0].Num;
    playFabClient.GetComponent<PlayFabClient>().
    StartClient();
}
```

The player may want to interrupt the matchmaking process, because it can take longer. You can implement a cancel method, which withdraws the matchmaking ticket:

```
public void CancelPlayFabMatchmaking()
{
    StopCoroutine(coroutine);
    CancelMatchmakingTicket();
}
private void CancelMatchmakingTicket()
{
    PlayFabMultiplayerAPI.CancelMatchmakingTicket(
    new CancelMatchmakingTicketRequest
    {
        QueueName = myQueueName,
        TicketId = ticketId,
    },
    this.OnTicketCanceled,
    this.OnMatchmakingError);
}

private void OnTicketCanceled(CancelMatchmakingTicket
Result obj)
{
    Debug.Log("Ticket cancelled.");
}
```

Extending the Control Panel

Let's extend the Control Panel by adding a button that starts the matchmaking process. You can also let the player cancel let the player cancel it:

```
bool playFabMatchmakingInProgress = false;
bool azureMatchmakingInProgress = false;

void OptionsWindow(int windowID)
{
    if (!playFabMatchmakingInProgress)
    {
        if (GUILayout.Button("Start PlayFab Matchmaking"))
        {
            playFab.GetComponent<PlayFabMatchmaking>().
            StartPlayFabMatchmaking();
            playFabMatchmakingInProgress = true;
        }
    }
    else if (playFabMatchmakingInProgress)
    {
        if (GUILayout.Button("Cancel PlayFab Matchmaking"))
        {
            playFab.GetComponent<PlayFabMatchmaking>().
            CancelPlayFabMatchmaking();
            playFabMatchmakingInProgress = false;
        }
    }
}
```

Testing

Start both of your game instances in two separate Unity Editors. Log in with both users and start the matchmaking process. The two players should find each other and automatically start the same game session.

Note   PlayFab's matchmaking also works without enabling server allocation, although it is very convenient to integrate them.

Compared to the result in the previous chapter, you now don't need to copy the `sessionId` to the second player. PlayFab's matchmaker process does this for you.

As you may have noticed, it is pretty easy and straightforward to implement matchmaking using a GBaaS. You'll now move on and create a custom matchmaker in Azure.

Azure

Matchmaking using pure cloud services is a more complex task and I advise that you do it only if you have strong fundamentals in the actual cloud technology. This section describes how to implement matchmaking with Azure cloud services. Before going into the details, it is important to note two aspects.

In contrast to PlayFab, there are practically endless ways to implement a matchmaking solution in Azure. There is nothing like "the" matchmaking architecture. My intention here is to show one way to implement it, which enables me to discuss the building blocks, execution flow, and the accompanying technologies.

We keep the implementation as simple as possible. You can add endless complexity to the architecture and optimize it. But my goal here is to show you the simplest possible solution so that you can learn about the concepts and technologies without getting lost in the complexity. Later, I give advice on how you could extend this implementation.

Building Blocks

Figure 4-3 illustrates the building blocks for this matchmaking solution.

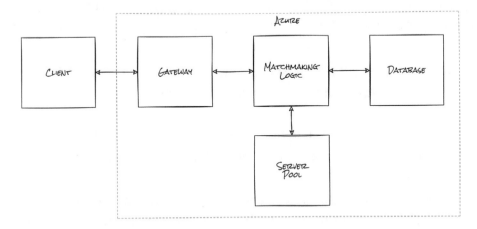

Figure 4-4. *Matchmaking building blocks*

It has the following parts:

- **Client.** The client, in this case Unity, starts the matchmaking process. We will use REST calls, as they are widely used and simple way to communicate.

- **Gateway.** An entry point to the cloud. In this case, the API Management service will expose the APIs to the clients. You can add monitoring and security features as well.

- **Matchmaking logic.** This is the core of the matchmaking solution. You need a piece of code that selects matching players according to predefined rules. You also need some kind of compute service in the cloud where this code can run.

- **Database.** Any time a new player intends to start or join an existing multiplayer session, it needs to send a request to the matchmaking service. You need to store these requests until you find matching players and they start a game.

- **Server pool.** This pool contains servers that are ready for use or already allocated to players. The matchmaker communicates with this component to getting a free, ready-to-use server and provides the address to the players.

When you implement any matchmaking solution, these are the basic building blocks you need. You can then decide which tools and technologies you will use. The next section shows an implementation with Azure.

Note   We use the same basic building blocks (client, gateway, logic, and database) in the following chapters. This makes easier to describe the idea and reduce complexity. This chapter discusses each implementation step in more detail.

Requirements

We tried to keep the requirements for your matchmaking service as simple as possible. As soon as you implement it, you can easily extend or change it and add more complex features.

Each authenticated player should be able to start or join a multiplayer game session. With their request, they should also submit their skill level.

The matchmaking algorithm will find another player at the same skill level and send both players the server address to play on. For the sake of simplicity, you should allow only two players in each game session.

Note that extending the matchmaking logic is very easy; the more challenging part is building the surrounding service.

Figure 4-5 shows what you'll want to achieve. Players 1 and 2 are already matched, as well as Players 3 and 5, because their skill levels are the same. They received a dedicated server from the matchmaker to play on. Players 4 and 6 are waiting for partners, as there are currently no players available at their skill levels.

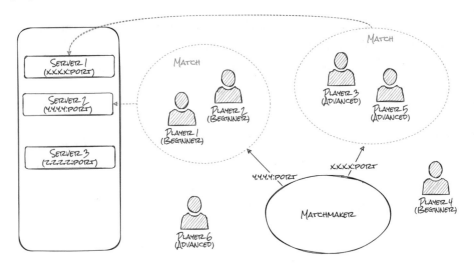

Figure 4-5. *The matchmaking scenario*

Azure Solution Overview

Figure 4-6 shows the matchmaking architecture you will build.

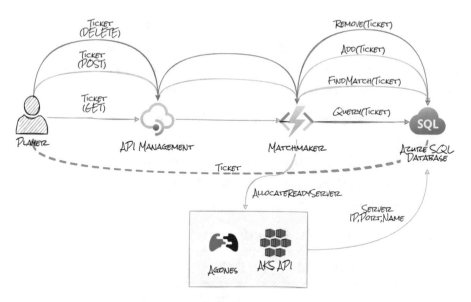

Figure 4-6. *Azure matchmaking solution*

You'll use the following Azure services:

- **Azure Functions.** Azure Functions is a serverless compute service that allows you to focus on your code and not on the underlying server infrastructure. You also only pay for what you consume and it scales up with increasing need.

- **Azure SQL Database for PostgreSQL.** A managed SQL database based on PostgreSQL that stores information about players and their assigned server addresses.

- **Azure API Management.** Publishes APIs for the clients so that they can submit matchmaking requests and poll assigned servers. It has a couple of additional features, such as ensuring security and monitoring traffic.

We'll implement a REST client in Unity, which has two functions: submitting new matchmaking requests and polling for matches. The API Management service forwards these requests to the respective Azure Functions. You will implement the following functions:

> **CreateTicket.** This function receives the request through HTTP REST and writes it to the database. It then directly triggers the Matchmaker function to check if there is a new match. Table 4-1 shows a possible content of your matchmaking table.

Table 4-1. *Matchmaking Records in the SQL Database*

Ticket ID	Skill Level	State	Server Address
T1	Beginner	Matched	y.y.y.y:port
T2	Beginner	Matched	y.y.y.y:port
T3	Advanced	Matched	x.x.x.x:port
T4	Beginner	Waiting	
T5	Advanced	Matched	x.x.x.x:port
T6	Advanced	Waiting	

> **DeleteTicket.** This receives a ticket ID and removes the related ticket from the database.

> **Matchmaker.** Calls the Matchmaker function directly after a client creates a new ticket. The Matchmaker function runs over all waiting tickets and tries to find a match in the database. If it finds one, it calls the GetReadyServer function.

GetReadyServer. Calls the Kubernetes API through a REST call to request a new ready server. It provides the IP and the port of the free server back to the Matchmaker function, which assigns this information to the matching tickets. You will integrate your matchmaking solution into Agones. By calling a Kubernetes API, you can allocate a server with the help of Agones.

GetServer. Receives from the client a ticket ID and queries the database based on this ID. It sends the server address to the client if there was a match.

In this example, you implement the core services that enable the matchmaking functionality. You can improve this solution by considering more non-functional aspects:

- **Security.** Although API Management provides some security, it is good practice to apply a firewall to decrease the risk of attacks. Be sure that you only open ports that are in use.

- **Response time.** You can implement this solution in multiple regions and put a Traffic Manager at the entry point. This service can distribute the incoming request to the closest location. This way, you can improve response time by bringing the solution closer to the users.

- **Scalability.** The number of connections to your database will run out with an increasing number of concurrent requests. You can buy a more expensive service tier or use an event hub that gathers the requests. You then process them in batches with fewer connections to the database.

- **Performance.** In the case of huge player base, you may find a faster way to store player data. For example, you can choose Azure CosmosDB or Azure Cache for Redis.

- **Maintainability.** You can apply various monitoring features in Azure to better see what is happening in your infrastructure. For example, getting alerted quickly when failures happen.

- **Efficiency.** Currently, the system implements a polling mechanism and keep asking the server if there is a match. It would be much more efficient to have a push mechanism, whereby the server informs the client.

Building Your Infrastructure

Let's create a separate module for the matchmaking resources. Create a new folder called matchmaker. Into the main.tf file of the root folder, you can refer to the matchmaker sources besides the Agones module:

```
module "agones" {
    source = "./agones"
}

module "matchmaker" {
    source = "./matchmaker"
}
```

You can also put the different resources into different files. Create a resource group for the matchmaking resources in resourcegroup.tf:

```
resource "azurerm_resource_group" "matchmaker" {
  name     = "matchmaker-resources"
  location = "West Europe"
}
```

Function App

First, you need to determine which cost plan you want to use for your functions. Azure Functions can run in an App Service plan, where you reserve *dedicated virtual machines* where your functions will run. Here you have to pay fix costs independently if you execute your functions.

The other option, what you see here, is the *consumption-based plan*. In that case, you only pay when the function is called. With the consumption plan, you can get one million free requests monthly. So you can experiment with Azure Functions without worrying about the cost.

Even if you choose the consumption plan, you need to create an App Service plan in Terraform. Use the Dynamic tier with Y1 size. That refers to the functions consumption plan. Create a file called `functionapp.tf`. You should put all the Azure Functions related resources there:

```
resource "azurerm_service_plan" "matchmaker" {
  name                = "matchmaker-azure-functions-
                        service-plan"
  location            = azurerm_resource_group.matchmaker.
                        location
  resource_group_name = azurerm_resource_group.matchmaker.name
  kind                = "FunctionApp"

  sku {
    tier = "Dynamic"
    size = "Y1"
  }
}
```

Azure Functions requires a storage account. Different types of storage accounts support different storage services, such as Blob, Queue, Table Storage, and Azure Files.

For the Azure Functions running in a consumption plan, you need a file share. In Terraform, you can choose from Standard or Premium account tiers. The Standard option contains the Azure Files option, so this is suitable for this scenario. Try the Locally-Redundant Storage (LRS), which provides moderate availability at a lower cost:

```
resource "azurerm_storage_account" "matchmaker" {
  name                     = "matchmakerfunctionsappsa"
  resource_group_name      = azurerm_resource_group.
                             matchmaker.name
  location                 = azurerm_resource_group.matchmaker.
                             location
  account_tier             = "Standard"
  account_replication_type = "LRS"
}
```

Finally, create the Azure Function App. Refer back to the earlier created resource group, App Service plan, and storage account. You also need to define the version of the Function App runtime, as it will otherwise default to ~1:

```
resource "azurerm_function_app" "matchmaker" {
  name                = "matchmaker-azure-functions"
  location            = azurerm_resource_group.
                        matchmaker.location
  resource_group_name = azurerm_resource_group.
                        matchmaker.name
  app_service_plan_id = azurerm_app_service_plan.
                        matchmaker.id
```

```
storage_account_name      = azurerm_storage_account.
                            matchmaker.name
storage_account_access_key = azurerm_storage_account.
                            matchmaker.primary_access_key
version                   = "~4"
}
```

Additionally, you need to allow the API Management service to access your Azure Function app. With the data block, you can fetch host keys to achieve this:

```
data "azurerm_function_app_host_keys" "matchmaker" {
  name                = azurerm_function_app.matchmaker.name
  resource_group_name = azurerm_resource_group.matchmaker.name
}
```

You are now ready with your Function app, at least the part you can create with Terraform. Later, you will develop your functions in this Function App, but first let's create some additional infrastructure resources.

Azure Database for PostgreSQL

You need a database to store and search for matchmaking tickets and the assigned server addresses. You have multiple options here.

This example uses the Azure Database for PostgreSQL, as it has an affordable cost plan. For development, you can even use the Flexible Server with Burstable B1MS instance, which is free for the first year.

As soon as you use it in a real setting, change to the General Purpose tier. In Terraform, you define this as the sku_name. Now create a new file called postgresqldb.tf and add the following code:

```
resource "azurerm_postgresql_flexible_server" "matchmaker" {
```

```
name                      = "matchmakerpostgresqlserver"
resource_group_name       = azurerm_resource_group.
                            matchmaker.name
location                  = azurerm_resource_group.matchmaker.
                            location
version                   = "12"
administrator_login       = "matchmakeradmin"
administrator_password    = "MatchmakerPassword99"
sku_name                  = "B_Standard_B1ms"
storage_mb                = 32768
zone                      = 2
}
```

Note   This example keeps things simple to focus on the main idea and not get lost in the details. You should never store administrator credentials in plain text.

You also need to create a database for the matchmaking information:

```
resource "azurerm_postgresql_flexible_server_database"
"matchmaker" {
  name      = "matchmaker-postgresql-database"
  server_id = azurerm_postgresql_flexible_server.matchmaker.id
}
```

When you go to production, you have to align the database type and choose the right tier carefully to make sure the database can manage the workload of your specific game requirements. There is no one type fits for all, and Azure provides diverse options to satisfy specific needs.

Now execute Terraform, which will generate the infrastructure on Azure:

```
terraform apply
```

Configure Your Infrastructure

In this section, you create a table in the database that will hold the information about the players' requests for matchmaking.

By default, TLS is enabled for communication between the client and the server. You should always keep the transport encrypted in production environments. For now, in development, you can disable this with the require_secure_transport server parameter:

```
az postgres flexible-server parameter set --name require_
secure_transport --value off --resource-group matchmaker-
resources --server-name matchmakerpostgresqlserver
```

When you're first creating a PostgreSQL server, Azure will grant public access to it. However, it restricts the access and allows it only for specified IPs. You need to create a firewall rule that allows the connection from your own IP:

Note   If you are unsure what your public IP is, you can use a service like www.whatsmyip.org/ to determine it.

```
az postgres flexible-server firewall-rule create --resource-
group matchmaker-resources --name matchmakerpostgresqlserver --
rule-name myclientaccess --start-ip-address <your current
public IP>
```

Now you can execute queries on your database. Create a file called
createtable.sql to store the SQL queries:

```
CREATE TABLE "Tickets" (
"TicketID" varchar(150) NOT NULL PRIMARY KEY,
"Skill_level" varchar(150) NOT NULL,
"State" varchar(150) NOT NULL,
"ServerAddress" varchar(150) NOT NULL,
"ServerName" varchar(150) NOT NULL)
```

Execute this query. You can also use your favorite SQL client. To keep it
simple, this example will execute it with Azure cli:

```
az postgres flexible-server execute --admin-user
matchmakeradmin --admin-password MatchmakerPassword99 --name
matchmakerpostgresqlserver --database-name matchmaker-
postgresql-database --file-path createtable.sql
```

Now that you have everything set up, you can start a simple SELECT
query to check the contents of the table:

```
az postgres flexible-server execute --admin-user
matchmakeradmin --admin-password MatchmakerPassword99 --name
matchmakerpostgresqlserver --database-name matchmaker-
postgresql-database --querytext "SELECT * FROM \"Tickets\""
-o table
```

Developing Matchmaking Logic

You need to implement and run your functions locally first. Then, if
everything works fine, you can publish them to Azure. For that, you will
use the Azure Functions Core Tools. The simplest way to install it is from
this URL:

```
https://docs.microsoft.com/en-us/azure/azure-functions/
functions-run-local?tabs=v4%2Cwindows%2Ccsharp%2Cportal%2Cbash
```
Then, check if you installed at least version 4:

```
func --version
4.0.3971
```

You also need at least .NET 6.0, so install it from here:
```
https://dotnet.microsoft.com/en-us/download/dotnet
```
Check if the correct version is available:

```
dotnet --version
6.0.101
```

Create a new functions project with the .NET runtime. The following command will create a new folder called MatchmakerFunctions and generate the configuration files:

```
func init MatchmakerFunctions --worker-runtime dotnet
```

Your First Azure Function

Go to the MatchmakerFunctions project folder and create a file called Matchmaker.cs. For the sake of simplicity, this example will puts all of the functions into this file. Of course, structure your code according to your actual requirements. Here, the goal is to show the concept as simply as possible. Let's start with the very basic functionality. You want the client to call the function using an HTTP POST request and have the function log this call.

It is a best practice to use asynchronous programming for serverless functions. For that, you use the async and the await keywords. The thread can then execute the actual method and exit when it arrives at an await keyword. Because the execution of the awaited method can take time, the thread is not blocked and can do something else useful. As soon as the response arrives from the awaited method, the original thread will come back to the function and continue the execution.

```csharp
using System.IO;
using System.Threading.Tasks;
using Microsoft.AspNetCore.Mvc;
using Microsoft.Azure.WebJobs;
using Microsoft.Azure.WebJobs.Extensions.Http;
using Microsoft.AspNetCore.Http;
using Microsoft.Extensions.Logging;

namespace MatchmakerFunctions {
    public class Matchmaker {

        [FunctionName("FirstFunction")]
        public async Task<IActionResult> FirstFunction (
            [HttpTrigger(AuthorizationLevel.Anonymous, "post",
            Route = null)] HttpRequest req,
            ILogger log)
        {
            string requestBody = await new StreamReader(req.
            Body).ReadToEndAsync();
            log.LogInformation(requestBody);
            string responseMessage = requestBody;
            return new OkObjectResult(responseMessage);
        }
    }
}
```

Now start it locally by using the func cli tool:

```
func start
```

You can test if this works with any REST client. With cURL, open a new terminal window and execute. You should see a "hello world" message in the response:

```
curl -X POST -d "hello world" http://localhost:7071/api/
FirstFunction
hello world
```

Connecting to the Database

You have to access the database from your functions. For that, you can store the connection string as an environment variable and refer to it from the function code.

You need to add it to your local.settings.json file and the ado.net version for local execution. The following command will show the connection string:

```
az postgres flexible-server show-connection-string -s
matchmakerpostgresqlserver -u matchmakeradmin -p
MatchmakerPassword99 -d matchmaker-postgresql-database
```

Let's set the database name in the connection string. In this example, it is matchmaker-postgresql-database. The local.settings.json file should look similar to this:

```
{
    "IsEncrypted": false,
    "Values": {
        "AzureWebJobsStorage": "UseDevelopmentStorage=true",
        "FUNCTIONS_WORKER_RUNTIME": "dotnet",
        "SqlConnectionString":"Server=matchmakerpostgresql
        server.postgres.database.azure.com;Database=postgres;
        Port=5432;User Id=matchmakeradmin;Password=Matchmaker
        Password99;"
    }
}
```

Now you can proceed with implementing the functions. You will apply the Entity Framework using dependency injection to integrate the database with your Azure Function. The Entity Framework allows you to manage data stored in your SQL database tables in objects. Create a file called Ticket.cs and implement the following class, which maps to the table defined in Table 4-1.

```
namespace MatchmakerFunctions
{
    public class Ticket
    {
        public string TicketID { get; set; }
        public string Skill_level { get; set; }
        public string State { get; set; }
        public string ServerAddress { get; set; }
        public string ServerName { get; set; }
    }
}
```

Note   The server name is included, which will be important later, when you deallocate servers that aren't needed.

Next, you need to create a context class, which will represent the session with the database. Add the Entity Framework package:

```
dotnet add package Microsoft.EntityFrameworkCore
```

Create a new class inherited from DbContext, including an entity set. The constructor must receive the connection string. Create a new file called MatchmakerContext.cs and add the following code:

```
using Microsoft.EntityFrameworkCore;

namespace MatchmakerFunctions
{
    public class MatchmakerContext : DbContext
    {
        public MatchmakerContext(DbContextOptions<Matchmaker
        Context> options) : base(options)
        {
        }          public DbSet<Ticket> Tickets { get; set; }
    }
}
```

You will inject MatchmakerContext into your function. Start by adding the required packages:

```
dotnet add package Microsoft.Azure.Functions.Extensions
dotnet add package Npgsql.EntityFrameworkCore.PostgreSQL
```

Create a Startup.cs file, including a class inherited from FunctionsStartup. This will run whenever the Function App starts. You need to override the Configure method to register the MatchmakerContext in the services, so that you can inject it later into your function. You can also pass the connection string from the environment variable, which is either defined in Azure or locally in the local.settings.json file.

```
using System;
using Microsoft.EntityFrameworkCore;
using Microsoft.Extensions.DependencyInjection;
using Microsoft.Azure.Functions.Extensions.DependencyInjection;

[assembly: FunctionsStartup(typeof(MatchmakerFunctions.StartUp))]
```

```
namespace MatchmakerFunctions
{
    public class StartUp : FunctionsStartup
    {
        public override void Configure(IFunctionsHostBuilder
        builder)
        {
            string connectionString = Environment.GetEnvironmen
            tVariable("SqlConnectionString");
            builder.Services.AddDbContext<MatchmakerContext>
            (options => options.UseNpgsql(connectionString));
        }
    }
}
```

Finally, inject the registered MatchmakerContext into your
Matchmaker class:

```
namespace MatchmakerFunctions {
    public class Matchmaker {

        private readonly MatchmakerContext matchmakerContext;
        public Matchmaker(MatchmakerContext matchmakerContext)
        {
            this.matchmakerContext = matchmakerContext;
        }
        ...
```

Writing into the Database

The next goal is to write a ticket into the database. For that, you simply
need to deserialize the request body, which is in JSON format. You can
generate a unique ticket ID and add a new record to the database. In the

response, provide the client the ticket ID, because the client will need this to request the server address. Let's change the earlier FirstFunction to the real Matchmaker function:

```
using System.IO;
using System.Threading.Tasks;
using Microsoft.AspNetCore.Mvc;
using Microsoft.Azure.WebJobs;
using Microsoft.Azure.WebJobs.Extensions.Http;
using Microsoft.AspNetCore.Http;
using Microsoft.Extensions.Logging;
using Newtonsoft.Json;
using System;

namespace MatchmakerFunctions
{
    public class Matchmaker
    {

        private readonly MatchmakerContext matchmakerContext;
        public Matchmaker(MatchmakerContext matchmakerContext)
        {
            this.matchmakerContext = matchmakerContext;
        }

        [FunctionName("Ticket")]
        public async Task<IActionResult> Ticket(
            [HttpTrigger(AuthorizationLevel.Anonymous, "post",
            "delete", "get", Route = null)] HttpRequest req,
            ILogger log)
        {
            string requestBody = await new StreamReader(req.
            Body).ReadToEndAsync();
```

```
var data = JsonConvert.DeserializeObject<Ticket>
(requestBody);
string responseMessage = "";
if (req.Method.Equals("POST"))
{
    var ticketID = Guid.NewGuid().ToString();
    var ticket = new Ticket { TicketID = ticketID,
    Skill_level = data.Skill_level, State =
    "Waiting", ServerAddress = "not available",
    ServerName = "not available" };

    matchmakerContext.Tickets.Add(ticket);
    matchmakerContext.SaveChanges();

    responseMessage = ticketID;
}
return new OkObjectResult(responseMessage);
        }
    }
}
```

Start an HTTP POST call with cURL and see if you get the ticketID:

```
curl -X POST -d "{Skill_level: 'advanced'}" http://
localhost:7071/api/Ticket
ba4a7833-cdbf-41cb-b1ed-d1088690462e
```

Now check if the ticket has arrived at the database:

```
az postgres flexible-server execute --admin-user
matchmakeradmin --admin-password MatchmakerPassword99 --name
matchmakerpostgresqlserver --database-name matchmaker-
postgresql-database --querytext "SELECT * FROM \"Tickets\"" -o
table
```

```
Successfully connected to matchmakerpostgresqlserver.
Ran Database Query: 'SELECT * FROM "Tickets"'
Retrieving first 30 rows of query output, if applicable.
Closed the connection to matchmakerpostgresqlserver
ServerAddress    ServerName    Skill_level    State
    TicketID
---------------  -------------  -------------  -------
------------------------------------
not available    not available  advanced       Waiting
    051459da-35a7-4713-aab6-02cc3a0ea040
```

Deleting Tickets

Players may on occasion decide to quit looking for a partner to play with. That means the client needs to remove the matchmaking request ticket from the database. You can extend a function by adding the DELETE request method to it. The player only needs to send the TicketID, which is the primary key in your database. Let's extend the Ticket function by adding a DELETE option:

```csharp
...
using System.Linq;
...
namespace MatchmakerFunctions
{
    public class Matchmaker
    {
        ...
        [FunctionName("Ticket")]
...
        {
...
```

```
if (req.Method.Equals("POST"))
{
    ...
}
else if (req.Method.Equals("DELETE"))
{
    string ticketID = req.Query["TicketID"];
    if (!String.IsNullOrEmpty(ticketID)) {
        var ticket = matchmakerContext.Tickets.
        Find(ticketID);

        matchmakerContext.Tickets.Remove(ticket);
        matchmakerContext.SaveChanges();

        var otherTicket = matchmakerContext.
        Tickets.Where(p => p.ServerName.
        Equals(ticket.ServerName)).
        SingleOrDefault();

        responseMessage = ticket.TicketID + " was
        deleted.";
    } else {
        responseMessage = "TicketID is not
        available.";
    }
}
```

Now check if your new functionality works, by using an existing ticket ID and sending it with the DELETE method to the function. Check the database to see if the function deleted the ticket.

```
curl -X DELETE http://localhost:7071/api/
Ticket?TicketID=43e92dd5-b633-4dbe-b5d6-ab701583af8e
```

Finding a Match

Create a file called Server.cs, which contains the following server information:

```
namespace MatchmakerFunctions
{
    public class Server
    {
        public string IP { get; set; }
        public string Port { get; set; }
        public string Name { get; set; }
    }
}
```

You will implement a FindMatch method, which goes through all the tickets and tries to find a matching one with the current ticket. This is the core of your matchmaking engine. You can create more complex rules to satisfy match criteria, but to keep it simple, this example will simply match two players with the same skill level. Add the FindMatch method to the Matchmaker class:

```
public void FindMatch(Ticket currentTicket)
{
    var tickets = matchmakerContext.Tickets;
    var CurrentTicket = matchmakerContext.Tickets.
    Find(currentTicket.TicketID);

    foreach (var ticket in tickets)
    {
        if (!ticket.TicketID.Equals(CurrentTicket.
        TicketID))
        {
            if (ticket.State.Equals("Waiting"))
```

```
        {
            if (ticket.Skill_level.
            Equals(CurrentTicket.Skill_level))
            {
                ticket.State = "Matched";
                CurrentTicket.State = "Matched";

                Server server = new Server();
                server.IP = "1.2.3.4";
                server.Port="9999";server.
                Name="mygame-server";
                ticket.ServerAddress = server.IP +
                ":" + server.Port;
                ticket.ServerName = server.Name;
                CurrentTicket.ServerAddress =
                server.IP + ":" + server.Port;
                CurrentTicket.ServerName =
                server.Name;
                break; // Only match 2 players
            }
        }
    }
}
matchmakerContext.SaveChanges();
}
```

Every time a new ticket arrives, it calls the matchmaking method (don't forget to extend the Ticket function with FindMatch(ticket)):

```
if (req.Method.Equals("POST"))
    {
```

...

```
        matchmakerContext.Tickets.Add(ticket);
        matchmakerContext.SaveChanges();

        FindMatch(ticket);
        responseMessage = ticketID;
    }
```

...

Note that you do not assign real server IP and port numbers. Let's just fill in those values with fake numbers for now. POST two new tickets with the same skill level and verify that they are matched in the database and that the function assigned server properties to them.

```
curl -X POST -d "{Skill_level: 'advanced'}" http://
localhost:7071/api/Ticket
0e0f198f-1e32-4a1c-bba2-479ce64d9c3b

curl -X POST -d "{Skill_level: 'advanced'}" http://
localhost:7071/api/Ticket
d66e5b7f-0ea4-412c-ac55-16cebff9262f

az postgres flexible-server execute --admin-user
matchmakeradmin --admin-password MatchmakerPassword99 --name
matchmakerpostgresqlserver --database-name matchmaker-
postgresql-database --querytext "SELECT * FROM \"Tickets\"" -o
table
Successfully connected to matchmakerpostgresqlserver.
Ran Database Query: 'SELECT * FROM "Tickets"'
Retrieving first 30 rows of query output, if applicable.
Closed the connection to matchmakerpostgresqlserver
```

```
ServerAddress     ServerName      Skill_level      State
TicketID
---------------   -------------   ------------     -------
----------------------------------
1.2.3.4:9999      mygame-server   advanced         Matched
0e0f198f-1e32-4a1c-bba2-479ce64d9c3b
1.2.3.4:9999      mygame-server   advanced         Matched
d66e5b7f-0ea4-412c-ac55-16cebff9262f
```

Getting a Ready Server

Finally, you need to add the server address to your matched tickets in the database. This is where you need the help of the system that manages the game servers.

In this case, it is Agones. Agones provides the server addresses of the ready servers by Game Server Allocation. As you saw in the last chapter, you can do this using the kubectl command, where you refer to an appropriately defined YAML file.

Note   You can also use another game server management platform and integrate it into your matchmaker solution.

You can also reach the Game Server Allocation through Kubernetes API. First, you allocate a server by calling the Kubernetes API with cURL. Then, you implement this call through your Azure Function.

After implementing the steps in the previous chapter, you can create running servers with the help of fleets:

```
kubectl get gs
```

```
NAME                             STATE    ADDRESS
    PORT    NODE                           AGE
simple-game-server-zwpbq-jv22m   Ready    20.123.136.188
    7065    aks-default-40919478-vmss000000   57s
simple-game-server-zwpbq-m5vv8   Ready    20.123.136.188
    7204    aks-default-40919478-vmss000000   57s
simple-game-server-zwpbq-mr8gp   Ready    20.123.136.188
    7221    aks-default-40919478-vmss000000   57s
```

Now you need access to the Kubernetes API. For that, you need to create a service account and assign it to your Kuberentes cluster with the role of a cluster admin:

```
kubectl create serviceaccount agonessa
kubectl create clusterrolebinding agonessa --
clusterrole=cluster-admin --serviceaccount=default:agonessa
```

You can then download the secret token with the help of the following commands. Save the token for later:

```
kubectl get secrets
kubectl describe secret agonessa-token-xxxxx
Name:          agonessa-token-8jdbb
Namespace:     default
Labels:        <none>
Annotations:   kubernetes.io/service-account.name: agonessa
               kubernetes.io/service-account.uid: 38ef2ed1-9db5-
               4130-8248-206f8ee59358
```

```
Type:   kubernetes.io/service-account-token
```

```
Data
====
namespace:   7 bytes
token:       <your token>
ca.crt:      1765 bytes
```

Using Azure CLI, request your Kubernetes API server address:

```
az aks show --name agones-cluster --resource-group agones-
resources --query=fqdn
"agones-b4c4cba3.hcp.westeurope.azmk8s.io"
```

Now you have everything to start a cURL request and allocate a server:

```
curl -k -d "{""apiVersion"":""allocation.agones.dev/v1"",""
kind"":""GameServerAllocation"",""spec"":{""required"":{""
matchLabels"":{""agones.dev/fleet"":""mygame-server""}}}}"
-H "Authorization: Bearer <your token>" -H "Content-Type:
application/json" -X POST https://agones-b4c4cba3.hcp.
westeurope.azmk8s.io/apis/allocation.agones.dev/v1/namespaces/
default/gameserverallocations
```

This request will allocate a server and come back with the server address:

```
{"kind":"GameServerAllocation","apiVersion":"allocation.agones.
dev/v1","metadata":{"name":"simple-game-server-zwpbq-jv22m","na
mespace":"default","creationTimestamp":"2022-01-31T14:37:03Z"},
"spec":{"multiClusterSetting":{"policySelector":{}},"required":
{"matchLabels":{"agones.dev/fleet":"simple-game-server"}},"sele
ctors":[{"matchLabels":{"agones.dev/fleet":"simple-game-server"
}}],"scheduling":"Packed","metadata":{}},"status":{"state":"All
ocated","gameServerName":"simple-game-server-zwpbq-jv22m","port
s":[{"name":"default","port":7065}],"address":"20.123.136.188",
"nodeName":"aks-default-40919478-vmss000000"}}
```

Now you can implement the same HTTP request in the Azure Function. The following steps are required for implementing the integration between Azure Functions and Agones:

1. Store both your Kubernetes API addresses and access tokens in the `local.settings.json` file for local execution. You'll refer to these values from the code with the `Environment. GetEnvironmentVariable` method.

```
{
    "IsEncrypted": false,
    "Values": {
        "AzureWebJobsStorage":
        "UseDevelopmentStorage=true",
        "FUNCTIONS_WORKER_RUNTIME": "dotnet",
        "SqlConnectionString" : "<connection_string>",
        "Kubernetes_API_Access_Token" : "<token>",
        "Kubernetes_API_Address_Game_Allocation" :
        "https://<kubernetes API FQDN>/apis/
        allocation.agones.dev/v1/namespaces/default/
        gameserverallocations",
        "Kubernetes_API_Address_Game_Server" :
        "https://<kubernetes API FQDN>/apis/agones.dev/
        v1/namespaces/default/gameservers/"
    }
}
```

2. The HTTP client will complain about the untrusted certificate. You need to bypass this validation with `HttpClientHandler`.

3. Similarly as with cURL, add the authorization token and the content type to your request header.

Because the result of your HTTP request is in JSON, you need to parse it and find the server and the port information in the response.

Let's add a new function to the Matchmaker class that allocates a ready server by calling the Kubernetes API:

```
using System.Net.Http;
using System.Text;
using System.Net.Http.Headers;
using Newtonsoft.Json.Linq;
...
            public async Task<Server> AllocateReadyServer()
        {
            const string data = @"{""apiVersion"":""allocation.
            agones.dev/v1"",""kind"":""GameServerAllocation"",
            ""spec"":{""required"":{""matchLabels"":{""agones.
            dev/fleet"":""mygame-server""}}}}";

            string kubernetesApiAccessToken = Environment.GetEn
            vironmentVariable("Kubernetes_API_Access_Token");
            string kubernetesApiAddress = Environment.GetEn
            vironmentVariable("Kubernetes_API_Address_Game_
            Allocation");

            HttpClientHandler clientHandler = new
            HttpClientHandler();
            clientHandler.
            ServerCertificateCustomValidationCallback =
            (sender, cert, chain, sslPolicyErrors) => { return
            true; };
```

```
HttpClient httpClient = new
HttpClient(clientHandler);
httpClient.DefaultRequestHeaders.Authorization
= new AuthenticationHeaderValue("Bearer",
kubernetesApiAccessToken);

var requestData = new StringContent(data, Encoding.
UTF8, "application/json");
var response = await httpClient.
PostAsync(kubernetesApiAddress, requestData);
var result = await response.Content.
ReadAsStringAsync();

JObject o = JObject.Parse(result);
Server server = new Server();

server.IP = (string)o.SelectToken("status.address");
server.Port = (string)o.SelectToken("status.
ports[0].port");
server.Name = (string)
o.SelectToken("metadata.name");

    return server;
}
```

Replace the fake server properties in this function call at the place in the code where you find a match:

```
if (ticket.Skill_level.Equals(CurrentTicket.Skill_level))
            {
                ticket.State = "Matched";
                CurrentTicket.State = "Matched";

                Server server =
                AllocateReadyServer().Result;
```

```
                              ticket.ServerAddress = server.IP +
                              ":" + server.Port;
                              ticket.ServerName = server.Name;
...
                    }
```

Now test this again by posting new tickets. Verify whether players with the same skill levels are matched and assigned the same real server parameters:

```
curl -X POST -d "{Skill_level: 'beginner'}" http://
localhost:7071/api/Ticket
07817b14-9c08-4a66-aa20-5adfdfc6e23a
curl -X POST -d "{Skill_level: 'beginner'}" http://
localhost:7071/api/Ticket
424088ee-32c7-462b-8e6a-ea83e275fcf3
kubectl get gs
NAME                          STATE      ADDRESS          PORT
   NODE                                  AGE
mygame-server-8hdln           Ready      20.126.133.167   7179
   aks-default-18801657-vmss000000   18h
mygame-server-jhfqs-62b7s     Ready      20.126.133.167   7333
   aks-default-18801657-vmss000000   17h
mygame-server-jhfqs-9mvfk     Allocated  20.126.133.167   7351
   aks-default-18801657-vmss000000   17h

az postgres flexible-server execute --admin-user
matchmakeradmin --admin-password MatchmakerPassword99 --name
matchmakerpostgresqlserver --database-name matchmaker-
postgresql-database --querytext "SELECT * FROM \"Tickets\""
-o table
Successfully connected to matchmakerpostgresqlserver.
Ran Database Query: 'SELECT * FROM "Tickets"'
```

Retrieving first 30 rows of query output, if applicable.
Closed the connection to matchmakerpostgresqlserver

```
ServerAddress          ServerName                  Skill_level
    State    TicketID
------------------     -------------------------   -------------
    -------   -------------------------------------
20.126.133.167:7351   mygame-server-jhfqs-9mvfk   beginner
    Matched   07817b14-9c08-4a66-aa20-5adfdfc6e23a
20.126.133.167:7351   mygame-server-jhfqs-9mvfk   beginner
    Matched   424088ee-32c7-462b-8e6a-ea83e275fcf3
```

Getting Your Server Address

In this section, you extend your `Ticket` function by adding a GET method to it, so that your clients can get the server IP and port to which they can connect. The clients can query the server address by providing their TicketIDs. Add the following GET method to the `Ticket` function of the `Matchmaker` class:

```
else if (req.Method.Equals("GET"))
{
    string ticketID = req.Query["TicketID"];
    if (!String.IsNullOrEmpty(ticketID)) {
        var currentTicket = matchmakerContext.
        Tickets.Find(ticketID);
        responseMessage = currentTicket.
        ServerAddress;
    } else {
        responseMessage = "TicketID is not
        available.";
    }
}
```

To test it, start a cURL GET request from the client side. It should return with the assigned server address:

```
curl -X GET http://localhost:7071/api/
Ticket?TicketID=07817b14-9c08-4a66-aa20-5adfdfc6e23a
20.126.133.167:7351
```

Deallocating Servers

You also need a mechanism to deallocate unused servers. This should happen when a server is no longer being used. It is an important feature, as the number of containers running on your virtual machine is limited. If you allocated more and more servers and didn't deallocate any of them, the virtual machine would run out of memory very quickly.

To deallocate unused servers, you again use the Kubernetes API and start a REST call with the DELETE method on a specific game server. This will shut down the game server and terminate the pod underneath.

To keep it simple, if a player leaves, the function will first delete the matchmaking ticket from the database. The function then will check if there is still someone using that server. If not, it will delete the game server.

This code is similar to the code used in the game server allocation. You don't send any data, but in the API URL, you specify the name of the server and call it with the DeleteAsync method. Let's extend the Matchmaker class:

```
public async Task<String> ShutdownServer(string
serverName)
    {
        string kubernetesApiAccessToken = Environment.GetEn
        vironmentVariable("Kubernetes_API_Access_Token");
        string kubernetesApiAddress = Environment.GetEnviro
        nmentVariable("Kubernetes_API_Address_Game_Server")
        + serverName;
```

```
HttpClientHandler clientHandler = new
HttpClientHandler();
clientHandler.
ServerCertificateCustomValidationCallback =
(sender, cert, chain, sslPolicyErrors) => { return
true; };

HttpClient httpClient = new
HttpClient(clientHandler);
httpClient.DefaultRequestHeaders.Authorization
= new AuthenticationHeaderValue("Bearer",
kubernetesApiAccessToken);

var response = await httpClient.DeleteAsync(kuberne
tesApiAddress);
var result = await response.Content.
ReadAsStringAsync();

return result;
    }
```

Also, you need to extend the DELETE block. You add a check to determine if there is any other ticket with the same server name in this database. If not, initiate the removal of the server:

```
...
var otherTicket = matchmakerContext.Tickets.Where(p =>
p.ServerName.Equals(ticket.ServerName)).SingleOrDefault();

                if (otherTicket==null) {
                    await ShutdownServer(ticket.
                    ServerName);
                }
```

```
            responseMessage = ticket.TicketID + " was
            deleted.";
...
```

Again, test it to see if it works. Add two new tickets, which will be matched, and verify that Agones allocated the server. Then remove the tickets one-by-one. After both are removed, verify that Agones deallocated the server.

With that, you have the complete functionality implemented in Azure Functions. Now you only need to implement the client in Unity. It will execute basically the same requests with the same parameters as the cURL tool.

Developing a REST Client in Unity

For the client side, you'll create something very similar to what you created for the PlayFab client. You need to implement the following methods:

- **CreateTicket.** This method starts a matchmaking request and sends all the player properties to the matchmaking service.

- **DeleteTicket.** If the player interrupts the matchmaking process or exits the game, you call this method to remove the request from the matchmaking database.

- **GetServerAddress.** This method sends the current ticket ID and, in the response, it waits for the respective server address if the matchmaker already assigned to it.

- **GetMatchmakingTicket.** Every six seconds (similar to PlayFab), you call this polling method as a coroutine, asking the matchmaking service if there is a match available. If there is, the client receives the server address and can start the game.

Create a new script file called AzureMatchmaking.cs and add it to the
Azure game object in Unity:

```
using UnityEngine;
using System.Net;
using System.IO;
using System.Text;
using System.Collections;

public class AzureMatchmaking : MonoBehaviour
{
    private IEnumerator coroutine;
    private string ticketID;

    public void StartAzureMatchmaking()
    {
        ticketID = CreateTicket("advanced");
        Debug.Log("New matchmaking ticket submitted, TicketID :
        " + ticketID);

        coroutine = WaitAndGetMatchingTicket(6.0f);
        StartCoroutine(coroutine);
    }

    string CreateTicket(string skill_level)
    {
        HttpWebRequest request = (HttpWebRequest)WebRequest.
        Create("http://localhost:7071/api/Ticket");
        request.Method = "POST";

        byte[] data = Encoding.ASCII.GetBytes("{Skill_level: '"
        + skill_level + "'}");
        request.ContentType = "application/json";
        request.ContentLength = data.Length;
```

```
        Stream requestStream = request.GetRequestStream();
        requestStream.Write(data, 0, data.Length);
        requestStream.Close();

        HttpWebResponse response = (HttpWebResponse)request.
        GetResponse();
        StreamReader reader = new StreamReader(response.
        GetResponseStream());
        string result = reader.ReadToEnd();
        return result;
    }
    string DeleteTicket(string ticketID)
    {
        HttpWebRequest request = (HttpWebRequest)WebRequest.
        Create("http://localhost:7071/api/Ticket?TicketID=" +
        ticketID);
        request.Method = "DELETE";

        HttpWebResponse response = (HttpWebResponse)request.
        GetResponse();
        StreamReader reader = new StreamReader(response.
        GetResponseStream());
        string result = reader.ReadToEnd();

        return result;
    }
    string GetServerAddress(string ticketID)
    {
        HttpWebRequest request = (HttpWebRequest)WebRequest.
        Create("http://localhost:7071/api/Ticket?TicketID=" +
        ticketID);
        request.Method = "GET";
```

```
        HttpWebResponse response = (HttpWebResponse)request.
        GetResponse();
        StreamReader reader = new StreamReader(response.
        GetResponseStream());
        string result = reader.ReadToEnd();
        return result;
}
private IEnumerator WaitAndGetMatchingTicket(float
waitTime)
{
    while (true)
    {
        Debug.Log("Waiting for mathing player...");
        GetMatchingTicket();
        yield return new WaitForSeconds(waitTime);
    }
}
void GetMatchingTicket()
{
    string serverAddress = GetServerAddress(ticketID);
    if (!serverAddress.Equals("not available") &&
    (!serverAddress.Equals("TicketID is not available.")))
    {
        Debug.Log("Matched! Server Address: " +
        serverAddress);
        StopCoroutine(coroutine);
    }

}
public void CancelAzureMatchmaking()
{
    Debug.Log(DeleteTicket(ticketID));
```

```
        StopCoroutine(coroutine);
    }
    void OnApplicationQuit()
    {
        CancelAzureMatchmaking();
        Debug.Log("Game ending after " + Time.time + "
        seconds");
    }
}
```

Extending the Control Panel

When you finish the client, test it locally to see if it works. To do that, you have to add a new button to your control panel (ControlPanel.cs), which allows you to start and cancel the matchmaking process:

```
bool azureMatchmakingInProgress = false;

void OptionsWindow(int windowID)
{
    if (!azureMatchmakingInProgress)
    {
        if (GUILayout.Button("Start Azure Matchmaking"))
        {
            azure.GetComponent<AzureMatchmaking>().
            StartAzureMatchmaking();
            azureMatchmakingInProgress = true;
        }
    }
    else if (azureMatchmakingInProgress)
    {
        if (GUILayout.Button("Cancel Azure Matchmaking"))
        {
```

```
azure.GetComponent<AzureMatchmaking>().
CancelAzureMatchmaking();
azureMatchmakingInProgress = false;
        }
    }
}
```

Start the functions locally:

```
func start
```

Then use multiple clients and see if they can submit a ticket, cancel a ticket, and get a match by polling the interface.

Publishing Matchmaker Functions to Azure

So far, your functions should work fine locally. Now you need to publish them to Azure and let the clients access them through an API Management service.

Publishing Azure Functions

You configured some environment variables in the local.settings.json file and referred to them from your code. These values must come into the Application Settings of the Azure Functions app. Using the CLI, you can set these values easily:

```
az functionapp config appsettings set -n matchmaker-azure-
functions -g matchmaker-resources --settings SqlConnectionStri
ng="Server=matchmakerpostgresqlserver.postgres.database.azure.
com;Database=matchmaker-postgresql-database;Port=5432;User
Id=matchmakeradmin;Password=MatchmakerPassword99;"
```

```
az functionapp config appsettings set -n matchmaker-azure-
functions -g matchmaker-resources --settings Kubernetes_API_
Access_Token="<your token>"
```

```
az functionapp config appsettings set -n matchmaker-azure-
functions -g matchmaker-resources --settings Kubernetes_
API_Address_Game_Allocation="https://agones-9e4c5ccf.hcp.
westeurope.azmk8s.io/apis/allocation.agones.dev/v1/namespaces/
default/gameserverallocations"
```

```
az functionapp config appsettings set -n matchmaker-azure-
functions -g matchmaker-resources --settings Kubernetes_API_
Address_Game_Server="https://agones-9e4c5ccf.hcp.westeurope.
azmk8s.io/apis/agones.dev/v1/namespaces/default/gameservers/"
```

Just as you did with your local address, you need to configure the firewall on the PostgreSQL to allow connections from the Function App. Each Function App has multiple outbound IP addresses. You don't know in advance which one will be used, so you have to add all of them to the whitelisted addresses. The following command will list the related outbound addresses:

```
az functionapp show -g matchmaker-resources -n matchmaker-
azure-functions --query outboundIpAddresses --output tsv
```

You either allow the connection for these outbound addresses, or you allow them from all Azure services by using the 0.0.0.0 address:

```
az postgres flexible-server firewall-rule create --resource-
group matchmaker-resources --name matchmakerpostgresqlserver --
rule-name AllAzureServices --start-ip-address 0.0.0.0
```

Now you can publish your function app to Azure with the Azure Core Tools:

```
func azure functionapp publish matchmaker-azure-functions --csharp
```

When you finish deploying the Function App to Azure, you can start a cURL POST request to test if it works fine locally. First, you'll get the function URL:

```
az functionapp function show --function-name Ticket --name matchmaker-azure-functions --resource-group matchmaker-resources --query "invokeUrlTemplate" --output tsv

https://matchmaker-azure-functions.azurewebsites.net/api/ticket
```

Finally, you can confirm that the function is working fine:

```
curl -X POST -d "{Skill_level: 'advanced'}" https://matchmaker-azure-functions.azurewebsites.net/api/ticket
df6cf5db-6b85-4702-a178-8a6cecac8217
```

Of course, you don't want just anyone to be able to call your matchmaking service REST interface. To resolve this, you could change the AuthorizationLevel from Anonymous to Function. Next, you'll learn how to put an API Management component in front of your functions. It will manage incoming requests.

Deploying Azure API Management

It is good practice to put the API Management Service in front of your Azure Functions. This way, the system can manage who can call the APIs and monitor the usage. In the consumption plan, you pay based on the number of executions. It's free up to 1 million calls. Create a new file called apim.tf with the following content:

```
resource "azurerm_api_management" "matchmaker" {
  name                 = "matchmaker-apim"
  location             = azurerm_resource_group.matchmaker.
                         location
  resource_group_name = azurerm_resource_group.matchmaker.name
  publisher_name       = "gamebackend.dev"
  publisher_email      = "mail@gamebackend.dev"
  sku_name             = "Consumption_0"
}
```

After you define the service, you have to describe the API. By default, a subscription is required. That means that the clients have to provide in their calls a key to access the API. You can turn this off for development and then use Azure Active Directory to decide if a client can access the API:

```
resource "azurerm_api_management_api" "matchmaker" {
  name                  = "matchmaker-api"
  resource_group_name   = azurerm_resource_group.
                          matchmaker.name
  api_management_name   = azurerm_api_management.
                          matchmaker.name
  revision              = "1"
  display_name          = "Matchmaker API"
  protocols             = ["https"]
  subscription_required = false
}
```

Multiple operations belong to the matchmaker API, and they are then mapped to backend services. In this case, they are Azure Functions. You need to define operations with POST, DELETE, and GET methods, which are implemented by the respective Azure Functions:

```
resource "azurerm_api_management_api_operation"
"matchmaker-post" {
  operation_id         = "matchmaker-post-ticket"
  api_name             = azurerm_api_management_api.
                         matchmaker.name
  api_management_name  = azurerm_api_management.matchmaker.name
  resource_group_name  = azurerm_resource_group.matchmaker.name
  display_name         = "POST Ticket"
  method               = "POST"
  url_template         = "/Ticket"
}
resource "azurerm_api_management_api_operation"
"matchmaker-get" {
  operation_id         = "matchmaker-get-ticket"
  api_name             = azurerm_api_management_api.
                         matchmaker.name
  api_management_name  = azurerm_api_management.matchmaker.name
  resource_group_name  = azurerm_resource_group.matchmaker.name
  display_name         = "GET Ticket"
  method               = "GET"
  url_template         = "/Ticket"
}

resource "azurerm_api_management_api_operation" "matchmaker-
delete" {
  operation_id         = "matchmaker-delete-ticket"
  api_name             = azurerm_api_management_api.
                         matchmaker.name
  api_management_name  = azurerm_api_management.matchmaker.name
  resource_group_name  = azurerm_resource_group.matchmaker.name
  display_name         = "DELETE Ticket"
  method               = "DELETE"
```

```
  url_template        = "/Ticket"
}
```

You also need to define the backend service to which the API Management Service should forward the requests. To describe your Azure Function App, you need to provide the URL, the ARM Resource ID, and the default App Key of your Function app:

```
resource "azurerm_api_management_backend" "matchmaker" {
  name                = "matchmaker-azure-functions-backend"
  resource_group_name = azurerm_resource_group.matchmaker.name
  api_management_name = azurerm_api_management.matchmaker.name
  protocol            = "http"
  url                 = "https://${azurerm_function_app.
                          matchmaker.default_hostname}/api/"
  resource_id         = "https://management.azure.com/
                          ${azurerm_function_app.matchmaker.id}"
  credentials {
    header = {
      x-functions-key = "${data.azurerm_function_app_host_keys.
                          matchmaker.default_function_key}"
    }
  }
}
```

The API Operation Policy is the glue between your operation and the backend. Assign a policy to the API, which points to the backend defined in the previous step:

```
resource "azurerm_api_management_api_policy" "matchmaker" {
  api_name            = azurerm_api_management_api.
                          matchmaker.name
  api_management_name = azurerm_api_management_api.matchmaker.
                          api_management_name
```

```
resource_group_name = azurerm_api_management_api.matchmaker.
                        resource_group_name

  xml_content = <<XML
<policies>
  <inbound>
    <set-backend-service id="apim-policy" backend-
    id="matchmaker-azure-functions-backend" />
  </inbound>
</policies>
XML
  depends_on = [
        azurerm_api_management_backend.matchmaker
  ]
}
```

After you deploy it successfully with Terraform, you can test if the API call works correctly:

```
curl -X POST -d "{Skill_level: 'advanced'}" https://matchmaker-
apim.azure-api.net/Ticket
f0918a5d-a8eb-4e82-92b3-5b7e2df17b76
```

Be aware that if you destroy your API Management, Azure will only "soft" delete it. That means that, with the next terraform apply, Terraform will complain that an API Management service with the same name exists. The following command removes the soft deleted API Management:

```
az rest --method delete --header "Accept=application/json" -u
"https://management.azure.com/subscriptions/<your subscription
id>/providers/Microsoft.ApiManagement/locations/westeurope/
deletedservices/matchmaker-apim?api-version=2020-06-01-preview"
```

Testing Clients with API Management

In your client code in Unity, AzureMatchmaking.cs, replace all instances of http://localhost:7071/api/ with the API Management address of https://matchmaker-apim.azure-api.net/.

Verify that both clients receive the same server address and that Agones allocates a game server for the session on the server side.

Putting It All Together

As the final step, integrate the results of the previous three chapters. Allow only authenticated players to start the matchmaking process and thus begin a multiplayer game session.

Integrate Matchmaking with Game Servers

Let's start the client by passing the server IP and port received from the matchmaking process to Mirror. Then start the Mirror client right away. To achieve this, you have to extend the AzureMatchmaking class with the following code:

```
using Mirror;
using kcp2k;

GameObject azureClient;

    public void StartAzureMatchmaking()
    {
        azureClient = GameObject.Find("AzureClient");

        ...

        void GetMatchingTicket()
    {

...
```

```
        StopCoroutine(coroutine);
        StartAzureClient(serverAddress);
    }
}

void StartAzureClient(string serverAddress)
{
    string serverIP = serverAddress.Substring(0,
    serverAddress.IndexOf(':'));
    string serverPort = serverAddress.
    Substring(serverAddress.IndexOf(':')+1, 4);
    azureClient.GetComponent<NetworkManager>().
    networkAddress = serverIP;
    azureClient.GetComponent<KcpTransport>().Port =
    (ushort)int.Parse(serverPort);
    azureClient.GetComponent<NetworkManager>().
    StartClient();
}
```

Verify whether the matchmaking works with multiple game clients. Up to this point, the clients are matched automatically and brought to a common game session.

Integrate Matchmaking with Authentication

Next, add the authentication process described earlier to the API Management. You need to extend the inbound policy on the API with a Validate JWT policy. The openid-config URL is your Azure B2C discovery document, the audience is the registered app ID, and the issuer URL is in the discovery document as well. You can extend your Terraform script with this policy:

```
resource "azurerm_api_management_api_policy" "matchmaker" {
```

```
  api_name             = azurerm_api_management_api.
                         matchmaker.name
  api_management_name = azurerm_api_management_api.
                         matchmaker.api_management_name
  resource_group_name = azurerm_api_management_api.
                         matchmaker.resource_group_name

  xml_content = <<XML
<policies>
  <inbound>
    <set-backend-service id="apim-policy" backend-
    id="matchmaker-azure-functions-backend" />

      <validate-jwt header-name="Authorization" failed-
      validation-httpcode="401" failed-validation-error-
      message="Unauthorized. Access token is missing or
      invalid.">
          <openid-config url="https://gamebackend2022.
          b2clogin.com/gamebackend2022.onmicrosoft.com/
          v2.0/.well-known/openid-configuration?p=B2C_1_
          SignInSignUp" />
          <audiences>
              <audience>e4d1e07d-81ff-45b8-
              b849-91bef09b5bbd</audience>
          </audiences>
          <issuers>
          <issuer>https://gamebackend2022.b2clogin.com/fe46bdde-
          805c-4a42-83c6-871e0f4278e7/v2.0/</issuer>
          </issuers>
      </validate-jwt>
  </inbound>
</policies>
XML
```

```
depends_on = [
    azurerm_api_management_backend.matchmaker
]
}
```

You have to apply this policy change using Terraform. You also have to extend your API calls in Unity with the authorization token. Simply add the token you received as a result of the authentication process to the request header of each API call:

```
...
request.Method = "POST";
request.Headers.Add("Authorization", "Bearer " +
GetComponent<AzureSettings>().token);
...
```

From now on, only logged-in players that have a token can call the matchmaking APIs and thus start an online multiplayer game.

Creating Shared Resources

In this chapter, you created several resources, which you can reuse in later chapters. To use them, you need to establish a new module called shared and put all reusable resources there.

Create a new folder called shared and refer it from the main.tf file:

```
module "shared" {
  source = "./shared"
}
```

Now create new files in the shared folder and copy each resource from the Matchmaker module. Start by creating a new resource group in the resourcegroup.tf file. All shared resources will belong to this resource group:

```
output "shared_resource_group_name" {
  value = azurerm_resource_group.shared.name
}

resource "azurerm_resource_group" "shared" {
  name     = "shared-resources"
  location = "West Europe"
}
```

Now you'll continue with the API Management. You want to use only one API Management Service, and multiple APIs and operations per service. You can create a shared resource and refer to it from the module. You have to expose the name of the API Management service with the help of the *output* block.

Create a file called apim.tf and add the following content:

```
output "api_management_name" {
  value = azurerm_api_management.shared.name
}

resource "azurerm_api_management" "shared" {
  name                = "shared-apim"
  location            = azurerm_resource_group.shared.location
  resource_group_name = azurerm_resource_group.shared.name
  publisher_name      = "gamebackend.dev"
  publisher_email     = "mail@gamebackend.dev"
  sku_name            = "Consumption_0"
}
```

Create another file called functionapp.tf to describe the storage account and the app service plan, which are common for all functions you create throughout this book. Move these parts from the Matchmaker module to this file:

```
output "app_service_plan_id" {
  value = azurerm_app_service_plan.shared.id
}

output "storage_account_name" {
  value = azurerm_storage_account.shared.name
}

output "storage_account_access_key" {
  value = azurerm_storage_account.shared.primary_access_key
}

resource "azurerm_storage_account" "shared" {
  name                     = "sharedfunctionsappsa"
  resource_group_name      = azurerm_resource_group.shared.name
  location                 = azurerm_resource_group.shared.
                             location
  account_tier             = "Standard"
  account_replication_type = "LRS"
}

resource "azurerm_app_service_plan" "shared" {
  name                = "shared-azure-functions-service-plan"
  location            = azurerm_resource_group.shared.location
  resource_group_name = azurerm_resource_group.shared.name
  kind                = "FunctionApp"
```

```
  sku {
    tier = "Dynamic"
    size = "Y1"
  }
}
```

You can also reuse the database for future features. Create a new file called postgresqldb.tf and move the content with some modifications to the shared folder:

```
resource "azurerm_postgresql_flexible_server" "shared" {
  name                    = "sharedpostgresqlserver"
  resource_group_name     = azurerm_resource_group.shared.name
  location                = azurerm_resource_group.shared.
                            location
  version                 = "12"
  administrator_login     = "sharedadmin"
  administrator_password  = "SharedPassword99"
  sku_name                = "B_Standard_B1ms"
  storage_mb              = 32768
  zone                    = 2

}

resource "azurerm_postgresql_flexible_server_database"
"shared" {
  name      = "shared-postgresql-database"
  server_id = azurerm_postgresql_flexible_server.shared.id
}
```

Any time you want to use these resources, you should hand over their parameters to each module. Modify the main.tf file:

```
module "matchmaker" {
  source                  = "./matchmaker"
```

```
api_management_name          = module.shared.api_
                               management_name
shared_resource_group_name = module.shared.shared_resource_
                               group_name
app_service_plan_id          = module.shared.app_
                               service_plan_id
storage_account_name         = module.shared.storage_
                               account_name
storage_account_access_key = module.shared.storage_account_
                               access_key
}
```

Finally, set the shared resources in the Matchmaker module. Go to the apim.tf file in the matchmaker folder and apply the following changes:

```
variable "api_management_name" {
    description = "Name of the API Management service"
}

variable "shared_resource_group_name" {
  description = "Shared resource group name"
}

resource "azurerm_api_management_api" "matchmaker" {
  resource_group_name    = var.shared_resource_group_name
  api_management_name    = var.api_management_name
...
}

resource "azurerm_api_management_api_operation"
"matchmaker-post" {
  api_management_name = var.api_management_name
```

```
  resource_group_name = var.shared_resource_group_name
...
}

resource "azurerm_api_management_api_operation" "matchmaker-
delete" {
  api_management_name = var.api_management_name
  resource_group_name = var.shared_resource_group_name
...
}

resource "azurerm_api_management_api_operation"
"matchmaker-get" {
  api_management_name = var.api_management_name
  resource_group_name = var.shared_resource_group_name
...
}

resource "azurerm_api_management_backend" "matchmaker" {
  resource_group_name = var.shared_resource_group_name
  api_management_name = var.api_management_name
...
}
```

Apply the changes in the functionapp.tf file as well:

```
variable "app_service_plan_id" {
  description = "AppService Plan ID"
}

variable "storage_account_name" {
  description = "Storage account name"
}
```

```
variable "storage_account_access_key" {
  description = "Storage account access key"
}

resource "azurerm_function_app" "matchmaker" {
  app_service_plan_id       = var.app_service_plan_id
  storage_account_name      = var.storage_account_name
  storage_account_access_key = var.storage_account_access_key
}
```

Also modify the client, since you call shared-apim (https://shared-apim.azure-api.net/matchmaker/Ticket) instead of matchmaker-apim (https://matchmaker-apim.azure-api.net/Ticket).

From now on, you can use these shared resources to more quickly implement additional features. Terraform code can become really complex as the infrastructure grows. You may need to restructure it regularly to complement your actual situation.

Summary

This chapter was built on previous topics in this book. It began with a basic introduction of tools and concepts, then introduced different ways to authenticate players. You explored how to provision servers in the cloud in order to host online multiplayer games. Finally, you learned about the Matchmaker function, which brings together authenticated players and lets them play each other.

Review Questions

1. What is the goal of matchmaking?

2. How do you integrate matchmaking with server allocation in PlayFab?

3. What is the function of rules in PlayFab matchmaking? Give an example.

4. How do you find out if there is a match to your PlayFab ticket?

5. What are the basic building blocks of a matchmaking solution in the cloud?

6. What is a Function App? Why do you need it to implement matchmaking?

7. How do you integrate a Function App with a database? What is the role of a database in the matchmaking process?

8. How do you test Function Apps on your local machine?

9. What is the role of API Management?

10. How do you add authentication to API calls?

CHAPTER 5

Leaderboards

This chapter introduces leaderboards and explains how to implement them in games. Leaderboards are important motivators for players. Achieving the highest rank, gathering the most items, or reaching the highest score all reinforce competition and encourage players to stay in the game longer.

Technically, you will implement a data table containing values assigned to players. A typical scenario is when the leaderboard contains the scores gathered by players. The game then shows the highest scores, and the players compete to be the best.

PlayFab provides a simple way to implement this feature, but you can also implement your own custom leaderboards in the cloud with little effort. This chapter shows, through a simple example, this idea and realization.

Components

Looking closer at leaderboards, you can see that they are basically data tables containing values assigned to players, as illustrated in Figure 5-1. A leaderboard also needs some data-manipulating algorithms to aggregate and sort values.

© Balint Bors 2023
B. Bors, *Game Backend Development*, https://doi.org/10.1007/978-1-4842-8910-5_5

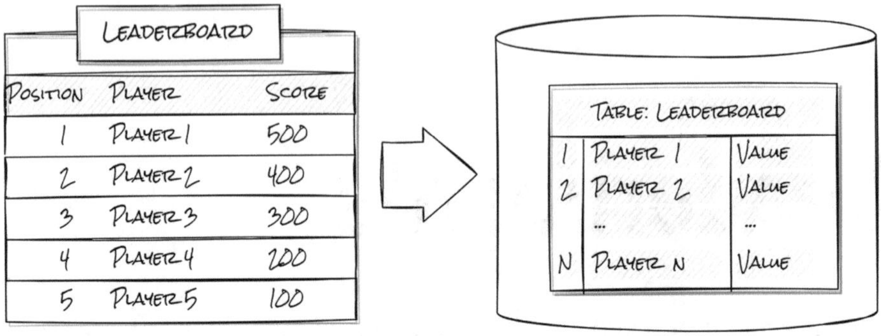

Figure 5-1. *Leaderboard*

A leaderboard gathers data from multiple players. You store this data in a central database and share it with players if their client requests it. You need to code both the client and the server side.

You need to implement at least the following functions on the client side:

- **Get leaderboard.** The clients want to download the actual leaderboard content and show it to the players. For that, you have to specify which leaderboard you are requesting and how many entries you need. A leaderboard can contain many more entries than the game can show, so such a limitation can restrict the traffic.

- **Update leaderboard.** The clients should be able to update the leaderboard with some values, such as the number of coins that specific player has gathered. This update will not affect other players and the values will be assigned to that specific player.

- **Show leaderboard.** This is the GUI part of the client, where it shows the downloaded leaderboard entries to the player.

On the server side, you need to implement at least the following functionality:

- **Interfaces and connection to the database.** The server side should be able to receive requests from the clients and query or update the database based on that.

- **Requested number of entries.** If the client only requests a subset of the entries in the leaderboard, the server should be able to filter them out and provide them to the client.

- **Sorting mechanism.** A leaderboard contains values assigned to players. When sending values to the client, you have to sort them according to some predefined criteria. For example, you want to send the client ten entries, starting with the highest score.

- **Implement some aggregation method.** You need to implement some method to manipulate the incoming player's values. As an example, for a high score leaderboard, you don't want to store all the scores a player achieved, only the highest one. So when a player sends an update with its actual score, you have three options: if no update came from that specific player, add the score as a new entry in the database. If there has been a lower score, overwrite it with the latest result. Otherwise, keep the older value and throw away the latest one.

You can also add functionality, just as PlayFab does, for example a reset frequency, where PlayFab wipes the tables regularly. Also, you can have multiple tables for different leaderboards. In the example here, you'll see how to implement the core functions.

PlayFab

PlayFab provides an easy and fast way to implement leaderboards. It refers to leaderboards as a type of player statistic. Statistics are any values assigned to different players that are typically unranked. On a leaderboard, you want to rank the entries based on some criteria, such as the highest score or the largest number of collected items.

Note   PlayFab is working on a second version of leaderboard, which is at this moment in private preview. It will extend the classic leaderboard with additional functionality, such as the ability to create child leaderboards.

Prerequisites

Before a player can update the leaderboard, it must be authenticated with PlayFab. You can assume that the DisplayName of the player is available, otherwise you would only have the PlayFabID to show on the leaderboard.

Configure PlayFab

Go to PlayFab's Game Manager and create a new leaderboard, as shown in Figure 5-2. Select Manually for the reset frequency, which means PlayFab will not periodically wipe the table. For the aggregation method, select Maximum (Always Use the Highest Value), because you want to store the highest value.

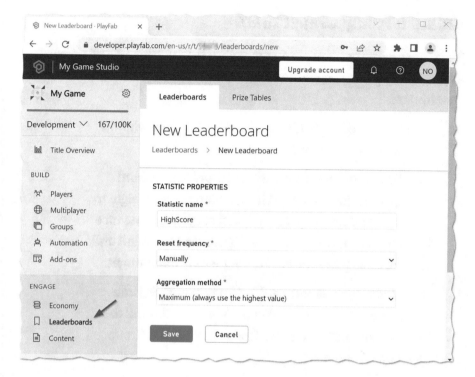

Figure 5-2. *Configuring a leaderboard in PlayFab*

Another important step is to allow clients to send player statistics to PlayFab. You can configure this in PlayFab's Game Manager, by clicking the gear wheel, choosing Title Settings ➤ API Features, and checking the Allow Client to Post Player Statistics checkbox. Click Save to save the settings.

Implement the Client

Now that you have a leaderboard in PlayFab, you need to access and manipulate it from your clients. For that, you need a GUI and the logic to use the PlayFab API to update and request the leaderboard.

Create a Fancy Leaderboard

You can skip this part and implement your own version of leaderboard, as this is very game specific. For this scenario, let's create a simple leaderboard.

1.   Create a Canvas (right-click the Hierarchy window and choose UI ➤ Canvas).

2.   Under the canvas, create an empty leaderboard game object. Set the Width to 300 and the Height to 200. Add an Image component to it, with some nice color. Also add a Shadow with Effect Distance 5 and -5, as well as a Vertical Layout Group component.

3.   Under the Leaderboard, add a new empty game object called Header. Set the Width to 300 and the Height to 30, and add a Horizontal Layout Group component to it.

4.   Under Header, add three empty game objects: PositionText, PlayerText, and ScoreText. Add a Text component to each with the related name in the Text field. Set the Font Size to 16 and the Alignment to Center.

5.   Duplicate (right-click the Hierarchy window and choose Duplicate) the Header game object, rename the resulted game object to Row, and create a prefab from it (by dragging-and-dropping into the Prefab folder in the Project window). You can now remove the row from the Hierarchy window, as you will generate the rows dynamically.

Now you have a basic leaderboard; you just need to fill it with data from the backend.

Updating the Leaderboard

In Unity Editor, create a new C# script called PlayFabLeaderboard.cs. Add this script to the PlayFab game object. By calling the PlayFab API, you can simply update the leaderboard.

```csharp
using System.Collections.Generic;
using UnityEngine;
using PlayFab;
using PlayFab.ClientModels;

public class PlayFabLeaderboard : MonoBehaviour
{
    public void UpdatePlayFabLeaderboard()
    {
        PlayFabClientAPI.UpdatePlayerStatistics(
            new UpdatePlayerStatisticsRequest
            {
                Statistics = new List<StatisticUpdate>
                {
                    new StatisticUpdate
                    {
                        StatisticName = "HighScore",
                        Value = UnityEngine.Random.Range(0,100)
                    }
                }
            },

            (UpdatePlayerStatisticsResult result) =>
            {
                Debug.Log("Leaderboard updated.");
            },

            (PlayFabError error) =>
```

```
        {
            Debug.LogError(error.GenerateErrorReport());
        });
    }
}
```

You will test this as soon as you implement a trigger button on the control panel. But first, let's implement the leaderboard reading method.

Getting the Leaderboard

Let's add the GetPlayFabLeaderboard() method to the PlayFabLeaderboard script, while keeping the UpdatePlayFabLeaderboard() method.

You need to call the PlayFab API with the name of the leaderboard (in PlayFab's terminology every leaderboard is a *statistic*), and the number of values you want to receive. You want to fill the leaderboard on the canvas with the result of the API call.

Don't forget to drag-and-drop the Leaderboard game object and the Row prefab into the PlayFabLeaderboard component in the Inspector. In this way, the GetPlayFabLeaderboard method can instantiate for each entry in the leaderboard a new row under the Leaderboard game object.

```
using UnityEngine.UI;

public class PlayFabLeaderboard : MonoBehaviour
{
    public Transform leaderboard;
    public GameObject leaderboardRow;
    GameObject[] leaderboardEntries;
    public GameObject canvas;

    public void GetPlayFabLeaderboard()
    {
```

```
PlayFabClientAPI.GetLeaderboard(
    new GetLeaderboardRequest
    {
        StatisticName = "HighScore",
        StartPosition = 0,
        MaxResultsCount = 6
    },

    (GetLeaderboardResult result) =>
    {
        canvas.SetActive(true);
        leaderboardEntries = new GameObject[result.
        Leaderboard.Count];
        for (int i = 0; i < result.Leaderboard.
        Count; i++)
        {
            leaderboardEntries[i] =
            Instantiate(leaderboardRow, leaderboard);
            Text[] texts = leaderboardEntries[i].GetCom
            ponentsInChildren<Text>();
            texts[0].text = result.Leaderboard[i].
            Position.ToString();
            texts[1].text = result.Leaderboard[i].
            DisplayName;
            texts[2].text = result.Leaderboard[i].
            StatValue.ToString();
        }
    },

    (PlayFabError error) =>
    {
```

```
            Debug.LogError(error.GenerateErrorReport());
        });
    }
}
```

Finally, implement a closing method, where you destroy all the row game objects, delete the values from the array, and turn off the leaderboard canvas. Add this method (while keeping the existing ones) to the PlayFabLeaderboard script as well:

```
using System;

public class PlayFabLeaderboard : MonoBehaviour
{
public void ClosePlayFabLeaderboard()
    {
        for (int i = 0; i < leaderboardEntries.Length; i++)
        {
            Destroy(leaderboardEntries[i]);
        }
        Array.Clear(leaderboardEntries, 0, leaderboardEntries.
        Length);
        canvas.SetActive(false);
    }
}
```

Extending the Control Panel

You need to extend the control panel and trigger the earlier described functions to see if everything is working fine:

```
public class ControlPanel : MonoBehaviour
{
```

```
public const int PLAYFAB_GETLEADERBOARD = 5;

void OnGUI()
{
    if (selection == PLAYFAB_GETLEADERBOARD)
        GUILayout.Window(0, new Rect(0, 0, 300, 0),
        GetPlayFabLeaderboard, "PlayFab Leaderboard");
}

void OptionsWindow(int windowID)
{
    if (GUILayout.Button("Get PlayFab Leaderboard"))
    {
        playFab.GetComponent<PlayFabLeaderboard>().
        GetPlayFabLeaderboard();
        selection = PLAYFAB_GETLEADERBOARD;
    }
}

void GetPlayFabLeaderboard(int windowID)
{
    if (GUILayout.Button("Update PlayFab Leaderboard"))
        playFab.GetComponent<PlayFabLeaderboard>().
        UpdatePlayFabLeaderboard();

    if (GUILayout.Button("Cancel"))
    {
        playFab.GetComponent<PlayFabLeaderboard>().
        ClosePlayFabLeaderboard();
        selection = ROOTMENU;
    }
}
}
```

With that, you see how easy to implement a leaderboard with the help of PlayFab. With very little effort, you can improve the player engagement and level up your game with this nice feature. Next, you see how to implement the same functionality using Azure.

Azure

You can implement a basic leaderboard using pure cloud services simply. As illustrated in Figure 5-3, you will only implement a GET and a POST HTTP request.

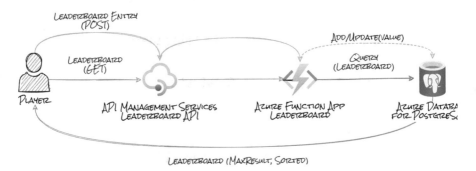

Figure 5-3. *Leaderboard on Azure*

You can use the same basic architecture, where the player calls a serverless function through the API Management service, which in turn updates or queries the database with the actual data.

Note that the implementation is very similar to the one involving matchmaking in Chapter 4. Refer to that section for a more detailed explanation.

Prerequisites

Similarly to PlayFab, this implementation also requires authenticated players. Otherwise, the client would not know the current player, and so the server cannot assign any values to it.

You will reuse the following shared components: API Management service, Azure Function App, and Azure Database for PostgreSQL.

Note   We defined the shared resources in Chapter 5. You will reuse those resources in this and the following chapters.

Initialize Terraform with New Resources

You'll add a new module to the existing Terraform scripts. Create a new folder called leaderboard and refer it from the main.tf file:

```
module "leaderboard" {
    source                     = "./leaderboard"
    api_management_name        = module.shared.api_
                                 management_name
    shared_resource_group_name = module.shared.shared_resource_
                                 group_name
    app_service_plan_id        = module.shared.app_
                                 service_plan_id
    storage_account_name       = module.shared.storage_
                                 account_name
    storage_account_access_key = module.shared.storage_account_
                                 access_key
}
```

Pass parameters of the shared components, such as the name of the API Management service to the leaderboard module. You will set these in variable blocks for each resource later. When you add a new module to Terraform, you have to reinitialize it with `terraform init`.

In the newly created `leaderboard` folder, create a new resource group for the leaderboard-specific resources. Create a new file called `resourcegroup.tf` and add the following code:

```
resource "azurerm_resource_group" "leaderboard" {
  name     = "leaderboard-resources"
  location = "West Europe"
}
```

Leaderboard Azure Functions

Create a new function app called `leaderboard-azure-functions`, which reuses your shared App Service Plan and Storage Account. You can create a new file called `functionapp.tf` in the leaderboard folder and add the following code:

```
variable "app_service_plan_id" {
  description = "AppService Plan ID"
}

variable "storage_account_name" {
  description = "Storage account name"
}

variable "storage_account_access_key" {
  description = "Storage account access key"
}

resource "azurerm_function_app" "leaderboard" {
  name                       = "leaderboard-azure-functions"
```

```
    location                      = azurerm_resource_group.
                                    leaderboard.location
    resource_group_name           = azurerm_resource_group.
                                    leaderboard.name
    app_service_plan_id           = var.app_service_plan_id
    storage_account_name          = var.storage_account_name
    storage_account_access_key    = var.storage_account_access_key
    version                       = "~4"
}

data "azurerm_function_app_host_keys" "leaderboard" {
    name                = azurerm_function_app.leaderboard.name
    resource_group_name = azurerm_resource_group.leaderboard.name
}
```

Creating a Leaderboard API

Update the API Management service with a new Leaderboard API and add
the two new operations (GET and POST) to it. These point to the respective
Function App functions, and they require authentication tokens through
the Azure AD. Create a new file called apim.tf and add the following
code to it:

```
variable "api_management_name" {
    description = "Name of the API Management service"
}

variable "shared_resource_group_name" {
  description = "Shared resource group name"
}

resource "azurerm_api_management_api" "leaderboard" {
    name                = "leaderboard-api"
```

```
    resource_group_name     = var.shared_resource_group_name
    api_management_name      = var.api_management_name
    revision                 = "1"
    path                     = "leaderboard"
    display_name             = "Leaderboard API"
    protocols                = ["https"]
    subscription_required    = false
}

resource "azurerm_api_management_api_operation"
"leaderboard-post" {
    operation_id           = "leaderboard-post"
    api_name               = azurerm_api_management_api.
                             leaderboard.name
    api_management_name    = var.api_management_name
    resource_group_name    = var.shared_resource_group_name
    display_name           = "POST Leaderboard"
    method                 = "POST"
    url_template           = "/Leaderboard"
}

resource "azurerm_api_management_api_operation"
"leaderboard-get" {
    operation_id           = "leaderboard-get-ticket"
    api_name               = azurerm_api_management_api.
                             leaderboard.name
    api_management_name    = var.api_management_name
    resource_group_name    = var.shared_resource_group_name
    display_name           = "GET Leaderboard"
    method                 = "GET"
    url_template           = "/Leaderboard"
}
```

```
resource "azurerm_api_management_backend" "leaderboard" {
  name                  = "leaderboard-azure-functions-backend"
  resource_group_name   = var.shared_resource_group_name
  api_management_name   = var.api_management_name
  protocol              = "http"
  url                   = "https://${azurerm_function_app.
                          leaderboard.default_hostname}/api/"
  resource_id           = "https://management.azure.
                          com/${azurerm_function_app.
                          leaderboard.id}"
  credentials {
    header = {
      x-functions-key = "${data.azurerm_function_app_host_keys.
                          leaderboard.default_function_key}"
    }
  }
}

resource "azurerm_api_management_api_policy" "leaderboard" {
  api_name              = azurerm_api_management_api.
                          leaderboard.name
  api_management_name   = azurerm_api_management_api.leaderboard.
                          api_management_name
  resource_group_name   = azurerm_api_management_api.leaderboard.
                          resource_group_name

  xml_content = <<XML
<policies>
  <inbound>
    <set-backend-service id="apim-policy" backend-
    id="leaderboard-azure-functions-backend" />
```

```
<validate-jwt header-name="Authorization" failed-
validation-httpcode="401" failed-validation-error-
message="Unauthorized. Access token is missing or
invalid.">
    <openid-config url="https://gamebackend2022.
    b2clogin.com/gamebackend2022.onmicrosoft.com/
    v2.0/.well-known/openid-configuration?p=B2C_1_
    SignInSignUp" />
    <audiences>
        <audience>e4d1e07d-81ff-45b8-
        b849-91bef09b5bbd</audience>
    </audiences>
    <issuers>
    <issuer>https://gamebackend2022.b2clogin.com/
    fe46bdde-805c-4a42-83c6-871e0f4278e7/v2.0/</issuer>
    </issuers>
</validate-jwt>
    </inbound>
</policies>
XML
    depends_on = [
        azurerm_api_management_backend.leaderboard
    ]
}
```

Note that the openid-config URL, audience, and the issuer should represent the actual values from your setup.

At this point, you can execute the Terraform script with terraform apply and verify that it runs without any issues.

Configure and Extend the Database

You have to do some configuration steps for the database. There are the same as in the previous chapter. You disable secure transport and add firewall rules so that you can access the database from your local machine and from Azure Functions.

```
az postgres flexible-server parameter set --name require_
secure_transport --value off --resource-group shared-resources
--server-name sharedpostgresqlserver
```

```
az postgres flexible-server firewall-rule create --resource-
group shared-resources --name sharedpostgresqlserver --rule-
name myclientaccess --start-ip-address <your local IP>
```

```
az postgres flexible-server firewall-rule create --resource-
group shared-resources --name sharedpostgresqlserver --rule-
name AllAzureServices --start-ip-address 0.0.0.0
```

You need to add a new table for the leaderboard to your existing shared PostgreSQL database. Create a file, for example createtable.sql, and add the following:

```
CREATE TABLE "Leaderboard" (
"PlayerID" varchar(150) NOT NULL PRIMARY KEY,
"Value" INT NOT NULL,
"DisplayName" varchar(150))
```

Execute it with Azure CLI:

```
az postgres flexible-server execute --admin-user sharedadmin
--admin-password SharedPassword99 --name sharedpostgresqlserver
--database-name shared-postgresql-database --file-path
createtable.sql
```

Finally, note the connection string:

217

```
az postgres flexible-server show-connection-string -s
sharedpostgresqlserver -u sharedadmin -p SharedPassword99 -d
shared-postgresql-database
```

Implement Azure Functions

In this section, you implement the leaderboard logic. You can find more details about implementing Azure Functions in Chapter 4.

Go to your leaderboards folder and run the following command with Azure Core Tools to create your new project:

```
func init LeaderboardFunctions --dotnet
```

Add the needed package references to LeaderboardFunctions.csproj:

```
<ItemGroup>
  <PackageReference Include="Microsoft.Azure.Functions.
  Extensions" Version="1.1.0" />
  <PackageReference Include="Microsoft.EntityFrameworkCore"
  Version="6.0.2" />
  <PackageReference Include="Microsoft.NET.Sdk.Functions"
  Version="4.0.1" />
  <PackageReference Include="Npgsql.EntityFrameworkCore.
  PostgreSQL" Version="6.0.3" />
</ItemGroup>
```

You will implement an entity framework to access and manipulate the database. First add the connection string to the local.settings.json file:

```
{
    "IsEncrypted": false,
    "Values": {
        "AzureWebJobsStorage": "UseDevelopmentStorage=true",
        "FUNCTIONS_WORKER_RUNTIME": "dotnet",
```

```
"SqlConnectionString" : "Server=sharedpostgresqlserver.
postgres.database.azure.com;Database=shared-postgresql-
database;Port=5432;User Id=sharedadmin;Password=SharedP
assword99;"
    }
}
```

Create a new LeaderboardContext.cs file:

```
using Microsoft.EntityFrameworkCore;

namespace LeaderboardFunctions
{
    public class LeaderboardContext : DbContext
    {
        public LeaderboardContext(DbContextOptions<LeaderboardC
        ontext> options) : base(options)
        {
        }           public DbSet<LeaderboardEntry> Leaderboard {
            get; set; }
    }
}
```

And create a StartUp class, which will start whenever the Function App starts:

```
using System;
using Microsoft.EntityFrameworkCore;
using Microsoft.Extensions.DependencyInjection;
using Microsoft.Azure.Functions.Extensions.DependencyInjection;

[assembly: FunctionsStartup(typeof(LeaderboardFunctions.
StartUp))]
```

```
namespace LeaderboardFunctions
{
    public class StartUp : FunctionsStartup
    {
        public override void Configure(IFunctionsHostBuilder
        builder)
        {
            string connectionString = Environment.GetEnvironmen
            tVariable("SqlConnectionString");
            builder.Services.AddDbContext<LeaderboardContext>
            (options => options.UseNpgsql(connectionString));
        }
    }
}
```

Create a LeaderboardEntry, which maps to each record in the database:

```
using System.ComponentModel.DataAnnotations;

namespace LeaderboardFunctions
{
    public class LeaderboardEntry
    {
        [Key]
        public string PlayerID { get; set; }
        public int Value { get; set; }
        public string DisplayName { get; set; }
    }
}
```

Finally, create the core function, which is triggered by HTTP calls from the client. You implemented two different HTTP methods:

- **HTTP GET.** You simply read all the records from the database into a list. Then you sort the list in descending order and send the requested number of entries in the response.

- **HTTP POST.** You check if there is a record with the same player ID. If yes, and if its value is smaller than the new value just arrived from the client, you update the record in the database. If the player ID does not yet exist in the database, you simply add to it.

Note that you can implement this in a lot of ways. The current way of implementation is just an example. Create a new file called Leaderboard. cs and add the following code to it:

```
using System.IO;
using System.Threading.Tasks;
using Microsoft.AspNetCore.Mvc;
using Microsoft.Azure.WebJobs;
using Microsoft.Azure.WebJobs.Extensions.Http;
using Microsoft.AspNetCore.Http;
using Microsoft.Extensions.Logging;
using Newtonsoft.Json;
using System.Linq;
using System.Collections.Generic;

namespace LeaderboardFunctions
{
    public class Leaderboard
    {

        private readonly LeaderboardContext leaderboardContext;
        public Leaderboard(LeaderboardContext
        leaderboardContext)
```

```
    {
        this.leaderboardContext = leaderboardContext;
    }

    [FunctionName("Leaderboard")]
    public async Task<IActionResult> LeaderboardEntry(
        [HttpTrigger(AuthorizationLevel.Anonymous,
        "post", "get", Route = null)] HttpRequest req,
        ILogger log)
    {
        string requestBody = await new StreamReader(req.
        Body).ReadToEndAsync();
        var data = JsonConvert.DeserializeObject<Leaderboar
        dEntry>(requestBody);

        string responseMessage = "";
        if (req.Method.Equals("POST"))
        {
            var leaderboardEntry = new LeaderboardEntry {
            PlayerID = data.PlayerID, Value = data.Value,
            DisplayName = data.DisplayName };
            var oldLeaderboardEntry = leaderboardContext.
            Leaderboard.Find(data.PlayerID);

            if (oldLeaderboardEntry!=null) {
                log.LogInformation("old: " +
                oldLeaderboardEntry.Value + " new: " +
                data.Value );
                if (oldLeaderboardEntry.Value < data.
                Value) {
                    leaderboardContext.
                    Entry(oldLeaderboardEntry).State
                    = Microsoft.EntityFrameworkCore.
                    EntityState.Detached;
```

```
            leaderboardContext.Leaderboard.
            Update(leaderboardEntry);
        }
    } else {
        log.LogInformation("add");
        leaderboardContext.Entry(leaderboardEntry).
        State = Microsoft.EntityFrameworkCore.
        EntityState.Detached;
        leaderboardContext.Leaderboard.
        Add(leaderboardEntry);
    }
    leaderboardContext.SaveChanges();
}
else if (req.Method.Equals("GET"))
{
    List<LeaderboardEntry> list = new
    List<LeaderboardEntry>();
    list = leaderboardContext.Leaderboard.ToList();

    list.Sort((s1, s2) => s1.Value.CompareTo(s2.
    Value));
    list.Reverse();

    int maxResultsCount = int.Parse(req.
    Query["MaxResultsCount"]);
    if (maxResultsCount > list.Count)
    maxResultsCount = list.Count;

    list = list.GetRange(0, maxResultsCount);

    string result = JsonConvert.
    SerializeObject(list);
    responseMessage = result;
}
```

```
        return new OkObjectResult(responseMessage);
    }
  }
}
```

You can now test if your functions and the database work correctly:

```
func start
```

```
curl -X POST -d "{PlayerID: 'abc', Value: '123'}" http://
localhost:7071/api/Leaderboard
```

```
curl -X GET http://localhost:7071/api/Leaderboard?
MaxResultsCount=6
```

Publishing Azure Functions

Now that the functions work fine locally, you need to publish them to
Azure. Set the connection string in the local settings. Let's upload it to
Azure as well:

```
az functionapp config appsettings set -n leaderboard-azure-
functions -g leaderboard-resources --settings SqlConnectionSt
ring="Server=sharedpostgresqlserver.postgres.database.azure.
com;Database=shared-postgresql-database;Port=5432;User Id=share
dadmin;Password=SharedPassword99;"
```

And then publish the functions:

```
func azure functionapp publish leaderboard-azure-functions
```

You can now test the function from the Azure Portal or by using cURL:

```
az functionapp function show --function-name Leaderboard --name
shared-azure-functions --resource-group shared-resources
--query "invokeUrlTemplate" --output tsv
```

```
curl -X POST -d "{PlayerID: 'abc', Value: '123'}" https://
leaderboard-azure-functions.azurewebsites.net/api/leaderboard
```

```
curl -X GET https://leaderboard-azure-functions.azurewebsites.
net/api/leaderboard?MaxResultsCount=6
```

Implement the Client in Unity

Similarly to PlayFab, you'll implement three functions for requesting, updating, and closing the leaderboard.

You will use simple HTTP calls. In the header, you always have to include the authorization token, otherwise the API Management service will refuse the request.

During the Azure login process, you stored the displayName and playerID values in the AzureSettings component. You can submit these in the update function with some random value to the leaderboard.

Create a new script called AzureLeaderboard.cs and add the UpdateAzureLeaderboard function to it:

```
using UnityEngine;
using System.Net;
using System.IO;
using System.Text;
public class AzureLeaderboard : MonoBehaviour
{
    public Transform leaderboard;
    public GameObject leaderboardRow;
    public GameObject canvas;
```

```
GameObject azure;
private void Start()
{
    azure = GameObject.Find("Azure");
}

public void UpdateAzureLeaderboard()
{
    HttpWebRequest request = (HttpWebRequest)WebRequest.
    Create("https://shared-apim.azure-api.net/leaderboard/
    Leaderboard");
    request.Method = "POST";

    request.Headers.Add("Authorization", "Bearer " +
    GetComponent<AzureSettings>().token);

    string displayName = azure.
    GetComponent<AzureSettings>().displayName;
    string playerID = azure.GetComponent<AzureSettings>().
    playerID;

    byte[] data = Encoding.ASCII.GetBytes("{PlayerID: '" +
    playerID + "', Value: '" + UnityEngine.Random.Range(0,
    100) + "', DisplayName: '" + displayName + "'}");
    request.ContentType = "application/json";
    request.ContentLength = data.Length;

    Stream requestStream = request.GetRequestStream();
    requestStream.Write(data, 0, data.Length);
    requestStream.Close();

    HttpWebResponse response = (HttpWebResponse)request.
    GetResponse();
```

```
    StreamReader reader = new StreamReader(response.
    GetResponseStream());
    string result = reader.ReadToEnd();
    Debug.Log("Update finished. " + result);
  }
}
```

When requesting the leaderboard, you convert the received JSON into a list and display the values for the player. Let's implement the GetAzureLeaderboard method:

```
using System.Collections.Generic;
using Newtonsoft.Json;
using UnityEngine.UI;

public class AzureLeaderboard : MonoBehaviour
{
    public Transform leaderboard;
    public GameObject leaderboardRow;
    GameObject[] leaderboardEntries;
    public GameObject canvas;

    GameObject azure;
    private void Start()
    {
        azure = GameObject.Find("Azure");
    }

    public void GetAzureLeaderboard()
    {
        HttpWebRequest request = (HttpWebRequest)WebRequest.
        Create("https://shared-apim.azure-api.net/leaderboard/
        Leaderboard?MaxResultsCount=6");
        request.Method = "GET";
```

```
request.Headers.Add("Authorization", "Bearer " +
GetComponent<AzureSettings>().token);

HttpWebResponse response = (HttpWebResponse)request.
GetResponse();
StreamReader reader = new StreamReader(response.
GetResponseStream());
string result = reader.ReadToEnd();

List<LeaderboardEntry> list = JsonConvert.DeserializeOb
ject<List<LeaderboardEntry>>(result);

canvas.SetActive(true);
leaderboardEntries = new GameObject[list.Count];
for (int i = 0; i < list.Count; i++)
{
    leaderboardEntries[i] = Instantiate(leaderboardRow,
    leaderboard);
    Text[] texts = leaderboardEntries[i].GetComponents
    InChildren<Text>();
    texts[0].text = i.ToString();
    texts[1].text = list[i].DisplayName;
    texts[2].text = list[i].Value.ToString();
}
    }
}

public class LeaderboardEntry
{
    public string PlayerID { get; set; }
    public int Value { get; set; }

    public string DisplayName { get; set; }
}
```

Finally, implement a `CloseAzureLeaderboard` method to clean up the array and hide the leaderboard panel:

```
using System;

public class AzureLeaderboard : MonoBehaviour
{
    public void CloseAzureLeaderboard()
    {
        for (int i = 0; i < leaderboardEntries.Length; i++)
        {
            Destroy(leaderboardEntries[i]);
        }
        Array.Clear(leaderboardEntries, 0, leaderboardEntries.
        Length);
        canvas.SetActive(false);
    }
}
```

With that, you have all the functions you need to communicate with the backend. In Unity, you can add the `AzureLeaderboard` component to the Azure game object in the Inspector. Then, drag-and-drop the Canvas, Leaderboard, and Row from the hierarchy to the `AzureLeaderboard` component.

Extending the Control Panel

Finally, you should also implement new buttons on the control panel to call these functions. Extend the `ControlPanel` script with the following code:

```
public class ControlPanel : MonoBehaviour
{
    public const int AZURE_GETLEADERBOARD = 6;
```

```
void OnGUI()
{
    if (selection == AZURE_GETLEADERBOARD)
        GUILayout.Window(0, new Rect(0, 0, 300, 0),
        GetAzureLeaderboard, "Azure Leaderboard");
}

void OptionsWindow(int windowID)
{
    if (GUILayout.Button("Get Azure Leaderboard"))
    {
        azure.GetComponent<AzureLeaderboard>().
        GetAzureLeaderboard();
        selection = AZURE_GETLEADERBOARD;
    }

}

void GetAzureLeaderboard(int windowID)
{
    if (GUILayout.Button("Update Azure Leaderboard"))
        azure.GetComponent<AzureLeaderboard>().
        UpdateAzureLeaderboard();

    if (GUILayout.Button("Cancel"))
    {
        azure.GetComponent<AzureLeaderboard>().
        CloseAzureLeaderboard();
        selection = ROOTMENU;
    }
}
}
```

To test this, log in through Azure, then update the leaderboard with values. You now have a working Azure-based leaderboard for your game.

Summary

In this chapter, we reviewed the leaderboard functionality and implemented it in PlayFab and Azure. You can see how much easier it is to use PlayFab and its API to implement this feature. However, it's also not difficult to implement basic leaderboards in Azure. You can use the same or similar building blocks and techniques as in the matchmaking solution. Leaderboards are important features and are great motivators for players to continue playing your game. They are easy to implement, but they add lots of additional value.

Review Questions

1. What is the benefit adding a leaderboard to a game?

2. Explain a typical leaderboard. How is the data stored?

3. Which functions do you need to implement for the client?

4. Which functionality should the server side cover?

5. How do you configure PlayFab to use a leaderboard?

6. Which PlayFab API calls are used to get and update leaderboards?

7. What is a prerequisite for a player to update a leaderboard?

8. Which building blocks do you need in Azure to implement leaderboards?

9. Why do you compare incoming and stored values in a leaderboard?

10. Why do you sort values in the leaderboard?

CHAPTER 6

Economy

A well-designed virtual game economy improves player engagement and is a very popular way to generate revenue.

In a virtual economy, there are virtual items to buy, typically with virtual currencies. You can also let your players purchase virtual currencies, items, features, or practically anything using real money. This is a great way to monetize your game and improve player engagement.

This chapter focuses on the realization of such an infrastructure to enable a virtual economy and in-app purchasing (IAP) in your game.

Components

Let's look more closely at the idea of a *virtual economy* and see what basic components you have to implement for this feature:

- **Items.** Anything that a player can buy in your game.

- **Catalog.** A list of all the items that a player can buy.

- **Virtual currencies.** Your game can support multiple currencies that are used to buy virtual items from the catalog. This is very game specific. This chapter's example uses the fictitious MyGame Coin (MC).

- **Player inventory.** When a player buys an item from the catalog, it will be added to their personal inventory.

- **Stores.** External third-party stores that allow in-app purchases and purchasing of virtual items for real money (not to be confused with PlayFab's Store definition).

Figure 6-1 shows the main functions you should implement for this virtual economy:

- **Get Catalog.** You want to allow players to see a list of items that they can purchase. You'll store this in the game backend in a data structure and the game client will show in it in game-specific representation.

- **Get Inventory.** Shows items purchased from the catalog that are stored in the backend. The same applies to the amount of virtual currencies the player owns.

- **Purchase Item.** The players can start a purchase, and as a result, the chosen item will appear in the player's inventory and the amount of virtual currency will be updated. If the player buys something for real money, that triggers the involvement of an external store.

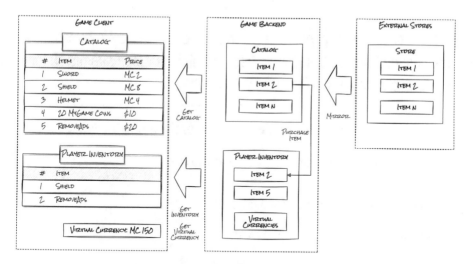

Figure 6-1. *Components and functions of a virtual economy*

In the following sections, you learn how to implement the backend components with both PlayFab and pure Azure services. You also learn how the game client can invoke the main functions to realize the virtual economy.

PlayFab

PlayFab provides a rich functionality to implement a game economy. It also simplifies this integration with multiple external stores, which can otherwise be a tedious task.

Economy GUI

Before going into the economy code, you need to create a simple window that will show the catalog and inventory items and the state of the virtual currency, and will allow players to start a purchase.

Note   This control panel is only required to demonstrate how to use the backend functionalities. It's best to build your own custom UI for managing catalogs and inventory items that fits your game.

Go to ControlPanel.cs and extend it with the following code:

```
public class ControlPanel : MonoBehaviour
{
    public const int PLAYFAB_ECONOMY = 7;

    string textArea = "\n\n\n\n";

    string economyTextAreaTitle = "";
    string itemToPurchase = "";
    string virtualCurrencyLabel = "";

    void OnGUI()
    {
        if (selection == PLAYFAB_ECONOMY)
            GUILayout.Window(0, new Rect(0, 0, 300, 0),
            PlayFabEconomyWindow, "PlayFab Economy");
    }

    void OptionsWindow(int windowID)
    {
        if (GUILayout.Button("PlayFab Economy"))
        {
            selection = PLAYFAB_ECONOMY;
        }
    }

    void PlayFabEconomyWindow(int windowID)
    {
```

```
if (economyTextAreaTitle != "")
    GUILayout.Label(economyTextAreaTitle);

textArea = ShopUI.GetTextArea();
textArea = GUILayout.TextArea(textArea, 200);

virtualCurrencyLabel = ShopUI.
GetVirtualCurrencyLabel();
if (virtualCurrencyLabel != "")
    GUILayout.Label(virtualCurrencyLabel);

GUILayout.Space(10);

if (GUILayout.Button("Get Catalog Items"))
{
    playFab.GetComponent<PlayFabEconomy>().
    GetCatalogItems();
    economyTextAreaTitle = "Catalog Items";
}

if (GUILayout.Button("Get Player Inventory + Virtual
Currency"))
{
    playFab.GetComponent<PlayFabEconomy>().
    GetInventory();
    economyTextAreaTitle = "Player Inventory";
}

GUILayout.Space(10);

if (GUILayout.Button("Purchase this item (number):"))
{
    playFab.GetComponent<PlayFabEconomy>().
    PurchaseItem(itemToPurchase);
```

```
        }

        itemToPurchase = GUILayout.
        TextField(itemToPurchase, 100);

        GUILayout.Space(10);

        if (GUILayout.Button("Buy from store"))
        {
            playFab.GetComponent<PlayFabEconomy>().
            BuyFromStore(itemToPurchase);
        }

        GUILayout.Space(10);

        if (GUILayout.Button("Cancel"))
        {
            selection = ROOTMENU;
        }
    }
}
```

Note that the PlayFabEconomy and the ShopUI classes are missing. You will create those in the next steps. Create a new class called ShopUI.cs, which manages and fills the text area:

```
using System.Collections.Generic;
using PlayFab.ClientModels;
public static class ShopUI
{
    private static string textArea = "\n\n\n\n\n";
    private static string virtualCurrencyLabel = "";
    public static void UpdateTextArea(List<ItemInstance> items)
    {
        string ta = "";
```

```
    int number = 0;
    foreach (ItemInstance item in items)
    {
        number++;
        ta += number + " | " + item.DisplayName + "\n";
    }

    for (int I = items.Count; I < 5; i++)
    {
        ta += "\n";
    }
    textArea = ta;
}

public static void UpdateVirtualCurrency(string VC_Name,
int VC_Amount)
{
    virtualCurrencyLabel = "You have " + VC_Amount + " " +
    VC_Name;
}

public static void UpdateTextArea(List<CatalogItem> items)
{
    string ta = "";
    int number = 0;
    foreach (CatalogItem item in items)
    {
        number++;
        ta += number + " | " + item.DisplayName + ".....";
        if (item.VirtualCurrencyPrices.Count != 0)
        {
            ta += item.VirtualCurrencyPrices["MC"] + " MC";
        }
```

```
            else
            {
                ta += "n/a";
            }
            ta += "\n";
        }

        for (int I = items.Count; I < 5; i++)
        {
            ta += "\n";
        }
        textArea = ta;
    }

    public static string GetVirtualCurrencyLabel()
    {
        return virtualCurrencyLabel;
    }
    public static string GetTextArea()
    {
        return textArea;
    }
}
```

Now that you have the GUI to display the items and related control buttons, let's move on to implementing the core functionality.

Catalog and Items

Figure 6-2 shows how to create a new catalog in PlayFab. Go to PlayFab's Game Manager, then choose ENGAGE ➤ Economy ➤ New Catalog.

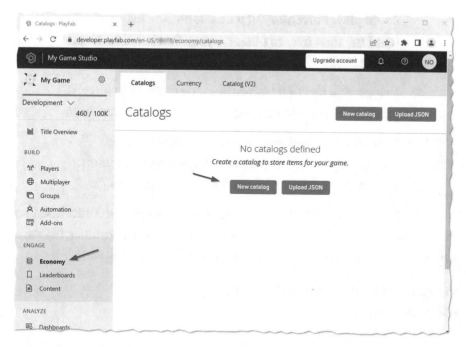

Figure 6-2. *Create a new catalog in PlayFab*

Name your catalog and click Save Catalog. This will create a catalog
with one item. To delete the primary catalog, remove all the items.

Now add some new items to the catalog, as shown in Figure 6-1. Here
are some options to choose from:

- **Durable or Consumable.** If your item is consumable,
  you can buy it repeatedly. You can also determine how
  many times the players can consume it and, optionally,
  determine the time between buying and consuming.
  For example, you can buy virtual currency for real
  money. Players can buy durable items only once. For
  example, removing advertisements.

- **Is stackable, tradable.** If an item is stackable, even if
  the player buys it several times, it will appear only once

241

in the player inventory. If it's tradable, the player can hand the item over to other players. Stackable items are not tradable.

- **Prices.** You can determine the price of the item after you define a virtual currency. You will do this step later.

- **Item class, tags, description, custom data...** You can specify many additional attributes for your items. Define those fields according to your game's needs.

Now that you have filled the catalog, you can go back to Unity and use the PlayFab API. You'll write the client code to access the catalog. Create a new file called PlayFabEconomy.cs and copy the following code:

```
using System.Collections.Generic;
using UnityEngine;
using PlayFab.ClientModels;
using PlayFab;

public class PlayFabEconomy : MonoBehaviour
{
    List<CatalogItem> catalogItems = new List<CatalogItem>();
    public void GetCatalogItems()
    {
        PlayFabClientAPI.GetCatalogItems(new
        GetCatalogItemsRequest()
        {
            CatalogVersion = "MyGame Catalog",
        },
        result =>
        {
            catalogItems.Clear();
```

```
        foreach (CatalogItem item in result.Catalog)
        catalogItems.Add(item);
        ShopUI.UpdateTextArea(catalogItems);
    },
    error =>
    {
            Debug.Log(error.GenerateErrorReport());
    });
    }
}
```

This will read all the catalog items and display them to the users using the ShopUI class.

Virtual Currency

It is time to create your virtual currency. You can do this in PlayFab's Game Manager, as shown in Figure 6-3.

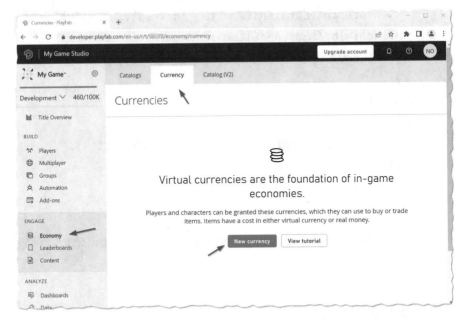

Figure 6-3. *Create a virtual currency*

Let's create the currency called MyGame Coin, with the currency code MC. Set the initial deposit to 100, which is what you'll grant to every user once.

Figure 6-4 shows where you can find the actual amount of virtual currency for a specific player.

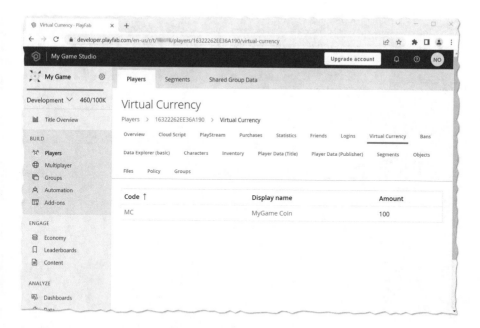

Figure 6-4. *Virtual currencies of a player*

Now that you have an official virtual currency, you can add some prices to your items in the catalog. Go back to your catalog (choose Economy ➤ MyGame Catalog) and, from Prices, add your prices in MC to each item.

Player Inventory

Next, you'll list the items a player owns. First, add some items to a player (for free) from the catalog, as shown in Figure 6-5.

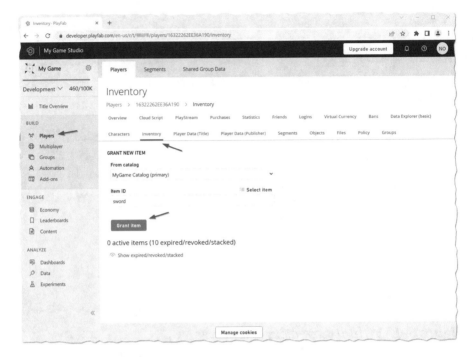

Figure 6-5. *Grant items to a player*

To read the actual items of a player, go to the `PlayFabEconomy.cs` class and add the following code to it. This will not only read the contents of the player's inventory, but will also list the available virtual currencies for buying additional items:

```
List<ItemInstance> playerInventoryItems = new
List<ItemInstance>();

    public void GetInventory()
    {
        PlayFabClientAPI.GetUserInventory(new
        GetUserInventoryRequest(),
        result =>
        {
```

```
    playerInventoryItems.Clear();
    foreach (ItemInstance item in result.Inventory)
    playerInventoryItems.Add(item);
    ShopUI.UpdateTextArea(playerInventoryItems);
    ShopUI.UpdateVirtualCurrency("MC", result.
    VirtualCurrency["MC"]);

  },
  error =>
  {
      Debug.Log(error.GenerateErrorReport());
  });
}
```

This example hard-codes the MC virtual currency, but of course you can align this code with your actual game. Note that the GetUserInventory API call will provide both the inventory items and the current state of the player's wealth.

Purchasing an Item

Letting players buy items is the main goal. PlayFab makes this really simple. You simply have to invoke the PurchaseItem method with the catalog name, item ID, price, and virtual currency type.

Extend the PlayFabEconomy.cs with the following code, which allows the players to buy a specific item using MC:

```
public void PurchaseItem(string itemToPurchase)
{
    int itemNumber = int.Parse(itemToPurchase) - 1;

    PlayFabClientAPI.PurchaseItem(new PurchaseItemRequest()
    {
```

```
            CatalogVersion = "MyGame Catalog",
            ItemId = catalogItems[itemNumber].ItemId,
            Price = (int)catalogItems[itemNumber].
            VirtualCurrencyPrices["MC"],
            VirtualCurrency = "MC"
        },
        result =>
        {
            Debug.Log("Purchase completed.");
        },
        error =>
        {
            Debug.Log(error.GenerateErrorReport());
        });
    }
```

If everything went fine, the item should appear in the player's inventory and the amount of virtual currency should decrease by the price of the item. Drag-and-drop the PlayFabEconomy component to the PlayFab game object in Unity and verify that it works. Comment out the BuyFromStore option, as you will implement it in the next section.

Bundles, Containers, Drop Tables, Stores

PlayFab provides several extra features to satisfy different game requirements. Bundles allow you to group items and grant them in a bundle to a player. A container is a group of items that's closed until the player opens it. With drop tables, you can reward players with items. Stores are subsets of catalogs, where you can override prices for the items.

In-App Purchasing

So far, you have implemented a solution to buy virtual items for virtual currencies. What if players could buy something for real money and that would cover your efforts in making a game? That's sounds good, but you need some additional components.

First, you need a real store that can manage purchasing with real credit cards. Each platform has its own store. For example, if you develop an Android game, you'll use the Google Play Store.

Second, Unity IAP helps you interface with those different stores. So you only have to set up your stores and then can easily communicate with them through Unity IAP.

Make sure that your catalog is in sync with the store's catalog. You have to add your relevant items to the store as well; otherwise, the store cannot refer to them when the purchasing request arrives.

After all, purchased items only make sense in your game. If the purchase was successful, the store provides a receipt. After validating the receipt, you have to make sure the item appears in the player's inventory.

To implement this, first turn on in-app purchasing in Unity. It is under the Services panel. It is also under the Edit ➤ Project Settings... ➤ Services ➤ In-App Purchasing menu.

Next, create a class in `UnityIAPManager.cs`. This uses the `UnityEngine.Purchasing` namespace and implements the `IStoreListener` interface. This way, you can receive Unity IAP events. You have to implement three functions:

1. **Initialize Unity IAP.** Here, configure Unity IAP and make it ready to execute purchases. Before calling the `Initialize` method, you upload the items from the catalog.

2. **Initiate a purchase.** It is only possible if you earlier
initialized the Unity IAP. If this is successfully
completed, it comes back with the receipt.

3. **Validate a receipt.** You have to make sure that the
player actually bought the product and paid for
it. PlayFab API provides a simple way to validate
receipts from different stores. For example, with
Google Play Store, you use `PlayFabClientAPI.`
`ValidateGooglePlayPurchase.`

Note   Unity IAP supports multiple stores (Google Play Store,
Microsoft Store, Amazon Store, Apple Store, etc.), but if you want to
use those stores, you need to register your game first. Instead, you
can create a Fake Store for developing activities. The drawback is
that receipt validation is not possible with this Fake Store scenario.

Copy the following code into the `UnityIAPManager.cs` file:

```
using UnityEngine;
using UnityEngine.Purchasing;
using System.Collections.Generic;
using PlayFab.ClientModels;

public class UnityIAPManager : IStoreListener
{
    private IStoreController controller;
    public UnityIAPManager(List<CatalogItem> catalog)
    {
        InitializeUnityIAP(catalog);
    }
    public void InitializeUnityIAP(List<CatalogItem> catalog)
```

```
{
    var module = StandardPurchasingModule.Instance();
    var builder = ConfigurationBuilder.Instance(module);

    foreach (var item in catalog)
    {
        builder.AddProduct(item.ItemId, ProductType.
        NonConsumable);
    }
    UnityPurchasing.Initialize(this, builder);
}

public void OnInitialized(IStoreController controller,
IExtensionProvider extensions)
{
    Debug.Log("Unity IAP is initialized. It is ready to
    make purchases.");
    this.controller = controller;
}

public void OnInitializeFailed(InitializationFailureRea
son error)
{
    Debug.Log("Initialization error: " + error);
}

public void PurchaseItem(string productId)
{
    controller.InitiatePurchase(productId);
}

public PurchaseProcessingResult ProcessPurchase(Purchase
EventArgs e)
{
```

```
    Debug.Log("Purchase completed. ProductId: " +
    e.purchasedProduct.definition.id + " Receipt: " +
    e.purchasedProduct.receipt);

    // TODO : receipt validation + grant item (only with
    real store / receipt)

    return PurchaseProcessingResult.Complete;
}

public void OnPurchaseFailed(Product i,
PurchaseFailureReason p)
{
    Debug.Log("Purchase failed. Reason: " + p);
}
}
```

Insert the Unity IAP initialization call into the requesting catalog items. Also, implement the BuyFromStore method to start a purchase. Go to PlayFabEconomy.cs and add the following code:

```
UnityIAPManager unityIAPManager;

public void GetCatalogItems()
{
    PlayFabClientAPI.GetCatalogItems(new
    GetCatalogItemsRequest()
    {
        CatalogVersion = "MyGame Catalog",
    },
    result =>
    {
        unityIAPManager = new
        UnityIAPManager(catalogItems);
```

```
        },
        error =>
        {
            Debug.Log(error.GenerateErrorReport());
        });
    }

    public void BuyFromStore(string itemToPurchase)
    {
        int itemNumber = int.Parse(itemToPurchase) - 1;
        unityIAPManager.PurchaseItem(catalogItems[itemNumber].
        ItemId);
    }
```

Now you should be able to buy items from the store by providing their number and clicking the Buy from Store button on the Control Panel. As a result, you get a receipt, which you can validate and add the item to your inventory.

In the next part, you will implement the same functionality with pure Azure services. That solution might be more flexible, but PlayFab provides a lot of features (receipt validation, coupons, etc.) that you have to implement by yourself.

Azure

You can use a similar architecture to the one used with other game backend features, when implementing a game economy in Azure. However, you need to take a slightly different approach than with other backend features.

Here, you need to store data for catalogs and player inventories. A player typically owns multiple items, and a catalog can contain several products. This requirement fits a document-oriented (NoSQL) database much better than a relational database.

In a document-oriented database, you can store each catalog in a separate document. In this example, you store all the items of the MyGame Catalog in a document:

```
{
        "_id" : ObjectId("62b9b009ea2970a0481ce3d4"),
        "CatalogId" : "MyGame Catalog",
        "Items" : [
                {
                        "ItemId" : "shield",
                        "DisplayName" : "Shield",
                        "Price" : 4,
                        "Currency" : "MC"
                },
                {
                        "ItemId" : "helmet",
                        "DisplayName" : "Helmet",
                        "Price" : 8,
                        "Currency" : "MC"
                },
                {
                        "ItemId" : "weapon",
                        "DisplayName" : "Weapon",
                        "Price" : 9,
                        "Currency" : "MC"
                }
        ]
}
```

You organize these documents into *collections*. For example, you can put different catalog documents in the Catalog collection.

Azure supports the implementation of such a document-oriented database through the Azure Cosmos DB account. Actually, you will use the MongoDB API to access and manipulate data.

As Figure 6-6 shows, you can use API Management Services to interface your clients with the Azure Function app. Only authenticated players can call the Economy API. The Azure Function App then queries and manipulates the data on the Cosmos DB.

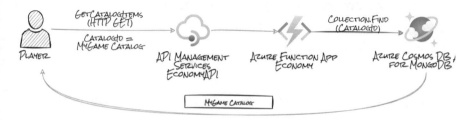

Figure 6-6. *Economy on Azure*

Building the Economy Backend

Again, you can reuse some shared resources, which were also required in other chapters of this book. Create a new subfolder called economy. You have to create a new economy module and provide the shared resources to it in the main.tf file:

```
module "economy" {
  source                     = "./economy"
  api_management_name        = module.shared.api_
                               management_name
  shared_resource_group_name = module.shared.shared_resource_
                               group_name
  app_service_plan_id        = module.shared.app_
                               service_plan_id
```

```
storage_account_name          = module.shared.storage_
                                account_name
storage_account_access_key = module.shared.storage_account_
                                access_key
}
```

Then, go to the economy folder and create a new resource group (in resourcegroup.tf), where you will put the new economy-related resources:

```
resource "azurerm_resource_group" "economy" {
  name     = "economy-resources"
  location = "West Europe"
}
```

Create a new file called functionapp.t, and add the Azure Function App resource to it. It refers to the shared App Service Plan and Storage Account. This will create an empty Azure Function App where you will upload your functions:

```
variable "app_service_plan_id" {
  description = "AppService Plan ID"
}

variable "storage_account_name" {
  description = "Storage account name"
}

variable "storage_account_access_key" {
  description = "Storage account access key"
}

resource "azurerm_function_app" "economy" {
  name                      = "economy-azure-functions"
```

```
  location                      = azurerm_resource_group.economy.
                                  location
  resource_group_name           = azurerm_resource_group.
                                  economy.name
  app_service_plan_id           = var.app_service_plan_id
  storage_account_name          = var.storage_account_name
  storage_account_access_key    = var.storage_account_access_key
  version                       = "~4"
}

data "azurerm_function_app_host_keys" "economy" {
  name                = azurerm_function_app.economy.name
  resource_group_name = azurerm_resource_group.economy.name
}
```

Now create the Azure Cosmos DB API for MongoDB. During the development phase, you can turn on the enable_free_tier option. This example uses the weakest consistency level, which you should change when moving to production. Create a new file called cosmosdb.tf and copy the following code into it:

```
resource "azurerm_cosmosdb_account" "economy" {
  name                = "mygame-cosmos-db"
  location            = azurerm_resource_group.economy.location
  resource_group_name = azurerm_resource_group.economy.name
  offer_type          = "Standard"
  kind                = "MongoDB"
  enable_free_tier    = true

  capabilities {
    name = "MongoDBv3.4"
  }
```

```
capabilities {
  name = "EnableMongo"
}

consistency_policy {
  consistency_level      = "Eventual"
}

geo_location {
  location              = azurerm_resource_group.economy.location
  failover_priority = 0
}
}

resource "azurerm_cosmosdb_mongo_database" "economy" {
  name                  = "mygame-cosmos-mongo-db"
  resource_group_name = azurerm_resource_group.economy.name
  account_name          = azurerm_cosmosdb_account.economy.name
}
```

Execute the terraform script (`terraform init`, `terraform apply`).
Note that you should comment out the api_management_name and
shared_resource_group_name variables, which you will define later with
the API Management Service. This will build the required infrastructure
components in Azure.

In the next step, you implement the functions that allow the access and
manipulation of data in the database.

Creating the Economy Functions

Using the Azure Core Tools, create a new dotnet project:

```
func init EconomyFunctions
```

Then, add the MongoDB packages to your project. This time you will use the MongoDB packages instead of the `EntityFramework`. Go to the `EntityFunctions` folder and execute the following commands:

```
dotnet add package MongoDB.Driver
dotnet add package MongoDB.Bson
```

Request the connection string of the MongoDB by providing the parameters of your database:

```
az cosmosdb keys list --type connection-strings -g economy-
resources --name mygame-cosmos-db
```

Copy the connection string into the `local.settings.json` file. This will allow you to test the functions locally:

```
{
    "IsEncrypted": false,
    "Values": {

        ...

        "MongoDBConnectionString" : "mongodb://mygame-cosmos-
        db:<password>==@mygame-cosmos-db.mongo.cosmos.azure.com
        :10255/?ssl=true&replicaSet=globaldb&retrywrites=false&
        maxIdleTimeMS=120000&appName=@mygame-cosmos-db@"
    }
}
```

Now start the implementation with the data structure. MongoDB uses BSON format, which is the binary form of JSON. Create a file called `Item.cs` and provide the following fields for each item:

```
using MongoDB.Bson;
using MongoDB.Bson.Serialization.Attributes;

namespace EconomyFunctions
{
```

```
    public class Item
    {

        [BsonElement("ItemId")]
        public string ItemId { get; set; }

        [BsonElement("DisplayName")]
        public string DisplayName { get; set; }

        [BsonElement("Price")]
        public int Price { get; set; }

        [BsonElement("Currency")]
        public string Currency { get; set; }
    }
}
```

You can obviously define any fields for one item. To each player, assign a list of items in PlayerInventory.cs:

```
using MongoDB.Bson;
using MongoDB.Bson.Serialization.Attributes;
using System.Collections.Generic;

namespace EconomyFunctions
{
    public class PlayerInventory {

        [BsonId]
        public ObjectId Id { get; set; }

        [BsonElement("PlayerId")]
        public string PlayerId { get; set; }

        [BsonElement("Items")]
```

```
        public List<Item> Items { get; set; }
    }
}
```

You can also create multiple catalogs, each with different items. Create a Catalog.cs file, which includes all the related fields:

```
using MongoDB.Bson;
using MongoDB.Bson.Serialization.Attributes;
using System.Collections.Generic;

namespace EconomyFunctions
{
    public class Catalog {

        [BsonId]
        public ObjectId Id { get; set; }

        [BsonElement("CatalogId")]
        public string CatalogId { get; set; }

        [BsonElement("Items")]
        public List<Item> Items { get; set; }
    }
}
```

Players can have different virtual currencies. You need to store the name of the virtual currency and the amount in VirtualCurrency.cs:

```
using MongoDB.Bson;
using MongoDB.Bson.Serialization.Attributes;

namespace EconomyFunctions
{
    public class VirtualCurrency {
```

```
    [BsonElement("VC_Amount")]
    public int VC_Amount { get; set; }

    [BsonElement("VC_Name")]
    public string VC_Name { get; set; }
  }
}
```

Finally, each player can get multiple virtual currencies. Define this in PlayerVirtualCurrency.cs:

```
using MongoDB.Bson;
using MongoDB.Bson.Serialization.Attributes;
using System.Collections.Generic;

namespace EconomyFunctions
{
    public class PlayerVirtualCurrency {

        [BsonId]
        public ObjectId Id { get; set; }

        [BsonElement("PlayerId")]
        public string PlayerId { get; set; }

        [BsonElement("VirtualCurrencies")]

        public List<VirtualCurrency> VirtualCurrencies {
        get; set; }
    }
}
```

Now that you have the data structures, you can create an Economy.cs file and add the Catalog function. This function is pretty long, so we break it into parts with some explanation:

```csharp
using System.IO;
using System.Threading.Tasks;
using Microsoft.AspNetCore.Mvc;
using Microsoft.Azure.WebJobs;
using Microsoft.Azure.WebJobs.Extensions.Http;
using Microsoft.AspNetCore.Http;
using Microsoft.Extensions.Logging;
using Newtonsoft.Json;
using System.Linq;

using MongoDB.Bson;
using MongoDB.Driver;

namespace EconomyFunctions
{
    public class Economy
    {

        [FunctionName("Catalog")]
        public async Task<IActionResult> Catalog(
                [HttpTrigger(AuthorizationLevel.Anonymous,
                "get", "post", "delete", Route = null)]
                HttpRequest req,
                ILogger log)
        {
            string requestBody = await new StreamReader(req.
            Body).ReadToEndAsync();
            Catalog data = JsonConvert.DeserializeObject<Catalo
            g>(requestBody);

            var client = new MongoClient(System.Environment.Get
            EnvironmentVariable("MongoDBConnectionString"));
            var database = client.GetDatabase("mygame-cosmos-
            mongo-db");
```

```
var collection = database.GetCollection<Catalog>("
Catalog");
```

...

In this first part, you implement a new function called `Catalog`, which is executed by receiving an HTTP request. This can be `GET`, `POST`, and `DELETE`. The incoming request comes in JSON format, which you need to deserialize to the earlier defined data structures. Also, you need to create a collection variable referring to the catalog collection in the database. This collection contains all the catalogs in document format.

...

```
string responseMessage = "";
if (req.Method.Equals("POST"))
{
    var catalogFilter = new BsonDocument { {
    "CatalogId", data.CatalogId } };
    var res = await collection.Find(catalogFilter).
    FirstOrDefaultAsync();
    if (res != null) // Catalog exists
    {
        bool itemExists = false;
        foreach (var item in data.Items)
        {
            var fittingVirtualCurrency = res.Items.
            Find(x => x.ItemId == item.ItemId);
            if (fittingVirtualCurrency != null)
            itemExists = true;
        }
        if (itemExists) // Item exists
        {
```

```
                responseMessage = "Item is already
                existing in the catalog.";

            }
            else // Item not exists
            {
                var filter = Builders<Catalog>.Filter.
                Where(x => x.CatalogId == data.
                CatalogId);
                foreach (var item in data.Items)
                {
                    var update = Builders<Catalog>.
                    Update.Push<Item>(x =>
                    x.Items, item);
                    var result = collection.
                    UpdateOneAsync(filter,
                    update).Result;
                }
                responseMessage = "There was no such
                item(s) in this catalog so far. Item(s)
                added.";
            }
        }
        else // Catalog not exists
        {
            collection.InsertOne(data);
            responseMessage = "This catalog hasn't
            existed so far. Added " + data.
            CatalogId + ".";
        }
    }

...
```

The POST request allows players to upload catalog items. This is analog to PlayFab's User Generated Content (UGC) option. Create a new catalog if the catalog doesn't exist. If the catalog does exist, verify that the item is available. If it's not, add it to the catalog. A player can add multiple items to the catalog at the same time. The data should arrive in JSON format.

```
...
    else if (req.Method.Equals("GET"))
            {
                string catalogId = req.Query["CatalogId"];
                var filter = new BsonDocument { { "CatalogId",
                catalogId } };
                var res = await collection.Find(filter).
                FirstOrDefaultAsync();
                if (res == null)
                {
                    responseMessage = "This catalog has no
                    items.";
                }
                else
                {
                    responseMessage = JsonConvert.
                    SerializeObject(res);
                }
            }
...
```

With HTTP GET request, you simply try to find the asked catalog in the collection and send the whole document to the player. The player provides the CatalogId in the URL.

```
...
else if (req.Method.Equals("DELETE"))
            {
```

```
foreach (var item in data.Items)
{
    var filter = Builders<Catalog>.Filter.
    Where(x => x.CatalogId == data.CatalogId &&
    x.Items.Any(i => i.ItemId == item.ItemId));
    var update = Builders<Catalog>.Update.
    Pull<Item>(x => x.Items, item);
    var result = collection.
    UpdateOneAsync(filter, update).Result;

    if (result.ModifiedCount > 0)
    {
        responseMessage += item.ItemId + " is
        deleted. ";
    }
    else if (result.ModifiedCount == 0)
    {
        responseMessage += item.ItemId + " is
        not existing. ";
    }

}
}
return (ActionResult)new OkObjectResult(response
Message);
}
}
}
```

You must also implement the DELETE method, which allows you to delete items from the catalog. Depending on your game, you can decide if your player can delete items from a catalog as well.

Implementing the Inventory and VirtualCurrency functions is almost the same as implementing Catalog. You can download the complete code including these functions from GitHub. We do not discuss them here to keep the chapter shorter.

Finally, it's time to see if the program works locally:

```
func start
```

In another window, send a new catalog item:

```
curl -X POST http://localhost:7071/api/Catalog -d
"{CatalogId: 'MyGame Catalog', Items: [{ItemId: 'sword',
DisplayName:'Sword', Price:2, Currency: 'MC'}]}"
```

Test if it arrived:

```
curl http://localhost:7071/api/Catalog?CatalogId=MyGame%20
Catalog
{"Id":"62bd50b4c1519dc85a319f7e","CatalogId":"MyGame Catalog","
Items":[{"ItemId":"sword","DisplayName":"Sword","Price":2,"Curr
ency":"MC"}]}
```

Next, you will publish the functions to Azure and make them accessible through an API.

Publishing the Functions to Azure

Start by updating your Application Settings in Azure with the connection string of the MongoDB.

```
az functionapp config appsettings set -n economy-
azure-functions -g economy-resources --settings
MongoDBConnectionString="<your connection string>"
```

Then, publish the functions with the help of the Azure Core Tools:

```
func azure functionapp publish economy-azure-functions
```

Send a new item to the catalog:

```
curl -X POST https://economy-azure-functions.azurewebsites.net/
api/catalog -d "{CatalogId: 'MyGame Catalog', Items: [{ItemId:
'shield', DisplayName:'Shield', Price:4, Currency: 'MC'}]}"
```

Finally, check if it arrived:

```
curl https://economy-azure-functions.azurewebsites.net/api/
catalog?CatalogId=MyGame%20Catalog
{"Id":"62bd50b4c1519dc85a319f7e","CatalogId":"MyGame Catalog","
Items":[{"ItemId":"sword","DisplayName":"Sword","Price":2,"Curr
ency":"MC"},{"ItemId":"shield","DisplayName":"Shield","Price":4
,"Currency":"MC"}]}
```

Implement Economy API

You'll use API Management Service again as an interface for your clients to the backend functions. It also ensures that only authenticated clients can call the function. Create an apim.tf file and add the following code:

```
variable "api_management_name" {
    description = "Name of the API Management service"
}

variable "shared_resource_group_name" {
    description = "Shared resource group name"
}

resource "azurerm_api_management_api" "economy" {
    name                  = "economy-api"
    resource_group_name   = var.shared_resource_group_name
    api_management_name   = var.api_management_name
    revision              = "1"
    path                  = "economy"
```

```
display_name           = "Economy API"
protocols              = ["https"]
subscription_required = false
}

resource "azurerm_api_management_api_operation" "economy-post-
catalog" {
  operation_id         = "economy-post-catalog"
  api_name             = azurerm_api_management_api.economy.name
  api_management_name = var.api_management_name
  resource_group_name = var.shared_resource_group_name
  display_name         = "POST Catalog"
  method               = "POST"
  url_template         = "/Catalog"
}
```

As an analog to the Catalog's POST method, define additional resources for Catalog (GET, DELETE), Inventory (GET, POST), and VirtualCurrency (GET, POST).

The backend definition should point to the published functions, and the API policy expects the access token before forwarding the request to the functions.

```
resource "azurerm_api_management_backend" "economy" {
  name                 = "economy-azure-functions-backend"
  resource_group_name = var.shared_resource_group_name
  api_management_name = var.api_management_name
  protocol             = "http"
  url                  = "https://${azurerm_function_app.
                         economy.default_hostname}/api/"
  resource_id          = "https://management.azure.
                         com/${azurerm_function_app.economy.id}"
  credentials {
```

```
  header = {
    x-functions-key = "${data.azurerm_function_app_host_keys.
    economy.default_function_key}"
  }
 }
}

resource "azurerm_api_management_api_policy" "economy" {
  api_name              = azurerm_api_management_api.economy.name
  api_management_name = var.api_management_name
  resource_group_name = var.shared_resource_group_name

  xml_content = <<XML
<policies>
  <inbound>
    <set-backend-service id="apim-policy" backend-id="economy-
    azure-functions-backend" />
    <validate-jwt header-name="Authorization" failed-
    validation-httpcode="401" failed-validation-error-
    message="Unauthorized. Access token is missing or
    invalid.">
        <openid-config url="https://gamebackend2022.b2clogin.
        com/gamebackend2022.onmicrosoft.com/v2.0/.well-known/
        openid-configuration?p=B2C_1_SignInSignUp" />
        <audiences>
            <audience>e4d1e07d-81ff-45b8-b849-91bef09b5bbd</
            audience>
        </audiences>
        <issuers>
            <issuer>https://gamebackend2022.b2clogin.com/fe46bd
            de-805c-4a42-83c6-871e0f4278e7/v2.0/</issuer>
        </issuers>
    </validate-jwt>
  </validate-jwt>
```

```
    </inbound>
</policies>
XML
```

```
}
```

Now you can enable the api_management_name and shared_resource_ group_name lines and execute the terraform script (terraform apply).

Developing the Client

Now we'll create a new file called AzureEconomy.cs in Unity and add it to the Azure game object. This will include all the logic required for calling the backend. We will use the same method as in other chapters, where we used HTTP requests to communicate with the backend.

In Unity, implement the same classes (Catalog, PlayerInventory, Item, VirtualCurrency, and PlayerVirtualCurrency) as in the backend. However, you don't need the BSON attributes and the ObjectId. To implement this, add the following code to the AzureEconomy.cs script:

```
public class Catalog
{
    public string CatalogId { get; set; }
    public List<Item> Items { get; set; }
}

public class PlayerInventory
{
    public string PlayerId { get; set; }
    public List<Item> Items { get; set; }
}

public class Item
{
```

```csharp
    public string ItemId { get; set; }
    public string DisplayName { get; set; }
    public int Price { get; set; }
    public string Currency { get; set; }
}
public class PlayerVirtualCurrency
{
    public string PlayerId { get; set; }
    public List<VirtualCurrency> VirtualCurrencies {
    get; set; }

}

public class VirtualCurrency
{
    public int VC_Amount { get; set; }
    public string VC_Name { get; set; }
}
```

Getting Items

Reading the Catalog requires a simple GET request. Add the following code to the AzureEconomy.cs file:

```csharp
using System.Collections.Generic;
using UnityEngine;
using System.Net;
using System.IO;
using Newtonsoft.Json;
using System.Text;

public class AzureEconomy : MonoBehaviour
{
```

```
Catalog catalog = new Catalog();
PlayerVirtualCurrency playerVirtualCurrency = new
PlayerVirtualCurrency();
UnityIAPManager unityIAPManager;

public void GetCatalogItems()
{
    HttpWebRequest request = (HttpWebRequest)WebRequest.
    Create("https://shared-apim.azure-api.net/economy/
    Catalog?CatalogId=MyGame%20Catalog");
    request.Method = "GET";

    request.Headers.Add("Authorization", "Bearer " +
    GetComponent<AzureSettings>().token);

    HttpWebResponse response = (HttpWebResponse)request.
    GetResponse();
    StreamReader reader = new StreamReader(response.
    GetResponseStream());
    string result = reader.ReadToEnd();

    catalog = JsonConvert.DeserializeObject<Catalog
    >(result);

    unityIAPManager = new UnityIAPManager(catalog);

    ShopUI.UpdateTextArea(catalog.Items);
}
...
```

Now update the UnityIAPManager class so that it accepts the non-PlayFab catalog type:

```
public class UnityIAPManager : IStoreListener
{
```

```
public UnityIAPManager(Catalog catalog)
{
    InitializeUnityIAP(catalog.Items);
}

public void InitializeUnityIAP(List<Item> catalog)
{
    var module = StandardPurchasingModule.Instance();
    var builder = ConfigurationBuilder.Instance(module);

    foreach (var item in catalog)
    {
        builder.AddProduct(item.ItemId, ProductType.
        NonConsumable);
    }
    UnityPurchasing.Initialize(this, builder);
}
}
```

Note that you need to update the ShopUI as well, but first, let's see how to finish the main AzureEconomy class.

Getting the Player's Inventory

The Inventory and VirtualCurrency classes work basically the same as GetCatalogItems. Add the following code to AzureEconomy.cs:

```
...
public void GetInventory()
{
    var playerId = this.gameObject.
    GetComponent<AzureSettings>().playerID;
```

```
    HttpWebRequest request = (HttpWebRequest)WebRequest.
    Create("https://shared-apim.azure-api.net/economy/
    Inventory?PlayerId=" + playerId);
    request.Method = "GET";

    request.Headers.Add("Authorization", "Bearer " +
    GetComponent<AzureSettings>().token);

    HttpWebResponse response = (HttpWebResponse)request.
    GetResponse();
    StreamReader reader = new StreamReader(response.
    GetResponseStream());
    string result = reader.ReadToEnd();
    Debug.Log(result);

    var inventory = JsonConvert.DeserializeObject<Player
    Inventory>(result);

    ShopUI.UpdateTextArea(inventory.Items);

    GetVirtualCurrency();
}

private void GetVirtualCurrency()
{
    var playerId = this.gameObject.
    GetComponent<AzureSettings>().playerID;
    HttpWebRequest request = (HttpWebRequest)WebRequest.
    Create("https://shared-apim.azure-api.net/economy/
    VirtualCurrency?PlayerId=" + playerId);
    request.Method = "GET";

    request.Headers.Add("Authorization", "Bearer " +
    GetComponent<AzureSettings>().token);
```

```
HttpWebResponse response = (HttpWebResponse)request.
GetResponse();
StreamReader reader = new StreamReader(response.
GetResponseStream());
string result = reader.ReadToEnd();
Debug.Log(result);

playerVirtualCurrency = JsonConvert.DeserializeObject<P
layerVirtualCurrency>(result);

ShopUI.UpdateVirtualCurrency(playerVirtualCurrency.
VirtualCurrencies[0].VC_Name, playerVirtualCurrency.
VirtualCurrencies[0].VC_Amount);
    }
...
```

Purchasing Items

If a player buys a new item, we'll read it from the catalog and post it to the player's inventory. To simplify the function, we'll check if the player already owns the item, and if they do not, we'll decrease the MC virtual currency by the price of the item. This example assumes that MC is first in the list of currencies to keep it simple.

Now implement the POST request, which changes the amount of virtual currency the player has, by adding the following code to AzureEconomy.cs:

```
...
    public void SetVirtualCurrency(string virtualCurrencyName,
    int virtualCurrencyAmount)
    {
        var playerId = this.gameObject.
        GetComponent<AzureSettings>().playerID;
```

```csharp
HttpWebRequest request = (HttpWebRequest)WebRequest.
Create("https://shared-apim.azure-api.net/economy/
VirtualCurrency");
request.Method = "POST";

request.Headers.Add("Authorization", "Bearer " +
GetComponent<AzureSettings>().token);

VirtualCurrency virtualCurrency = new VirtualCurrency()
{
    VC_Name = virtualCurrencyName,
    VC_Amount = virtualCurrencyAmount
};

PlayerVirtualCurrency playerVirtualCurrency = new
PlayerVirtualCurrency()
{
    PlayerId = playerId,
    VirtualCurrencies = new List<VirtualCurrency>() {
    virtualCurrency }
};

var json = JsonConvert.SerializeObject(playerVirtual
Currency);

byte[] data = Encoding.ASCII.GetBytes(json);

request.ContentType = "application/json";
request.ContentLength = data.Length;

Stream requestStream = request.GetRequestStream();
requestStream.Write(data, 0, data.Length);
requestStream.Close();
```

```
HttpWebResponse response = (HttpWebResponse)request.
GetResponse();
StreamReader reader = new StreamReader(response.
GetResponseStream());

string result = reader.ReadToEnd();

GetVirtualCurrency();

Debug.Log(result);
    }
```

Next, implement the PurchaseItem method in the AzureEconomy.cs
file using the following code:

...

```
    public void PurchaseItem(string itemToPurchase)
    {
        int itemNumber = int.Parse(itemToPurchase) - 1;
        var playerId = this.gameObject.
GetComponent<AzureSettings>().playerID;

        HttpWebRequest request = (HttpWebRequest)WebRequest.
Create("https://shared-apim.azure-api.net/economy/
Inventory");
        request.Method = "POST";

        request.Headers.Add("Authorization", "Bearer " +
GetComponent<AzureSettings>().token);

        PlayerInventory playerInventory = new PlayerInventory()
        {
            PlayerId = playerId,
            Items = new List<Item>() { catalog.
            Items[itemNumber] }
        };
```

```
var json = JsonConvert.SerializeObject(playerI
nventory);

byte[] data = Encoding.ASCII.GetBytes(json);

request.ContentType = "application/json";
request.ContentLength = data.Length;

Stream requestStream = request.GetRequestStream();
requestStream.Write(data, 0, data.Length);
requestStream.Close();

HttpWebResponse response = (HttpWebResponse)request.
GetResponse();
StreamReader reader = new StreamReader(response.
GetResponseStream());

string result = reader.ReadToEnd();
Debug.Log(result);

if (result != "Item is already existing in the
inventory.")
{
    SetVirtualCurrency("MC", playerVirtualCurrency.
    VirtualCurrencies[0].VC_Amount - catalog.
    Items[itemNumber].Price);
}
}
...
```

Buying from the Store

You can simply reuse the UnityIAPManager that you implemented in the PlayFab section to enable in-app purchasing. Finalize the AzureEconomy class using the following method:

...

```
    public void BuyFromStore(string itemToPurchase)
    {
        int itemNumber = int.Parse(itemToPurchase) - 1;
        unityIAPManager.PurchaseItem(catalog.Items[itemNumber].
        ItemId);
    }
}
```

Economy GUI

Similar to what you did in PlayFab, you will create a simple user interface that allows you to use the functions you implemented in the previous part. First extend the control panel with the following code:

```
public class ControlPanel : MonoBehaviour
{
    public const int AZURE_ECONOMY = 8;

    void OnGUI()
    {
        if (selection == AZURE_ECONOMY)
            GUILayout.Window(0, new Rect(0, 0, 300, 0),
            AzureEconomyWindow, "Azure Economy");
    }

    void OptionsWindow(int windowID)
    {
        if (GUILayout.Button("Azure Economy"))
        {
            selection = AZURE_ECONOMY;
        }
    }
}
```

```
void AzureEconomyWindow(int windowID)
{
    if (economyTextAreaTitle != "")
        GUILayout.Label(economyTextAreaTitle);

    textArea = ShopUI.GetTextArea();
    textArea = GUILayout.TextArea(textArea, 200);

    virtualCurrencyLabel = ShopUI.
    GetVirtualCurrencyLabel();
    if (virtualCurrencyLabel != "")
        GUILayout.Label(virtualCurrencyLabel);

    GUILayout.Space(10);

    if (GUILayout.Button("Get Catalog Items"))
    {
        azure.GetComponent<AzureEconomy>().
        GetCatalogItems();
        economyTextAreaTitle = "Catalog Items";
    }
    if (GUILayout.Button("Get Player Inventory + Virtual
    Currency"))
    {
        azure.GetComponent<AzureEconomy>().GetInventory();
        economyTextAreaTitle = "Player Inventory";
    }

    GUILayout.Space(10);

    if (GUILayout.Button("Grant Virtual Currency"))
    {
```

```
        azure.GetComponent<AzureEconomy>().
        SetVirtualCurrency("MC", 100);
    }

    GUILayout.Space(10);

    if (GUILayout.Button("Purchase this item (number):"))
    {
        azure.GetComponent<AzureEconomy>().
        PurchaseItem(itemToPurchase);

    }

    itemToPurchase = GUILayout.
    TextField(itemToPurchase, 100);

    GUILayout.Space(10);

    if (GUILayout.Button("Buy from store"))
    {
        azure.GetComponent<AzureEconomy>().
        BuyFromStore(itemToPurchase);
    }
    }
}
```

The ShopUI file needs some extensions. This static class must update the text area on the GUI. In the case of Azure, you can use the Item class instead of CatalogItem:

```
public static class ShopUI
{
    public static void UpdateTextArea(List<Item> items)
    {
        string ta = "";
```

```
        int number = 0;
        foreach (var item in items)
        {
            number++;
            ta += number + " | " + item.DisplayName + ".....";
            ta += item.Price + " " + item.Currency;
            ta += "\n";
        }

        for (int i = items.Count; i < 5; i++)
        {
            ta += "\n";
        }
        textArea = ta;
    }
}
```

With that, you have implemented the same calls from Unity as from the command line with cURL. Add the AzureEconomy script as a new component to the Azure game object. Then test the client with the API Management Service URL. If there is an issue, you can use the local URL to see the error messages in the backend.

Summary

In this chapter, you learned how to implement a game economy using PlayFab and a custom Azure solution. PlayFab provides rich options and opportunities to integrate third-party stores. It is flexible and easy to use. If you decide to create a custom solution, prepare to write a considerable amount of custom code. But you have more flexibility and even more options than with PlayFab. NoSQL database is better than a relational database for implementing this feature.

Review Questions

1. What are the benefits of implementing an economy into your game?

2. What are the basic components of virtual economies?

3. What are the basic functions you should implement in a game economy?

4. What are the typical properties of items in a virtual economy?

5. What is in-app purchasing (IAP)?

6. What kind of database do you use to implement an economy?

7. What are documents and collections in MongoDB?

8. How do you add new items to a catalog or an inventory?

9. How do you enforce player authentication before using the API?

10. When would you use PlayFab and when would you implement a custom economy solution?

CHAPTER 7

Game Analytics

You have published your game and players have downloaded it. You even see in the server logs that they are joining multiplayer sessions. But you have almost no information about the players' behavior. You should know if players leave the game after a while because of some nerve-racking challenge. Or, if most of your players cannot succeed to the next level.

Game analytics allow you to react to players' behavior and provide your players with the best experience. For example, you can remove hurdles so that the players can proceed easier through levels.

This chapter explains how to implement game analytics by PlayFab and also using pure cloud services.

Building Blocks

You need to know what is happening during gameplay and how players behave when interacting with your game. You also need to know if there are problems or performance issues.

To analyze these concerns, you need to gather data. The more data you gather from the clients, the better insights you will have. If your player performs some action, gathers some item, buys something, starts or leaves the game, these are all events and they provide valuable information.

You need to gather such events from the clients and store them. With the help of data analytic tools, you can explore and visualize this data, getting answers to your questions about the occurrences in your game.

© Balint Bors 2023
B. Bors, *Game Backend Development*, https://doi.org/10.1007/978-1-4842-8910-5_7

You can break this process down into the following building blocks:

- **Event generation.** You have to implement an event generation mechanism in your game clients. An event should include all the data needed for analysis, triggered at a certain point during gameplay. For example, you want to generate an event when the player leaves the game and include the level number. You have to carefully plan the number of generated events and observe only the important aspects.

- **Event aggregation.** You can have millions of players, and each player can generate thousands of events. You need a robust event-processing backend to cope with the continuous flow of huge amount of events.

- **Event storage.** You have to store the events for non-real time analysis. An important concern here is the data retention time. You should keep the data as long as it is relevant for analysis.

- **Exploration and visualization.** You need powerful tools. Also, don't underestimate the data analytic skills required to implement the right queries for getting information from the huge amount of data you gather from your clients.

The next section explains how to implement these functionalities with both PlayFab and Azure. With PlayFab, you get an out-of-the-box game analytics service. If you choose to build your own solution, Azure provides the needed services, although the effort to build and maintain is much higher than with PlayFab.

PlayFab

PlayFab makes it really simple to implement game analytics for your games. It provides you all the above four building blocks. You don't have to implement any of them.

For event generation, you can use methods from PlayFab's API, and PlayFab generates certain events automatically. These automated events are, for example, `player_logged_in` and `player_created`.

Automatic Events

Let's start by observing the automatic events. If you go to PlayFab, you have two options for checking incoming events:

- **PlayStream Monitor.** In your game's Title Overview, you can observe the incoming events under the PlayStream Monitor tab. On a world map, you can see live where players log into your game.

- **Analyze ➤ Data.** In the Data Explorer, you can analyze the received data from the clients and execute queries to get insights into your player's behavior.

Try to log in to your game client and see how the `player_logged_in` event appears in the PlayStream Monitor.

If you click Settings and select Fade Out Logins After ➤ Never, you can observe the players' locations after they log in.

PlayFab generates a lot of automatic events, which you can use with no additional code or configuration. But what if you want to analyze a specific behavior?

Creating Custom Events

You can also generate custom events by using PlayFab API calls. Consider a hypothetical scenario. You want to know when most players leave the game. If it's during a specific level, maybe because that's because it's too difficult.

Let's create an event—let's call it `player_exited`. This event will include the level number. You can also further refine it, for example, by adding the position of the character. Create a new script in Unity called PlayFabGameAnalytics.cs and add the following code to it:

```
using System.Collections.Generic;
using UnityEngine;
using PlayFab;
using PlayFab.ClientModels;

public class PlayFabGameAnalytics : MonoBehaviour
{
    public void CreatePlayerExitedEvent(int Level)
    {
        Dictionary<string, object> EventBody = new
        Dictionary<string, object>
            {
                { "Level", Level }
            };

        CreateEvent("player_exited", EventBody);
    }

    void CreateEvent(string EventName, Dictionary<string,
    object> EventBody)
    {
        PlayFabClientAPI.WritePlayerEvent(new
        WriteClientPlayerEventRequest
```

```
    {
        EventName = EventName,
        Body = EventBody
    },
    (WriteEventResponse result) => Debug.Log("Event sent"),
    (PlayFabError error) => Debug.LogError(error.
    GenerateErrorReport()));
    }
}
```

Add a new button to the control panel and trigger a `player_exited`
event with a random level value:

```
public class ControlPanel : MonoBehaviour
{
    void OptionsWindow(int windowID)
    {
        if (GUILayout.Button("Send PlayFab Event"))
        {
            playFab.GetComponent<PlayFabGameAnalytics>().Create
            PlayerExitedEvent(UnityEngine.Random.Range(1, 10));
        }
    }
}
```

If you execute this event, you can observe your appearing custom
event in the PlayStream Monitor, similar to automatic events.

Analyzing the Events

Now that you have gathered a lot of useful data about your player's
behavior, you want to define and execute queries and get insights about
what is happening during gameplay. You can either go to the Data Explorer
in PlayFab or download Kusto Explorer to your local machine:

```
https://docs.microsoft.com/en-us/azure/data-explorer/kusto/
tools/kusto-explorer
```

After you start Kusto Explorer, configure it to access the game data through PlayFab Insights. Click Add Connection and configure it, as shown in Figure 7-1.

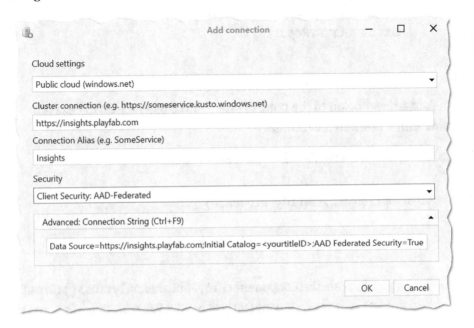

Figure 7-1. *Configure Kusto Explorer to PlayFab*

To explore your data, you have to use the Kusto Query Language (KQL). It is a simple but powerful language to explore your data. The following example filters out the `player_exited` events, extracts the `Level` value from the event data, and counts the number of `player_exited` events for each level.

```
['events.all']
| where FullName_Name == "player_exited"
| extend Level = tostring(parse_json(EventData).Level)
| summarize Exited = count() by Level
| order by Level asc
```

In Kusto Explorer you can create fancy charts to see the result. For this example, it came out that most players leave the game during level eight. You can see this in the chart in Figure 7-2.

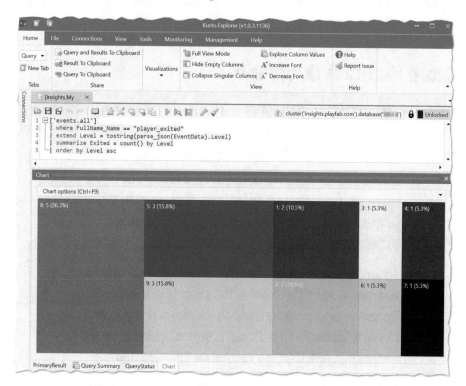

Figure 7-2. *Game analytics with Kusto Explorer*

The following section explains how to implement the same functionality, but you'll build your own infrastructure on Azure.

Azure

There are a lot of ways to implement game analytics backend on Azure. This section shows one possible way.

You can use the free or at least cheap services to learn and experiment. As soon as you go into production or the number of players increases, you'll need to align the service types and architecture.

When implementing game analytics, one of the biggest challenge is to process the huge amount of incoming data. You have to care scale your infrastructure properly.

Azure Solution Overview

In this section, you reuse components from earlier chapters to simplify the implementation as far as possible. You will implement the four game analytics building blocks with the following services:

- **Event generation.** We use standard HTTP POST methods to submit an event. The player has to log in first, and the event will contain all the data in JSON format.

- **Event aggregation.** Azure API Management receives the events from the clients. It forwards to the Azure Function App backend, which forwards to the event hubs. With the help of Event Capture, Azure copy the events periodically into the Azure Blob Storage.

- **Event storage.** Azure Blob Storage can store a large amount of event data for longer time.

- **Exploration and visualization.** Azure Data Explorer can read and query files containing the events. It can also generate charts for better representation of data.

Figure 7-3 shows the flow of events from the generation to the analysis. Using this solution, you can capture and store game analytics data and get insight about what is happening in your game.

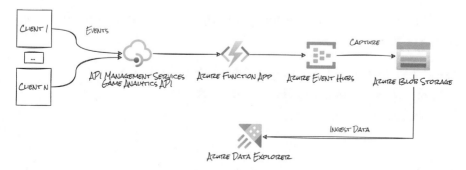

Figure 7-3. *Game analytics on Azure*

Build Your Own Game Analytics Backend

This section explains how to build the solution with the help of Terraform. You will reuse and extend the Azure API Management and Azure Functions services. For better structure, you can put each service in different .tf files.

Start by creating a new module in Terraform. Create a new folder called gameanalytics and add the following code to the main.tf file:

```
module "gameanalytics" {
  source                    = "./gameanalytics"
  api_management_name       = module.shared.api_
                              management_name
  shared_resource_group_name = module.shared.shared_resource_
                              group_name
  app_service_plan_id       = module.shared.app_
                              service_plan_id
  storage_account_name      = module.shared.storage_
                              account_name
```

```
    storage_account_access_key = module.shared.storage_account_
                                 access_key
}
```

Create a new resource group by putting the following code into
resourcegroup.tf:

```
resource "azurerm_resource_group" "gameanalytics" {
  name     = "gameanalytics-resources"
  location = "West Europe"
}
```

Configure API Management

You add the game analytics API to the Azure API Management service. This
is the interface for the clients to the event-processing backend. You then
implement a POST operation and let only clients with access tokens submit
events. Then create a new file called apim.tf and add the following code:

```
variable "api_management_name" {
  description = "Name of the API Management service"
}

variable "shared_resource_group_name" {
  description = "Shared resource group name"
}

resource "azurerm_api_management_api" "gameanalytics" {
  name                = "gameanalytics-api"
  resource_group_name = var.shared_resource_group_name
  api_management_name = var.api_management_name
  revision            = "1"
  path                = "gameanalytics"
  display_name        = "GameAnalytics API"
```

```
  protocols              = ["https"]
  subscription_required = false
}

resource "azurerm_api_management_api_operation"
"gameanalytics-post" {
  operation_id          = "gameanalytics-post-event"
  api_name              = azurerm_api_management_api.
                          gameanalytics.name
  api_management_name   = var.api_management_name
  resource_group_name   = var.shared_resource_group_name
  display_name          = "POST Event"
  method                = "POST"
  url_template          = "/GameAnalyticsFunc"
}

resource "azurerm_api_management_backend" "gameanalytics" {
  name                  = "gameanalytics-azure-functions-backend"
  resource_group_name   = var.shared_resource_group_name
  api_management_name   = var.api_management_name
  protocol              = "http"
  url                   = "https://${azurerm_function_app.
                          gameanalytics.default_hostname}/api/"
  resource_id           = "https://management.azure.
                          com/${azurerm_function_app.
                          gameanalytics.id}"
  credentials {
    header = {
      x-functions-key = "${data.azurerm_function_app_host_keys.
                          gameanalytics.default_function_key}"
    }
  }
}
```

```
resource "azurerm_api_management_api_operation_policy"
"gameanalytics-post" {
  api_name              = azurerm_api_management_api_operation.
                          gameanalytics-post.api_name
  api_management_name = azurerm_api_management_api_operation.
                          gameanalytics-post.api_management_name
  resource_group_name = azurerm_api_management_api_operation.
                          gameanalytics-post.resource_group_name
  operation_id          = azurerm_api_management_api_operation.
                          gameanalytics-post.operation_id

  xml_content = <<XML
<policies>
  <inbound>
    <set-backend-service id="apim-policy" backend-
    id="gameanalytics-azure-functions-backend" />
    <validate-jwt header-name="Authorization" failed-
    validation-httpcode="401" failed-validation-error-
    message="Unauthorized. Access token is missing or
    invalid.">
        <openid-config url="https://gamebackend2022.b2clogin.
        com/gamebackend2022.onmicrosoft.com/v2.0/.well-known/
        openid-configuration?p=B2C_1_SignInSignUp" />
        <audiences>
            <audience>e4d1e07d-81ff-45b8-b849-91bef09b5bbd</
            audience>
        </audiences>
        <issuers>
            <issuer>https://gamebackend2022.b2clogin.com/fe46bd
            de-805c-4a42-83c6-871e0f4278e7/v2.0/</issuer>
        </issuers>
```

```
    </validate-jwt>
  </inbound>
</policies>
XML
}
```

Azure Blob Storage

Let's continue at the end of the solution, because you have to refer to the storage from the event hub. With the help of Terraform, you can create a new storage account and a blob storage container to archive events. You can have up to 12 months 5GB storage for free. Create a new file called storage.tf and add the following code to it:

```
resource "azurerm_storage_account" "gameanalytics" {
  name                     = "gameanalyticssa"
  resource_group_name      = azurerm_resource_group.
                             gameanalytics.name
  location                 = azurerm_resource_group.
                             gameanalytics.location
  account_tier             = "Standard"
  account_replication_type = "LRS"
}

resource "azurerm_storage_container" "gameanalytics" {
  name                  = "eventhubarchive"
  storage_account_name  = azurerm_storage_account.
                          gameanalytics.name
  container_access_type = "private"
}
```

Event Hubs

This is the core component of the solution. Note that you need the Event Hubs Capture feature, because it allows you to copy events to the Azure Blob Storage. This feature is only available with the Standard SKU. Note that this service is not free.

You can increase the retention up to seven days, but don't use event hubs for permanent data storage.

By increasing the number of partitions, you can increase the throughput of events. In this way, you can scale up if the amount of incoming events increases considerably.

You can configure how often the Event Hubs Capture should copy the events to the storage. You can also set a size window for triggering event archiving. By setting skip_empty_archives, you allow it to archive only when events occurred. The capture destination is the Azure Blob Storage. Event hubs will generate AVRO files, which is a big data file format. Create a new file called eventhub.tf and add the following code to it:

```
resource "azurerm_eventhub_namespace" "gameanalytics" {
    name                = "GameAnalyticsEventHubNamespace"
    location            = azurerm_resource_group.gameanalytics.
                          location
    resource_group_name = azurerm_resource_group.
                          gameanalytics.name
    sku                 = "Standard"
    capacity            = 1
}

resource "azurerm_eventhub" "gameanalytics" {
    name                = "GameAnalyticsEventHub"
    namespace_name      = azurerm_eventhub_namespace.
                          gameanalytics.name
    resource_group_name = azurerm_resource_group.
                          gameanalytics.name
```

```
partition_count     = 2
message_retention   = 1

capture_description {
  enabled  = true
  encoding = "Avro"
  skip_empty_archives = true
  interval_in_seconds = 60

  destination {
    name = "EventHubArchive.AzureBlockBlob"
    archive_name_format = "{Namespace}/{EventHub}/
    {PartitionId}/{Year}/{Month}/{Day}/{Hour}/{Minute}/
    {Second}"
    blob_container_name = "${azurerm_storage_container.
    gameanalytics.name}"
    storage_account_id  = "${azurerm_storage_account.
    gameanalytics.id}"
  }
}
}
```

Also add an authorization rule, so that your Azure Function can send
events to the events hub:

```
resource "azurerm_eventhub_authorization_rule"
"gameanalytics" {
  name                = "MyAuthRule"
  namespace_name      = azurerm_eventhub_namespace.
                        gameanalytics.name
  eventhub_name       = azurerm_eventhub.gameanalytics.name
  resource_group_name = azurerm_resource_group.
                        gameanalytics.name
  listen              = false
```

```
  send              = true
  manage            = false
}
```

Implement Azure Function

You need a new Function App, which is assigned to the existing App Service Plan and Storage Account. Create a new file called functionapp.tf and add the following code to it:

```
variable "app_service_plan_id" {
  description = "AppService Plan ID"
}

variable "storage_account_name" {
  description = "Storage account name"
}

variable "storage_account_access_key" {
  description = "Storage account access key"
}

resource "azurerm_function_app" "gameanalytics" {
  name                       = "gameanalytics-azure-functions"
  location                   = azurerm_resource_group.
                               gameanalytics.location
  resource_group_name        = azurerm_resource_group.
                               gameanalytics.name
  app_service_plan_id        = var.app_service_plan_id
  storage_account_name       = var.storage_account_name
  storage_account_access_key = var.storage_account_access_key
  version                    = "~4"
}
```

```
data "azurerm_function_app_host_keys" "gameanalytics" {
  name                = azurerm_function_app.gameanalytics.name
  resource_group_name = azurerm_resource_group.
                        gameanalytics.name
}
```

When you have the Function App, create a simple dotnet function with the help of Azure Function Core Tools:

```
func init GameAnalyticsFunctions
```

Now, create the GameAnalytics.cs file, place it in a new folder, and copy the following code into it:

```
using System.IO;
using System.Threading.Tasks;
using Microsoft.Azure.WebJobs;
using Microsoft.Azure.WebJobs.Extensions.Http;
using Microsoft.AspNetCore.Http;
using Microsoft.Extensions.Logging;

namespace GameAnalyticsFunctions
{
    public class GameAnalytics
    {
        [FunctionName("GameAnalyticsFunc")]
        [return: EventHub("outputEventHubMessage", Connection =
        "EVENTHUB_CONNECTION_STRING")]
        public async Task<string> Run(
                [HttpTrigger(AuthorizationLevel.Anonymous,
                "post", Route = null)] HttpRequest req,
                ILogger log)
        {
```

```
            string requestBody = await new StreamReader(req.
            Body).ReadToEndAsync();
            return requestBody;
        }
    }
}
```

In the GameAnalyticsFunctions.csproj file, add a new package reference:

```
<PackageReference Include="Microsoft.Azure.WebJobs.
Extensions.EventHubs" Version="5.1.0" />
```

Use the Azure CLI to get the event hub's connection string:

```
az eventhubs eventhub authorization-rule keys list --
resource-group gameanalytics-resources --namespace-
name GameAnalyticsEventHubNamespace --eventhub-name
gameanalyticseventhub --name MyAuthRule --query="primaryConnect
ionString"
```

Copy the connection string into the local.settings.json file:

```
{
    "IsEncrypted": false,
    "Values": {
        "AzureWebJobsStorage": "UseDevelopmentStorage=true",
        "FUNCTIONS_WORKER_RUNTIME": "dotnet",
        "EVENTHUB_CONNECTION_STRING": "Endpoint=sb://
        gameanalyticseventhubnamespace.servicebus.windows.net/;
        SharedAccessKeyName=MyAuthRule;SharedAccessKey=<yourkey>;
        EntityPath=gameanalyticseventhub"
    }
}
```

Configure the connection string in Azure:

```
az functionapp config appsettings set -n gameanalytics-azure-
functions -g gameanalytics-resources --settings EVENTHUB_
CONNECTION_STRING="Endpoint=sb://gameanalyticseventhubnamespace.
servicebus.windows.net/;SharedAccessKeyName=<yourkey>;
EntityPath=gameanalyticseventhub"
```

And finally, publish the function to Azure:

```
func azure functionapp publish gameanalytics-azure-functions
```

Testing Your Backend

You should verify that everything is working fine. Start your function locally to see if there is an error message.

```
func start
```

Open another terminal window and submit some events to your Azure Function:

```
curl -X POST http://localhost:7071/api/GameAnalyticsFunc -d
"{\"eventname\":\"player_exited\", \"Level\": 123 }"
```

Check if the Azure Function has any problems. Then go to the Azure Portal and check if the event arrived at the event hubs. You can see this if you go directly to your event hubs instance and query the event hub under Process Data. Then go to your storage container and check if there are AVRO files available.

Finally, verify that you can submit an event through the Azure API Management service. Temporarily remove the authorization check and test it with cURL:

```
curl -X POST https://shared-apim.azure-api.net/gameanalytics/
GameAnalyticsFunc -d "{\"eventname\":\"player_exited\",
\"Level\": 321 }"
```

If you can see that the event arrived at the event hub and is written into the storage, you can proceed to the next step. You have to do the same HTTP POST from Unity at the right moment.

Sending Events from the Clients

In Unity, you implement the HTTP POST method to submit an event to the backend. The event data contains the name of the event and any additional data you want to gather. In Unity, create a new script called AzureGameAnalytics.cs and add the following code:

```
using UnityEngine;
using System.Net;
using System.IO;
using System.Text;

public class AzureGameAnalytics : MonoBehaviour
{
    GameObject azure;
    private void Start()
    {
        azure = GameObject.Find("Azure");
    }
    public void CreatePlayerExitedEvent(int Level)
    {
        string Eventbody = "\"eventname\":\"player_exited\",
        \"Level\": " + Level;
        CreateAzureEvent(Eventbody);
    }

    public void CreateAzureEvent(string Eventbody)
    {
```

```
HttpWebRequest request = (HttpWebRequest)WebRequest.
Create("https://shared-apim.azure-api.net/
gameanalytics/GameAnalyticsFunc");
request.Method = "POST";

request.Headers.Add("Authorization", "Bearer " +
GetComponent<AzureSettings>().token);

string playerID = azure.GetComponent<AzureSettings>().
playerID;

byte[] data = Encoding.ASCII.GetBytes("{\"PlayerID\":
\"" + playerID + "\", " + Eventbody + "}");
request.ContentType = "application/json";
request.ContentLength = data.Length;

Stream requestStream = request.GetRequestStream();
requestStream.Write(data, 0, data.Length);
requestStream.Close();

HttpWebResponse response = (HttpWebResponse)request.
GetResponse();
StreamReader reader = new StreamReader(response.
GetResponseStream());
string result = reader.ReadToEnd();
Debug.Log("Event sent " + result);
    }
}
```

Now add a button to the control panel. When this button is clicked, it invokes the event sending function:

```
public class ControlPanel : MonoBehaviour
{
```

```
void OptionsWindow(int windowID)
{
    if (GUILayout.Button("Send Azure Event"))
    {
        azure.GetComponent<AzureGameAnalytics>().CreatePlay
        erExitedEvent(UnityEngine.Random.Range(1, 10));
    }
}
}
```

Drag-and-drop `AzureGameAnalytics` to the Azure game object as a
new component and verify that the event was sent.

Getting Insights Into Your Data

You have all the gathered events in Azure Blob Storage, stored in AVRO
format. Azure Data Explorer can read this format, and you can start queries
from the web interface. Fortunately, Microsoft provides a free version of it,
which you can use for experimenting.

Start Azure Data Explorer from here:

`https://aka.ms/kustofree`

Create a free cluster and ingest the data from the Azure Blob Storage.
Select From Blob Container as the source type and copy the storage
connection string to the Link to Source field. You can do this by clicking
the Generate SAS token and URL in Azure Portal and then choosing
Storage Accounts ➤ gameanalyticssa ➤ eventhubarchive ➤ Shared Access
Tokens. Don't forget to grant Read and List permissions before generating
the URL. Then you need to copy the Blob SAS URL to the Link to Source
field in Azure Data Explorer. It is also important to set the data format to
Apache Avro in the Schema settings.

When the data ingestion is done, you can query your data. First, check if your events have arrived:

```
MyTable
| take 100
```

If you see that your events have been received from your Unity client, you can finally see which level most players left the game, as shown in Figure 7-4:

```
MyTable
| where parse_json(Body).eventname == "player_exited"
| extend Level = tostring(parse_json(Body).Level)
| summarize Exited = count() by Level
| order by Level asc
```

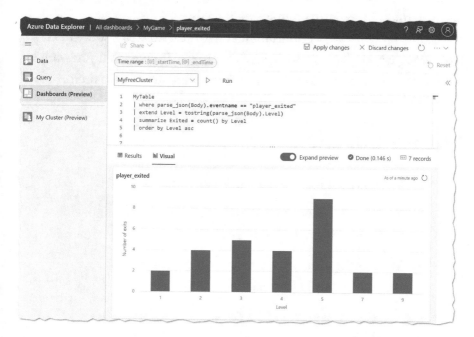

Figure 7-4. *Azure Data Explorer with game play insights*

You can also use Kusto Explorer to investigate your data from the local machine. Simply add the cluster URI from Azure Data Explorer as a new connection to Kusto Explorer, and you can start queries against the data.

Summary

In this chapter, you learned about the purpose of implementing game analytics. You investigated two ways for realization. PlayFab provides an out-of-the-box solution with minimal implementation efforts. On the other hand, if you want to build your own game analytics infrastructure, you should count on considerable effort.

You implemented a simple architecture that can process numerous incoming events. Rethink the architecture for large-scale deployments. For example, extending it with Azure Databricks or Azure HDInsight allows data scientists to perform complex data analysis.

Game analytics is an important feature if you want to know what is happening when players are playing your game. Define what you want to know, your questions, and gather the data to find answers to them.

Review Questions

1. What is the function of game analytics?

2. What are the basic building blocks when implementing game analytics?

3. What is the difference between automatic and custom events in PlayFab?

4. How can you explore and visualize event data in PlayFab?

5. Which services can you use for event aggregation in Azure?

6. Why should you archive events from event hubs?

7. Which feature allows you to copy events from event hubs to Azure Blob Storage?

8. How can you submit events from your game clients?

9. What is KQL and how do you write a query to get ten elements of a table?

10. How do you ingest data into Azure Data Explorer?

CHAPTER 8

Party, Chat, AI

This chapter explains how to implement the chat functionality in your game. Chatting is a basic feature in modern multiplayer games. It very often belongs to a specific game session or lobby, when groups of players are communicating with each other.

This implementation focuses on the core chat functionality in a client-server based architecture. The server will send the received messages from specific clients to all other clients.

Modern infrastructure vendors also provide sophisticated AI (Artificial Intelligence) or cognitive services, such as translation and moderation. You can easily invoke these services and provide a better experience for your players. In this example, you will implement automatic translation, which allows the program to translate incoming messages from any language to English.

Introduction

Let's start with breaking down the topic of "chatting" into its main functional building blocks, as shown in Figure 8-1. This chapter focuses on implementing these core features:

- **Creating a chatroom.** You need a place where a group of players can communicate with each other. You can decide to have a global chatroom for all players, a chatroom for each game session, or let

© Balint Bors 2023
B. Bors, *Game Backend Development*, https://doi.org/10.1007/978-1-4842-8910-5_8

players gathering in a lobby to chat with each other. In this example, you will let players create explicitly a chatroom. But this can also happen automatically as part of, for example, the matchmaking process.

- **Joining a chatroom.** Players can request to be part of a group where they can communicate with others. Similarly to creating a chatroom, this can happen automatically when, for example, joining a game session. In this example, you will implement joining a chatroom explicitly by providing a chatroom ID.

- **Sending text messages.** Players send their text or data messages to a server.

- **Receiving text messages.** The backend provides an interface to receive messages from authenticated players and process these text or data messages.

- **Message broadcasting.** A way to process messages on the server. You send the incoming messages to all the players. This is how a group chat works, where you send messages to the whole group.

- **AI services.** More and more cognitive services become available with the help of artificial intelligence. You can easily extend your chat service with intelligent functions. We will implement and see the translation service in practice.

You can also extend these with features depending on your game's requirements:

- **Sending to a specific person.** Instead of message broadcasting, the server sends the message to one specific player.

- **Speech-to-text/text-to-speech.** You can improve accessibility by transcribing voice to text or convert incoming messages to voice.

- **Peer-to-peer communication.** This allows direct communication between the clients without using the costly resources of the server.

- **Voice/video chat.** Many games have live communication capabilities, so the backend services allow relatively easy implementation. This is not as common as simple text messaging.

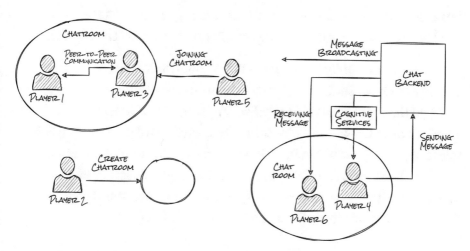

Figure 8-1. *Chat functionalities*

When you want to add a chatroom to your game, besides building the backend, it is important to plan time to implement a suitable user interface. Compared to other backend features, such as matchmaking or game analytics, chat has more implementation effort on the frontend.

PlayFab

PlayFab helps you develop a chat function for your game using the solution called Azure PlayFab Party. In development mode, Party includes 10,000 free minutes, so you can experiment without worrying about cost.

You need to download an additional PlayFab Party Unity SDK, because the standard PlayFab SDK does not contain the Party features:

`https://github.com/PlayFab/PlayFabPartyUnity/releases`

When you first install the Party SDK, the following error may come up:

```
Assets\PlayFabPartySDK\Source\Scripts\
PartyXboxLiveSDKCSharpSource\XBLSDK.cs(253,37): error CS0227:
Unsafe code may only appear if compiling with /unsafe. Enable
"Allow 'unsafe' code" in Player Settings to fix this error.
```

To fix this, in Unity Editor, go to File ➤ Build Settings... ➤ Player Settings ➤ Other Settings and check Allow 'unsafe' Code.

Add the `PlayFabMultiplayerManager` script from Assets ➤ PlayFabPartySDK ➤ Source ➤ Scripts ➤ PartyUnitySDK to the PlayFab game object in your hierarchy. That way, the engine executes it at startup.

Also, Party uses `PlayFabSharedSettings` under Assets ➤ PlayFabSDK ➤ Shared ➤ Public ➤ Resources to get the Title ID and the Developer Secret Key, so copy these from PlayFab's Game Manager.

Enable PlayFab Party

If you want to use the PlayFab Party feature in your title, you have to enable it in PlayFab. Go to PlayFab's Game Manager, choose Multiplayer ➤ Party, and click Enable. After that, you can see the usage statistics of the Party service.

Create a Simple Chat UI

In this section, you will create a simple chat user interface and reuse it for the PlayFab and the custom Azure solutions. Obviously, you can skip this step if you have your own solution that allows players to send and receive messages.

Using the GUILayout component in Unity, you can create a window with a text area where the messages appear, a text field for typing your own message, and a Send button to send messages. You can also add a toggle button to enable or disable translation. And finally, you'll add two buttons for the two core functions: creating a new chat room and joining an existing one. Let's extend the ControlPanel with the following code:

```
public class ControlPanel : MonoBehaviour
{
    public const int PLAYFAB_CHAT = 9;

    string chatMessage = "";
    bool isTranslated = false;

    void OnGUI()
    {
        if (selection == PLAYFAB_CHAT)
            GUILayout.Window(0, new Rect(0, 0, 300, 0),
            PlayFabChatWindow, "PlayFab Chat");
    }
```

```
void OptionsWindow(int windowID)
{
    if (GUILayout.Button("PlayFab Chat"))
    {
        selection = PLAYFAB_CHAT;
    }
}

void PlayFabChatWindow(int windowID)
{
    textArea = ChatUI.GetTextArea();
    textArea = GUILayout.TextArea(textArea, 200);

    chatMessage = GUILayout.TextField(chatMessage, 100);

    if (GUILayout.Button("Send Message"))
    {
        playFab.GetComponent<PlayFabChat>().
        SendChatMessage(chatMessage);
        chatMessage = "";
    }

    isTranslated = GUILayout.Toggle(isTranslated,
    "Translate Messages");
    playFab.GetComponent<PlayFabChat>().doTranslateMessage
    = isTranslated;

    GUILayout.Space(10);

    if (GUILayout.Button("Create PlayFab Party"))
        playFab.GetComponent<PlayFabChat>().StartParty();

    if (GUILayout.Button("Join PlayFab Party"))
        playFab.GetComponent<PlayFabChat>().JoinParty();
```

```
GUILayout.Space(10);

if (GUILayout.Button("Cancel"))
    selection = ROOTMENU;
    }
}
```

You will add the PlayFabChat class in the next step.

Now we'll prepare a simple static class to manipulate UI elements. In this case, you want to roll up the previous messages in the text area when a new message arrives. Create a new script called ChatUI and copy the following code:

```
public static class ChatUI
{
    private static string textArea = "\n\n\n\n\n";
    private static string[] chatRows = new string[5];
    public static void UpdateTextArea(string displayName,
    string message)
    {
        for (int i = 0; i < 4; i++)
        {
            chatRows[i] = chatRows[i + 1];
        }
        chatRows[4] = displayName + ": " + message;

        string ta = "";

        for (int i = 0; i < 5; i++)
        {
            if (chatRows[i] == null)
            {
                ta += "\n";
```

```
            }
            else
            {
                ta += chatRows[i] + "\n";
            }
        }
        textArea = ta;
    }

    public static string GetTextArea()
    {
        return textArea;
    }
}
```

As a next step, we will implement each chat building block, in this case by using Party API calls.

Creating a New Chatroom

Create a new script, called PlayFabChat.cs, where you store all the Party related invocations. You will break up this file in the next sections. Finally, add this as a new component to the PlayFab game object, just as you did for PlayFabMultiplayerManager.

CreateAndJoinNetwork creates a new chatroom and when it is ready, it fires the OnNetworkJoined event. With this event, the client receives the network ID. This is what other clients need if they want to join the same chatroom.

Any time a new message appears, the OnChatMessageReceived event is raised, providing the receiver the sender's PlayFab ID and the message. It would be better to have the sender's display name, however, the current API does not provide this. To resolve this, you can implement a CloudScript that translates PlayFab IDs to display names. We come back to this in the next chapter.

```
using UnityEngine;
using PlayFab.Party;
using PlayFab;
using PlayFab.ServerModels;

public class PlayFabChat : MonoBehaviour
{
        public bool doTranslateMessage { get; set; }
        public void StartParty()
    {
        PlayFabMultiplayerManager.Get().CreateAndJoinNetwork();

        PlayFabMultiplayerManager.Get().OnNetworkJoined +=
        OnNetworkJoined;
        PlayFabMultiplayerManager.Get().OnChatMessageReceived
        += OnChatMessageReceived;
        PlayFabMultiplayerManager.Get().OnRemotePlayerJoined +=
        OnRemotePlayerJoined;
        PlayFabMultiplayerManager.Get().OnRemotePlayerLeft +=
        OnRemotePlayerLeft;
        PlayFabMultiplayerManager.Get().OnError += OnError;
    }

    private void OnNetworkJoined(object sender, string
    networkId)
    {
        Debug.Log("Joined to network: " + networkId);
        SetTitleData(networkId);
    }
```

```
private void OnChatMessageReceived(object sender,
PlayFabPlayer from, string message, ChatMessageType type)
{
    PlayFabMultiplayerManager.Get().TranslateChat =
    doTranslateMessage;
    ChatUI.UpdateTextArea(from.EntityKey.Id, message);
}
private void OnRemotePlayerJoined(object sender,
PlayFabPlayer player)
{
    Debug.Log("Joined new player: " + player.EntityKey.Id);
}
private void OnRemotePlayerLeft(object sender,
PlayFabPlayer player)
{
    Debug.Log("Player left: " + player.EntityKey.Id);
}
public void OnError(object sender,
PlayFabMultiplayerManagerErrorArgs args)
{
    Debug.Log("An error occured: " + args.Message);
}
```

After you have created a new party, you have to provide the network ID to other players so that they can join. There are a lot of different ways to solve this depending on your actual chat implementation. You could, for example, distribute this automatically between players belonging to the same game session or lobby.

Here, for the sake of simplicity, you will store it in title data, which is a shared place that players can reach. You can call this method directly after you create a new party, so that other players can access the network ID:

```
public void SetTitleData(string networkId)
{
    PlayFabServerAPI.SetTitleData(
        new SetTitleDataRequest
        {
            Key = "PartyNetworkId",
            Value = networkId
        },
        result => Debug.Log("Setting TitleData was
        successful."),
        error =>
        {
            Debug.Log("Error setting TitleData: " + error.
            GenerateErrorReport());
        }
    );
}
```

Now that you have a party and its network ID is stored in a reachable place for other players, you can implement how others can join the chatroom.

Joining a Chatroom

When a client intends to join a party, it needs to get the network ID, in our example, from the Title Data. With a simple API call, you can read this information out, and then call the JoinNetwork method with the network ID to join that specific party:

```
public void JoinParty()
{
    PlayFabClientAPI.GetTitleData(new PlayFab.ClientModels.
    GetTitleDataRequest(),
```

```
        result =>
        {
            PlayFabMultiplayerManager.Get().
            JoinNetwork(result.Data["PartyNetworkId"]);
            PlayFabMultiplayerManager.Get().OnNetworkJoined
            += OnNetworkJoined;
            PlayFabMultiplayerManager.Get().
            OnChatMessageReceived += OnChatMessageReceived;
            PlayFabMultiplayerManager.Get().
            OnRemotePlayerJoined += OnRemotePlayerJoined;
            PlayFabMultiplayerManager.Get().
            OnRemotePlayerLeft += OnRemotePlayerLeft;
            PlayFabMultiplayerManager.Get().OnError +=
            OnError;
        },
        error =>
        {
            Debug.Log("Error getting TitleData: " + error.
            GenerateErrorReport());
        }
    );
}
```

Sending Messages

After you have a party and people join it, they can send messages to each
other. In this example, you broadcast messages to all players with the
SendChatMessageToAllPlayers method. But you could also use a recipient
list by using SendChatMessage:

```
public void SendChatMessage(string message)
{
```

```
ChatUI.UpdateTextArea(this.gameObject.
GetComponent<PlayFabSettings>().displayName, message);
PlayFabMultiplayerManager.Get().SendChatMessageToAllPla
yers(message);
    }
}
```

As the result of this, all players except the sender will receive a message with the OnChatMessageReceived event, including the sender's PlayFab ID.

With this method, you can close the PlayFabChat class. Verify that you can create a new party and join it from another Unity client.

Translate Messages

PlayFab provides an easy way to translate messages. By using the Party Unity SDK, you simply have to change the boolean value of TranslateChat. This will automatically recognize the language the sender uses and translate it into English. With the toggle button on the UI, you can enable and disable this chat translation. The TranslateChat method determines if an incoming message is translated, which you configure in the OnChatMessageReceived:

```
private void OnChatMessageReceived(object sender,
PlayFabPlayer from, string message, ChatMessageType type)
{
    PlayFabMultiplayerManager.Get().TranslateChat =
    doTranslateMessage;
    ChatUI.UpdateTextArea(from.EntityKey.Id, message);
}
```

You can experiment further with other features of the PlayFab Party API, such as with text moderation, or the Text-to-Speech functions. But this chapter moves on and explains how to implement a custom chat solution on Azure.

Azure

Implementing chat functionality on Azure is more challenging than with PlayFab, but the advantage is that you can customize it more easily to your game's requirements. A group chat is typically a publish-subscribe scenario. Someone sends (publishes) a message, and those who requested to receive messages when they appear (with other word, subscribed) will receive it.

Fortunately, Azure has a service providing this functionality out-of-the box. This is the Azure Web PubSub service, and it sends messages to subscribed clients. It uses WebSocket, which keeps the connection alive between the client and the server.

Both sides can start message transfers to the other, as long as the connection is living. This is very different compared to an HTTP connection, where the client starts a request, receives a response from the server, and the connection is terminated.

You want clients connected to the server to receive messages from each other through the server in real time. Otherwise, you should always send HTTP request to the server asking: do you have new messages for me? This would be a so-called *polling mechanism*.

Figure 8-2 shows the architecture of a chat solution you will implement on Azure. The following steps have to be implemented to send and receive chat messages:

1. Player authentication. This is the first step, because you want to be sure that only authenticated users can communicate via your chat service.

2. With the access token, the client goes to the API Management Service, and through this service, it tries to access your Azure Function App. The client needs a connection URL to access the Azure Web PubSub service. Note that this is an HTTP GET request. Other clients can also request a connection URL, and thus subscribe to messages through that connection.

3. If the API Management Service accepts the access token, it forwards the request to the Azure Function App, which sends the connection URL back to the client.

4. The client opens a WebSocket connection to the Azure Web PubSub service using the connection URL received in the previous step. Then, it sends a message.

5. The Web PubSub service triggers the Azure Function App and forwards the message through input binding.

6. Through output binding, the Azure Function App instructs the Web PubSub service to send the message to all subscribers.

7. The Web PubSub service sends the message to all subscribers that have the connection URL and have a live WebSocket connection to it.

8. The client sends the message to the translator service to translate the message to the chosen language.

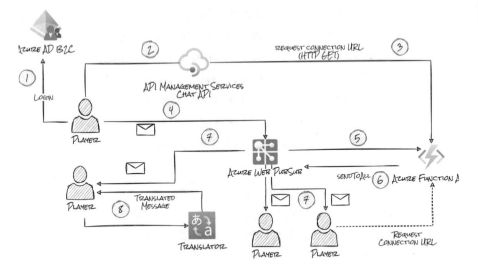

Figure 8-2. *Azure chat solution*

Building Your Chat Infrastructure

You will build your infrastructure with the help of Terraform. To avoid repeating tasks, you will reuse and extend some of the shared resources from Chapter 4. These are the API Management Service (you will add a new Chat API to it), the Azure App Service Plan, and the Storage Account.

Let's start by creating a new chat module. You'll create a new chat folder and extend your main.tf file. You provide the module as input to some parameters of your shared resources:

```
module "chat" {
  source                     = "./chat"
  api_management_name         = module.shared.api_
                               management_name
  shared_resource_group_name = module.shared.shared_resource_
                               group_name
```

```
app_service_plan_id        = module.shared.app_
                             service_plan_id
storage_account_name       = module.shared.storage_
                             account_name
storage_account_access_key = module.shared.storage_account_
                             access_key
}
```

In the chat folder, create a new resourcegroup.tf file, which will create a resource group for all resources belonging to the chat functionality:

```
resource "azurerm_resource_group" "chat" {
  name     = "chat-resources"
  location = "West Europe"
}
```

Now that you have the base structure, you can build your chat specific infrastructure. Let's build them step-by-step with Terraform.

Handle Messages with Azure Function App

Create a new file called functionapp.tf in the chat folder and add the following code to it. Note that you refer to and use your shared App Service Plan and Storage Account. The host keys will be necessary for the API Management Service, so that it can reach your functions.

```
variable "app_service_plan_id" {
  description = "AppService Plan ID"
}

variable "storage_account_name" {
  description = "Storage account name"
}
```

```
variable "storage_account_access_key" {
  description = "Storage account access key"
}

resource "azurerm_function_app" "chat" {
  name                         = "chat-azure-functions"
  location                     = azurerm_resource_group.chat.
                                 location
  resource_group_name          = azurerm_resource_group.chat.name
  app_service_plan_id          = var.app_service_plan_id
  storage_account_name         = var.storage_account_name
  storage_account_access_key   = var.storage_account_access_key
  version                      = "~4"
}

data "azurerm_function_app_host_keys" "chat" {
  name                = azurerm_function_app.chat.name
  resource_group_name = azurerm_resource_group.chat.name
}
```

If you apply your Terraform script, you will see the chat-azure-functions created in Azure. Comment out the api_management_name and shared_resource_group_name rows from the chat module, initialize Terraform with the new module (terraform init), and run the scripts from the root folder (terraform apply). This will create the so far described infrastructure.

Next, you'll fill this with content using the Azure Functions Core Tools. From the chat folder, execute the following command:

```
func init ChatFunctions
```

This will create a new folder with initial settings. Add the required package to the ChatFunctions.csproj file:

```
<PackageReference Include="Microsoft.Azure.WebJobs.
Extensions.WebPubSub" Version="1.2.0" />
```

Create a new file, called Chat.cs, and implement the publish and the subscribe functions. To keep it as simple as possible, they really do nothing else but return a connection URL and instruct the Web PubSub service to distribute the message:

```
using System;
using System.Threading.Tasks;
using Microsoft.AspNetCore.Http;
using Microsoft.Azure.WebJobs;
using Microsoft.Azure.WebJobs.Extensions.Http;
using Microsoft.Azure.WebJobs.Extensions.WebPubSub;
using Microsoft.Azure.WebPubSub.Common;
using Microsoft.Extensions.Logging;

namespace ChatFunctions
{
    public class Chat
    {
        [FunctionName("Subscribe")]
        public WebPubSubConnection Subscribe(
            [HttpTrigger(AuthorizationLevel.Anonymous, "get",
            Route = null)] HttpRequest req,
            [WebPubSubConnection(Hub = "chat")]
            WebPubSubConnection connection, ILogger log)
        {
            return connection;
        }
```

```
[FunctionName("Publish")]
public async Task Publish(
    [WebPubSubTrigger("chat", WebPubSubEventType.User,
    "message")]
    UserEventRequest request, BinaryData data,
    WebPubSubDataType dataType,
    Ilogger log,
    [WebPubSub(Hub = "chat")] IasyncCollector<WebPubSub
    Action> actions)
{
    await actions.AddAsync(WebPubSubAction.
    CreateSendToAllAction(request.Data.ToString(),
    WebPubSubDataType.Text));
}

}
}
```

At this point, you have to build the Azure Web PubSub service, so that you can give the connection string of it to your functions. Note that you do not test your functions locally, because the Web PubSub service cannot trigger the publishing service on your machine.

Creating Azure Web PubSub Service

Create a new file called pubsub.tf in the chat folder and add the following content to it. Again, we will use the free version, which allows 20 connections. For production, scale up to standard tier. Enabling the live trace can be helpful to see what is happening inside of your Web PubSub service. For example, to see new connections and messages. Create a new file called pubsub.tf and add the following code:

```
resource "azurerm_web_pubsub" "chat" {
  name                = "chat-webpubsub"
  location            = azurerm_resource_group.chat.location
  resource_group_name = azurerm_resource_group.chat.name

  sku      = "Free_F1"
  capacity = 1

  public_network_access_enabled = true

  live_trace {
    enabled                   = true
    messaging_logs_enabled    = true
    connectivity_logs_enabled = true
  }
}
```

After you apply it with Terraform, you can get the connection string. You can get it simply by using the Azure CLI:

```
az webpubsub key show --name chat-webpubsub --resource-group
chat-resources --query=primaryConnectionString
"Endpoint=https://chat-webpubsub.webpubsub.azure.
com;AccessKey=<your_key>
```

Add this connection string to your local.settings.json file, so that you can run your functions locally without error:

```
{
    "IsEncrypted": false,
    "Values": {
        "AzureWebJobsStorage": "UseDevelopmentStorage=true",
```

```
    "AzureWebJobsSecretStorageType": "files",
    "FUNCTIONS_WORKER_RUNTIME": "dotnet",
    "WebPubSubConnectionString": "Endpoint=https://chat-
    webpubsub.webpubsub.azure.com;AccessKey=<your_key>
  }
}
```

Also add it to Application Settings in Azure:

```
az functionapp config appsettings set -n chat-azure-
functions -g chat-resources --settings WebPubSubConnectio
nString="Endpoint=https://chat-webpubsub.webpubsub.azure.
com;AccessKey=<your_key>"
```

One final step is missing. You have to create and configure an Azure Web PubSub hub. A *hub* is a set of client connections. This is where you define the event handler. In your case, the Function App.

First publish your Function App with the Azure Functions Core Tools:

```
func azure functionapp publish chat-azure-functions
```

Then you can query your Web PubSub extension key:

```
az functionapp keys list --name chat-azure-functions --
resource-group chat-resources --query=systemKeys.webpubsub_
extension
```

You have to provide this key to the Web PubSub hub's event handler, so that it can communicate with your Function App. Add the following code to the pubsub.tf script of the Web PubSub hub resource and execute it with Terraform:

```
resource "azurerm_web_pubsub_hub" "chat" {
  name          = "chat"
  web_pubsub_id = azurerm_web_pubsub.chat.id
```

```
event_handler {
  url_template         = "https://chat-azure-functions.
                         azurewebsites.net/runtime/webhooks/
                         webpubsub?code=<your_webpubsub_
                         extension_key>"
  user_event_pattern = "*"
}

anonymous_connections_enabled = true

depends_on = [
  azurerm_web_pubsub.chat
]
}
```

Testing the Core Infrastructure

Now you have the complete publish-subscribe mechanism implemented on Azure. Let's test it to see if it works. Start with the subscribe:

```
curl https://chat-azure-functions.azurewebsites.net/api/
subscribe
{"baseUrl":"wss://...","url":"wss://...","accessToken":"..."}
```

This is fine. Use the URL to connect the WebSocket to the Web PubSub service. You can use your favorite WebSocket client, such as Postman, or you can use an online client, for example https://websocketking.com/.

After connecting to the Web PubSub service, you can send a message, which should come back to you. Try multiple clients and confirm that your publishing function works fine and broadcasts the messages to the clients.

API Management Service

Of course, you want to protect your Function App, so that just not anyone can subscribe to your game's chat. The player has to log in before being able to request the connection URL for the WebSocket. You can put an API Management Service between your client and server to protect the backend from unauthenticated clients.

Create a new file called apim.tf in the chat folder and add the following content to it:

```
variable "api_management_name" {
    description = "Name of the API Management service"
}

variable "shared_resource_group_name" {
  description = "Shared resource group name"
}

resource "azurerm_api_management_api" "chat" {
  name                  = "chat-api"
  resource_group_name   = var.shared_resource_group_name
  api_management_name   = var.api_management_name
  revision              = "1"
  path                  = "chat"
  display_name          = "chat API"
  protocols             = ["https"]
  subscription_required = false
}

resource "azurerm_api_management_api_operation" "chat-get" {
  operation_id        = "subscribe"
  api_name            = azurerm_api_management_api.chat.name
  api_management_name = var.api_management_name
  resource_group_name = var.shared_resource_group_name
  display_name        = "GET subscribe"
  method              = "GET"
  url_template        = "/Subscribe"
}
```

```
resource "azurerm_api_management_backend" "chat" {
  name                 = "chat-azure-functions-backend"
  resource_group_name  = var.shared_resource_group_name
  api_management_name  = var.api_management_name
  protocol             = "http"
  url                  = "https://${azurerm_function_app.chat.
                            default_hostname}/api/"
  resource_id          = "https://management.azure.
                            com/${azurerm_function_app.chat.id}"
  credentials {
    header = {
      x-functions-key = "${data.azurerm_function_app_host_keys.
                            chat.default_function_key}"
    }
  }
}

resource "azurerm_api_management_api_operation_policy"
"chat-get" {
  api_name             = azurerm_api_management_api_operation.
                            chat-get.api_name
  api_management_name  = azurerm_api_management_api_operation.
                            chat-get.api_management_name
  resource_group_name  = azurerm_api_management_api_operation.
                            chat-get.resource_group_name
  operation_id         = azurerm_api_management_api_operation.
                            chat-get.operation_id

  xml_content = <<XML
<policies>
  <inbound>
```

```xml
    <set-backend-service id="apim-policy" backend-id="chat-
    azure-functions-backend" />
    <validate-jwt header-name="Authorization" failed-
    validation-httpcode="401" failed-validation-error-
    message="Unauthorized. Access token is missing or invalid.">
        <openid-config url="https://gamebackend2022.b2clogin.
        com/gamebackend2022.onmicrosoft.com/v2.0/.well-known/
        openid-configuration?p=B2C_1_SignInSignUp" />
        <audiences>
            <audience>e4d1e07d-81ff-45b8-b849-91bef09b5bbd
            </audience>
        </audiences>
        <issuers>
            <issuer>https://gamebackend2022.b2clogin.com/fe46bd
            de-805c-4a42-83c6-871e0f4278e7/v2.0/</issuer>
        </issuers>
    </validate-jwt>
  </inbound>
</policies>
XML
```

}

This is very similar to what you implemented, for example, for the matchmaking solution in Chapter 4. For details, refer to that chapter.

Let's remove the comments from the lines at api_management_name and shared_resource_group_name in the main.tf file and execute the Terraform script.

To test if you can access the function through the API Management Service, you also have to provide the access token in your request:

```
curl https://shared-apim.azure-api.net/chat/subscribe
{ "statusCode": 401, "message": "Unauthorized. Access token is
missing or invalid." }
```

Let's continue implementing the Unity client, which can already authenticate the player and provide the access token to your API Management Service.

Implementing the Unity Chat Client

Going back to Unity to implement your own game client. Create a new C# script called AzureChat.cs and add it to the Azure game object in the hierarchy. In the next sections, you will add code only to this file. You will also reuse your chat UI from the PlayFab part of this chapter.

To use WebSockets in Unity, you need to use an external library. You can use the Native WebSocket client for Unity. Download this project in Unity Editor by going to Window ➤ Package Manager ➤ + ➤ Add Package from Git URL…, and copy the location of the library: https://github.com/endel/NativeWebSocket.git#upm.

Getting the Connection URL

First, you need to get the connection URL to the WebSocket on the Web PubSub service.

Implement a simple HTTP GET request to your API Management Service. This should include the access token. From the JSON response, you have to extract the URL that you will use to connect to the WebSocket. Add the following code to the AzureChat script:

```
using UnityEngine;
using System.Net;
using System.IO;
using Newtonsoft.Json;
using NativeWebSocket;

public class AzureChat : MonoBehaviour
{
```

```csharp
    public void ConnectToChat()
    {
        ConnectToWebSocket(GetClientAccessUrl());
    }

    public string GetClientAccessUrl()
    {
        HttpWebRequest request = (HttpWebRequest)WebRequest.
        Create("https://shared-apim.azure-api.net/chat/
        Subscribe");
        request.Method = "GET";

        request.Headers.Add("Authorization", "Bearer " +
        GetComponent<AzureSettings>().token);

        HttpWebResponse response = (HttpWebResponse)request.
        GetResponse();
        StreamReader reader = new StreamReader(response.
        GetResponseStream());
        string result = reader.ReadToEnd();

        var accessData = JsonConvert.DeserializeObject<AccessDa
        ta>(result);
        return accessData.url;
    }
public class AccessData
{
    public string baseUrl { get; set; }
    public string url { get; set; }
    public string accessToken { get; set; }
}
}
```

Connecting to the WebSocket

Now that you have the WebSocket URL, you can connect to it. First, implement a ChatData class, which you will use to deserialize incoming JSON messages. You can specify your own message format, which can include any information. Just make sure you use the same structure when you send the message.

```
public class ChatData
{
    public string DisplayName { get; set; }
    public string Message { get; set; }
}
```

With Unity's update method, you keep on dispatching queued messages when the connection between the client and the server is open.

```
using NativeWebSocket;
public class AzureChat : MonoBehaviour
{
WebSocket websocket;
private bool isConnected = false;
void Update()
    {
#if !UNITY_WEBGL || UNITY_EDITOR
        if (isConnected)
            websocket.DispatchMessageQueue();
#endif
    }
}
```

Then implement the connection to the WebSocket. Connect to the WebSocket asynchronously to avoid blocking the thread. When a message appears, you can deserialize using the chatData object and show the sender and the message on your UI.

```
public class AzureChat : MonoBehaviour
{
    public void ConnectToChat()
    {
        ConnectToWebSocket(GetClientAccessUrl());
    }

    async void ConnectToWebSocket(string clientAccessUrl)
    {
        websocket = new WebSocket(clientAccessUrl);

        websocket.OnOpen += () =>
        {
            Debug.Log("Connection open!");
            isConnected = true;
        };

        websocket.OnError += (e) =>
        {
            Debug.Log("Error! " + e);
        };

        websocket.OnClose += (e) =>
        {
            Debug.Log("Connection closed!");
            isConnected = false;
        };

        websocket.OnMessage += (bytes) =>
        {
```

```
ChatData chatData = JsonConvert.Deserialize
Object<ChatData>(System.Text.Encoding.UTF8.
GetString(bytes));

ChatUI.UpdateTextArea(chatData.DisplayName,
chatData.Message);

    };

    await websocket.Connect();
    }
}
```

When leaving your application, close the WebSocket.

```
public class AzureChat : MonoBehaviour
{
    private async void OnApplicationQuit()
    {
        await websocket.Close();
    }
}
```

Sending Chat Messages

If the connection is alive with the server, you can send messages. You will send them in JSON format and will include the sender's display name and the message.

```
public class AzureChat : MonoBehaviour
{
    public async void SendChatMessage(string message)
    {
            string jsonMessage = "{\"DisplayName\": \"" + this.
            gameObject.GetComponent<AzureSettings>().displayName
            + "\", \"Message\": \"" + message + "\"}";
```

```
        await websocket.SendText(jsonMessage);
    }
}
```

Testing the Chat Client

Let's extend the control panel with a very simple test client:

```
public class ControlPanel : MonoBehaviour
{
    public const int AZURE_CHAT = 10;

    void OnGUI()
    {
        if (selection == AZURE_CHAT)
            GUILayout.Window(0, new Rect(0, 0, 300, 0),
                AzureChatWindow, "Azure Chat");
    }

    void OptionsWindow(int windowID)
    {
        if (GUILayout.Button("Azure Chat"))
        {
            azure.GetComponent<AzureChat>().ConnectToChat();
            selection = AZURE_CHAT;
        }
    }

    void AzureChatWindow(int windowID)
    {
        textArea = ChatUI.GetTextArea();
        textArea = GUILayout.TextArea(textArea, 200);
```

```
chatMessage = GUILayout.TextField(chatMessage, 100);

if (GUILayout.Button("Send Message"))
{
azure.GetComponent<AzureChat>().
SendChatMessage(chatMessage);
    chatMessage = "";
}

GUILayout.Space(10);

if (GUILayout.Button("Cancel"))
    selection = ROOTMENU;
}
}
```

Right away, when you open your chat window, invoke the ConnectToChat method. You can then assign the SendChatMessage to your Send Message button on the chat UI and test if you can send and receive messages. Don't forget to log in before trying to subscribe to the chat service.

Azure Translator

Finally, you can add a cognitive service to your chat functionality to create a better user experience. You need to create a Cognitive Account in Azure, which translates text to other languages.

Building the Cognitive Backend

Create a new file called cognitive.tf in the chat folder and add the following Terraform content to it:

```
resource "azurerm_cognitive_account" "chat" {
  name                = "cognitive-account"
  location            = azurerm_resource_group.chat.location
  resource_group_name = azurerm_resource_group.chat.name
  kind                = "TextTranslation"

  sku_name = "F0"
}
```

You can apply this with Terraform, which will create a free tier translator service on your Azure subscription. To the API Management Service's apim.tf file, add the new chat-translate operation. Be aware when configuring the backend. The backend points to the Translator service, which requires the following information in each request's header:

- **Ocp-Apim-Subscription-Key.** This is the access key of the Cognitive account. Fortunately, you can get this through the Terraform script.

- **Ocp-Apim-Subscription-Region.** You can query this information with Azure CLI:

  ```
  az cognitiveservices account show --name
  cognitive-account --resource-group chat-resources --
  query=location
  ```

- **Content-Type.** This should be application/json.

- **Query parameter.** You should always add "api-version" = "3.0"

You can again only accept requests that include the access token in their headers:

```
resource "azurerm_api_management_api_operation" "chat-
translate" {
  operation_id        = "translate"
  api_name            = azurerm_api_management_api.chat.name
  api_management_name = var.api_management_name
  resource_group_name = var.shared_resource_group_name
  display_name        = "POST translate"
  method              = "POST"
  url_template        = "/Translate"
}

resource "azurerm_api_management_backend" "chat-translate" {
  name                = "translator-backend"
  resource_group_name = var.shared_resource_group_name
  api_management_name = var.api_management_name
  protocol            = "http"
  url                 = "${azurerm_cognitive_account.chat.
                        endpoint}"
  credentials {
    header = {
      Ocp-Apim-Subscription-Key = "${azurerm_cognitive_account.
                                  chat.primary_access_key}"
      Ocp-Apim-Subscription-Region = "westeurope"
      Content-Type = "application/json"
    }
    query = {
      "api-version" = "3.0"
    }
  }
}
```

```
resource "azurerm_api_management_api_operation_policy" "chat-
translate" {
  api_name             = azurerm_api_management_api_operation.
                         chat-translate.api_name
  api_management_name  = azurerm_api_management_api_operation.
                         chat-translate.api_management_name
  resource_group_name  = azurerm_api_management_api_operation.
                         chat-translate.resource_group_name
  operation_id         = azurerm_api_management_api_operation.
                         chat-translate.operation_id

  xml_content = <<XML
<policies>
  <inbound>
    <set-backend-service id="apim-policy" backend-
    id="translator-backend" />
    <validate-jwt header-name="Authorization" failed-
    validation-httpcode="401" failed-validation-error-
    message="Unauthorized. Access token is missing or invalid.">
        <openid-config url="https://gamebackend2022.b2clogin.
        com/gamebackend2022.onmicrosoft.com/v2.0/.well-known/
        openid-configuration?p=B2C_1_SignInSignUp" />
        <audiences>
            <audience>e4d1e07d-81ff-45b8-b849-91bef09b5bbd
            </audience>
        </audiences>
        <issuers>
            <issuer>https://gamebackend2022.b2clogin.com/fe46bd
            de-805c-4a42-83c6-871e0f4278e7/v2.0/</issuer>
        </issuers>
    </validate-jwt>
    <set-header name="Authorization" exists-action="delete" />
```

```
</inbound>
</policies>
XML
```

}

Implementing the Client

Implement the HTTP GET call, where you provide the target language as a query parameter (in this case English, to=en). Now add the following code to the AzureChat class:

```
using System.Text;

public class AzureChat : MonoBehaviour
{
private string TranslateMessage(string message)
    {
        HttpWebRequest request = (HttpWebRequest)WebRequest.
        Create("https://shared-apim.azure-api.net/chat/
        Translate?to=en");
        request.Method = "POST";

        request.Headers.Add("Authorization", "Bearer " +
        GetComponent<AzureSettings>().token);

        byte[] data = Encoding.ASCII.GetBytes("[{\"text\":
        \"" + message + "\"}]");
        request.ContentType = "application/json";
        request.ContentLength = data.Length;

        Stream requestStream = request.GetRequestStream();
        requestStream.Write(data, 0, data.Length);
        requestStream.Close();
```

```
        HttpWebResponse response = (HttpWebResponse)request.
                                    GetResponse();
        StreamReader reader = new StreamReader(response.
                                    GetResponseStream());

        string result = reader.ReadToEnd();
        return result;
    }
}
```

You get a response in JSON format from the Translator service. To deserialize it, you have to create the following classes (add them to AzureChat.cs as well):

```
using System.Collections.Generic;

public class DetectedLanguage
{
    public string language { get; set; }
    public double score { get; set; }
}

public class Translation
{
    public string text { get; set; }
    public string to { get; set; }
}

public class Root
{
    public DetectedLanguage detectedLanguage { get; set; }
    public List<Translation> translations { get; set; }
}
```

Let's add the Translation service call to every incoming message. If the toggle button is on, you send the incoming message to the Translator service. Then, you deserialize the JSON response and update the UI with the translated message. To achieve this, first define doTranslateMessage:

```
public class AzureChat : MonoBehaviour
{
    public bool doTranslateMessage { get; set; }
}
```

Then, search the AzureChat class for the ConnectToWebSocket method and modify it by adding the translation service:

```
websocket.OnMessage += (bytes) =>
    {
        ChatData chatData = JsonConvert.Deserialize
        Object<ChatData>(System.Text.Encoding.UTF8.
        GetString(bytes));

        if (doTranslateMessage)
        {
            string json = TranslateMessage(chatData.
            Message);
            Root[] azureTranslatorResponse = JsonConvert.De
            serializeObject<Root[]>(json);
            chatData.Message = azureTranslatorResponse[0].
            translations[0].text;
        }

        ChatUI.UpdateTextArea(chatData.DisplayName,
        chatData.Message);
    };
```

Now test it to see if it works by slightly modifying the control panel. You want the players to be able to turn the translation on and off. To achieve this, create a simple toggle button, which switches the doTranslateMessage boolean value to true and false:

```
public class ControlPanel : MonoBehaviour
{
    void AzureChatWindow(int windowID)
    {
        textArea = ChatUI.GetTextArea();
        textArea = GUILayout.TextArea(textArea, 200);

        chatMessage = GUILayout.TextField(chatMessage, 100);

        if (GUILayout.Button("Send Message"))
        {
            azure.GetComponent<AzureChat>().
            SendChatMessage(chatMessage);
            chatMessage = "";
        }

        isTranslated = GUILayout.Toggle(isTranslated,
        "Translate Messages");
        azure.GetComponent<AzureChat>().doTranslateMessage =
        isTranslated;

        GUILayout.Space(10);

        if (GUILayout.Button("Cancel"))
            selection = ROOTMENU;
    }
}
```

Test the translation to see if it's working when the players activate it. With that, you learned how to apply cognitive services in Azure.

Summary

PlayFab Party API is already GA (generally available) and provides an easy way to implement chat in your game. Microsoft keeps improving the Unity SDK to cover more and more Party features on Unity as well.

On the other hand, you may want more flexibility and a custom solution better suited to your specific requirements. If so, you can implement your own chat backend solution on Azure.

A good example is when you don't want to transmit the player ID, but instead the display name of the sender. If PlayFab does not provide this data by its API, you have to implement a custom solution. By building your own custom solution on the cloud, you can implement whatever you want.

The next chapter reviews how to use CloudScripts to get the display name of other players by providing their PlayFab IDs.

Review Questions

1. What can a chat functionality include and how does it contribute to user engagement?

2. What are the main building blocks of a chat solution?

3. How can you use cognitive services to improve user experiment?

4. What is the chat solution of PlayFab and how is it used in Unity?

5. How do you know if a new message is available in PlayFab?

6. Which messaging pattern is typically used to implement chat?

7. How does WebSocket differ from HTTP communication?

8. How do you connect Azure Functions to the Web PubSub service?

9. How do you translate chat messages using Azure?

10. In which case would you prefer to use PlayFab, and when would you build your own solutions when implementing chat functionality?

CHAPTER 9

CloudScript and Azure Functions

PlayFab introduced CloudScript to implement server-side logic, which provides endless opportunities to customize your game's backend. The CloudScript code runs on PlayFab-managed servers and has access to the PlayFab API.

PlayFab recently deprecated JavaScript-based CloudScript and introduced Azure Functions as the preferred way for implementing custom game backend logic. This provides both the easy API access of PlayFab and the powerful features of the Azure cloud.

This chapter shows you how to implement custom game backend code with CloudScript and Azure Functions.

Serverless Computing

Serverless computing has become popular in the past years because of its flexibility and cost-effectiveness. It allows you to focus only on your application code and not worry about the servers underneath. The cloud service provider takes over all the infrastructure scaling and management tasks.

© Balint Bors 2023

B. Bors, *Game Backend Development*, https://doi.org/10.1007/978-1-4842-8910-5_9

Typically, serverless functions implement only short-running tasks. Figure 9-1 shows a simple example. You can develop and deploy server-side application logic to the cloud. Then a trigger—for example, a client call or a scheduler—lets the cloud execute the code.

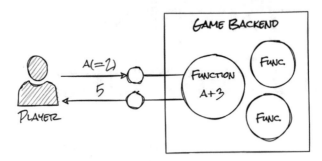

***Figure 9-1.** Serverless functions*

When the execution finishes, the function provides the result or triggers another service. The provider charges you according to your consumption. So if you don't use it, you don't pay for it.

Often, your requirements will stretch the capabilities of what your game backend service provides. You can only use features that you can access through the given API. On the one hand, it is an easy and convenient way to access sophisticated infrastructures and features through an API. On the other hand, you can only have exactly those capabilities that the API allows.

By introducing server-side coding, you have endless opportunities to extend the capabilities of a game backend service provider. Even for pure cloud backends, it is a great opportunity to implement and deploy small functions easily.

You can also deploy the same code on a server, but then you have to build and operate the server, which can be considerable overhead. With serverless computing, you can focus only on your code and let the cloud provider handle the infrastructure.

PlayFab

PlayFab implements serverless functions under the feature PlayFab Automation. It provides the opportunity to host and run backend code snippets on PlayFab infrastructure as well as use automatized triggers:

- **PlayStream rules.** In the case of a specific PlayStream event, you can trigger the execution of a CloudScript. For example, you can send a notification to yourself at a new player's login.

- **Scheduled tasks.** You can execute CloudScripts anytime manually or make them regularly recurring. For example, you can remove inactive player accounts after a certain period of time.

Now you'll implement the missing piece from the previous chapter. The PlayFab chat solution with PlayFab Party could not provide the display name of the other players. You want the chat window, instead of the entity ID, to show the real name of the players.

Unfortunately, PlayFab Party only provides the sender's entity ID (title player account ID) and the message. As a solution, you can write a CloudScript that provides the PlayFabId (master account Id) that belongs to a certain entity ID. You can see this in Figure 9-2.

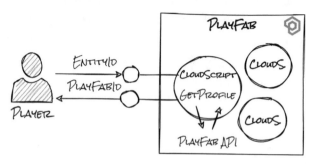

Figure 9-2. *PlayFab's CloudScript (legacy)*

After the client receives the PlayFabId, it can request the player profile of the other player, which also includes the display name. This sounds cumbersome, but it is fine to learn the implementation of CloudScripts.

Implementing CloudScript

Let's start by implementing the server-side code. Go to PlayFab's Game Manager, and on your title, go to BUILD ➤ Automation ➤ CloudScript ➤ Revisions (Legacy). You will find a lot of example code, which you can remove and put the following ECMAScript 6 (JavaScript) code into it:

```
handlers.GetPlayFabIdFromEntityId = function(args,context) {
    var request = {
            "Entity": {
                "Id": args.Id,
                "Type": "title_player_account"
            }
    };

    var result = entity.GetProfile(request);
    return result.Profile.Lineage.MasterPlayerAccountId;
}
```

This code, simply by using the current logged-in entity, calls the GetProfile method and requests the profile of another entity. You then pass the entity ID as an argument from Unity. This CloudScript will return the master player account ID, which is the PlayFabId. Let's deploy it and continue with the client side.

Implementing the Client

Note that to implement this example, you will reuse the code from the earlier chapter about implementing a chat feature for your game. Before starting this example, you may want to review that chapter.

Let's create a new script file, called PlayFabCloudScript.cs, in Unity. As every call to the backend has some latency and cost, let's create a cache to store the display name. Start the PlayFabCloudScript with the following code and you will continue in the later steps:

```
using System.Collections.Generic;
using UnityEngine;
using PlayFab;
using PlayFab.ClientModels;

public class PlayFabCloudScript : MonoBehaviour
{
    IDictionary<string, string> displayNamesCache = new
    Dictionary<string, string>();
    public string GetDisplayNameFromCache(string entityId)
    {
        string displayName;
        if (displayNamesCache.TryGetValue(entityId, out
        displayName)) return displayName;
        else return null;
    }
}
```

Now you'll change the earlier chat code (PlayFabChat.cs). Originally, when a new message arrived, you displayed the entity ID and the message to the chat window. Check if the entity ID has a corresponding display name in the cache. If so, you'll use it; otherwise, you'll start a request to CloudScript to find it:

```
private void OnChatMessageReceived(object sender,
PlayFabPlayer from, string message, ChatMessageType type)
{
    PlayFabMultiplayerManager.Get().TranslateChat =
    doTranslateMessage;

    var displayName = this.GetComponent<PlayFabCloudScri
    pt>().GetDisplayNameFromCache(from.EntityKey.Id);
    if (displayName != null)
    {
        ChatUI.UpdateTextArea(displayName, message);
    } else
    {
        ChatUI.UpdateTextArea(from.EntityKey.Id, message);
        this.GetComponent<PlayFabCloudScript>().
        UpdateDisplayNameCache(from.EntityKey.Id);
    }
}
```

You can implement the UpdateDisplayNameCache method
with pure CloudScript or by using Azure Functions. Add it to the
PlayFabCloudScript class:

```
public void UpdateDisplayNameCache(string entityId)
{
    ExecuteCloudScript(entityId); // with CloudScript
                                  (legacy)
    // ExecuteCloudScriptFunctions(entityId);
    // with CloudScript Functions
}
```

Now you'll implement a simple call of the previously created
CloudScript in the PlayFabCloudScript class:

```
private void ExecuteCloudScript(string entityId)
{
    PlayFabClientAPI.ExecuteCloudScript(new
    ExecuteCloudScriptRequest()
    {
        FunctionName = "GetPlayFabIdFromEntityId",
        FunctionParameter = new { Id = entityId },
    },
    result =>
    {
        GetDisplayName(result.FunctionResult.ToString());
    },
    error =>
    {
        Debug.Log(error.GenerateErrorReport());
    });
}
```

If the API call is successful, the client gets the PlayFabId and uses it to get the player's profile. Add this to the PlayFabCloudScript, and with that, you have finished the class:

```
private void GetDisplayName(string playFabId)
{
    PlayFabClientAPI.GetPlayerCombinedInfo(new
    GetPlayerCombinedInfoRequest
    {
        PlayFabId = playFabId,
        InfoRequestParameters = new
        GetPlayerCombinedInfoRequestParams
        {
            GetUserAccountInfo = true,
```

```
                ProfileConstraints = new
                PlayerProfileViewConstraints
                {
                    ShowDisplayName = true
                }
            }
        },
        result =>
        {
            var displayName = result.InfoResultPayload.
            AccountInfo.TitleInfo.DisplayName;
            var entityId = result.InfoResultPayload.
            AccountInfo.TitleInfo.TitlePlayerAccount.Id;

            displayNamesCache[entityId] = displayName;
            ChatUI.UpdateDisplayName(entityId, displayName);
        },
        error =>
        {
            Debug.Log(error.GenerateErrorReport());
        });
    }
}
```

When you receive the display name to the corresponding entity ID, you can exchange it in the chat window. To achieve this, add this method to the earlier created ChatUI.cs script as part of the ChatUI class:

```
public static void UpdateDisplayName(string entityId,
string displayName)
{
    textArea = textArea.Replace(entityId, displayName);
```

```
chatRows[4] = chatRows[4].Replace(entityId,
    displayName);
}
```

This is definitely not perfect, as the entity ID will still show up initially for a short period on the chat window. The main idea here is to introduce how to implement CloudScript and how to call it from your client. Each game has a different UI, and to keep the example simple, this solution is fine for now.

Drag-and-drop the `PlayFabCloudScript` file to the PlayFab game object as a new component. Verify with multiple Unity clients that the display name appears in the chat window instead of the player's ID.

In this example, you can see how easy it is to implement and call CloudScripts with PlayFab. You create and deploy a revision of the JavaScript code in PlayFab's Game Manager and call it with `PlayFabClientAPI.ExecuteCloudScript`, providing the name of the script and the parameters. As PlayFab is deprecating this, let's review the Azure Function-based CloudScript solution.

Azure

So far in this book, you have implemented features provided by PlayFab, and then implemented the same on Azure. In this case, Azure extends PlayFab, so for the first time, the two worlds meet. This is great, because through PlayFab, you now have direct access to a lot of powerful features of Azure cloud.

Figure 9-3 shows the sequence of steps to implement this example scenario.

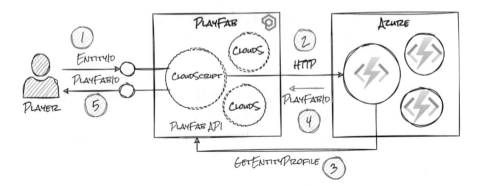

Figure 9-3. *CloudScript using Azure Functions*

Again, the goal is to get the PlayFab ID from the entity ID, so that you can query the display name of certain player. Here are the steps:

1. The client starts an API request toward PlayFab providing the entity ID.

2. PlayFab forwards the request with a simple HTTP call toward the Azure Function.

3. The Azure Function can execute the PlayFab API calls. It requests from PlayFab the entity profile of the entity ID.

4. As the entity profile contains the PlayFabId, the Azure Function sends it back to the caller in the HTTP response.

5. The client receives the PlayFab Id, and with that ID, it can request the display name from PlayFab.

There are advantages to using Azure Functions, compared to the earlier CloudScript solution:

- Now that you have access to the infinite features of Azure through the PlayFab API, there is no need to implement an additional access layer, such as an API Management Service.

- You can use C# to implement your server-side code as well, which is convenient if you are used to it in Unity.

- You can develop and debug your serverless code locally.

However, you also have to consider some disadvantages when using Azure Functions with PlayFab:

- You need a subscription to Azure besides your PlayFab account.

- You still have to build and manage some infrastructure on your own. That requires knowledge of Azure.

Building Infrastructure for Serverless

You will again start by building the infrastructure backend. You only need the Azure Function App and some supporting resources. Let's create a new folder called cloudscript and add it to the main.tf file:

```
module "cloudscript" {
  source                     = "./cloudscript"
  app_service_plan_id        = module.shared.app_
                               service_plan_id
  storage_account_name       = module.shared.storage_
                               account_name
  storage_account_access_key = module.shared.storage_account_
                               access_key
}
```

You can reuse the earlier defined App Service Plan and the Storage Account. You need both of these to implement the serverless function.

Create a new file called resourcegroup.tf in the cloudscript folder:

```
resource "azurerm_resource_group" "cloudscript" {
  name     = "cloudscript-resources"
  location = "westeurope"
}
```

PlayFab suggests using West US locations for the functions to reduce latency. Let's use Western Europe here; otherwise you have to build the shared resources in West US too.

Finally, create a functionapp.tf file, which describes the Azure Function App resource:

```
variable "app_service_plan_id" {
  description = "AppService Plan ID"
}

variable "storage_account_name" {
  description = "Storage account name"
}

variable "storage_account_access_key" {
  description = "Storage account access key"
}

resource "azurerm_function_app" "cloudscript" {
  name                = "cloudscript-azure-functions"
  location            = azurerm_resource_group.
                        cloudscript.location
  resource_group_name = azurerm_resource_group.
                        cloudscript.name
  app_service_plan_id = var.app_service_plan_id
```

```
storage_account_name        = var.storage_account_name
storage_account_access_key  = var.storage_account_access_key
version                     = "~4"
}
```

Now that you have described the target infrastructure, you can apply it with Terraform:

```
terraform apply
```

Developing Azure Function

Go to your `cloudscript` folder and let the Azure Core Tools create your dotnet project in the `CloudScriptFunctions` subfolder:

```
func init CloudScriptFunctions
```

PlayFab Integration

Before developing the server-side code, you have to make sure it will work with PlayFab. For that, add the PlayFab SDK package reference:

```
dotnet add package PlayFabAllSDK
```

Also download these helper classes so that you can access the execution context:

```
curl https://raw.githubusercontent.com/PlayFab/PlayFab-Samples/
master/Samples/CSharp/AzureFunctions/CS2AFHelperClasses.cs -o
CS2AFHelperClasses.cs
```

The Core Function

Create a new file called `CloudScript.cs`, which includes the code that translates the entity ID to the PlayFab ID:

```csharp
using System;
using System.Threading.Tasks;
using Microsoft.Azure.WebJobs;
using Microsoft.Azure.WebJobs.Extensions.Http;
using Microsoft.AspNetCore.Http;
using Microsoft.Extensions.Logging;
using Newtonsoft.Json;
using PlayFab;
using PlayFab.ProfilesModels;
using PlayFab.Samples;

namespace CloudScriptFunctions
{
    public class CloudScript
    {
        [FunctionName("GetPlayFabIdFromEntityId")]
        public async Task<dynamic> Run(
                [HttpTrigger(AuthorizationLevel.Function, "get",
                "post", Route = null)] HttpRequest req,
                ILogger log)
        {
            FunctionExecutionContext<dynamic> context =
            JsonConvert.DeserializeObject<FunctionExecutionCont
            ext<dynamic>>(await req.ReadAsStringAsync());
            dynamic args = context.FunctionArgument;

            PlayFab.PlayFabSettings.staticSettings.TitleId
            = Environment.GetEnvironmentVariable("PLAYFAB_
            TITLE_ID");
            PlayFab.PlayFabSettings.staticSettings.
            DeveloperSecretKey = Environment.
            GetEnvironmentVariable("PLAYFAB_DEV_SECRET_KEY");
```

```
var entityResponse = await
PlayFabAuthenticationAPI.GetEntityTokenAsync(new
PlayFab.AuthenticationModels.
GetEntityTokenRequest());

EntityKey entityKey = new EntityKey {
    Id = args["entityId"],
    Type = "title_player_account"
};

var request = new GetEntityProfileRequest { Entity
= entityKey };
var getProfileAsyncResult = await PlayFab.
PlayFabProfilesAPI.GetProfileAsync(request);

return getProfileAsyncResult.Result.Profile.
Lineage.MasterPlayerAccountId;
    }
  }
}
```

Let's look at this code a bit closer:

- The code uses the HTTP trigger with function-level authorization to avoid others being able to call the function. This means that you have to provide additional code to the function URL in PlayFab.

- The code uses FunctionExecutionContext from the PlayFab.Samples namespace to read the input arguments of the function. You will submit the entity ID in this way to the function. The context also contains useful information about the caller, but you will not use it now.

- In PlayFabSettings, you have to provide the title ID and the development secret key. You can get these values from your PlayFab's Game Manager. Let's store these values in Application Settings or in the local. settings.json for local execution.

- Request an entity token for authentication.

- Request the entity profile of the provided entity Id from the PlayFabProfilesAPI. This will come back with the complete profile, and you select the master player account ID to send the response.

Publish the Code

You have to add the title ID and the development secret key to the Application Settings in Azure:

```
az functionapp config appsettings set -n cloudscript-azure-
functions -g cloudscript-resources --settings PLAYFAB_TITLE_
ID=" <your title Id>"

az functionapp config appsettings set -n cloudscript-azure-
functions -g cloudscript-resources --settings PLAYFAB_DEV_
SECRET_KEY="<your developer secret key>"
```

Then, publish the code to Azure:

```
func azure functionapp publish cloudscript-azure-functions
...
Functions in cloudscript-azure-functions:
    GetPlayFabIdFromEntityId - [httpTrigger]
        Invoke url: https://cloudscript-azure-functions.
        azurewebsites.net/api/getplayfabidfromentityid?code=<
        your_code>
```

If everything works fine, you'll see the invoke URL including the code as a result of the publishing process. Copy this and move to the next step.

Configure PlayFab to Integrate with Azure Functions

Go to PlayFab's Game Manager and register your Azure Function, as shown in Figure 9-4. The function name should be the same as your Azure Function. Paste your Function URL from the previous step.

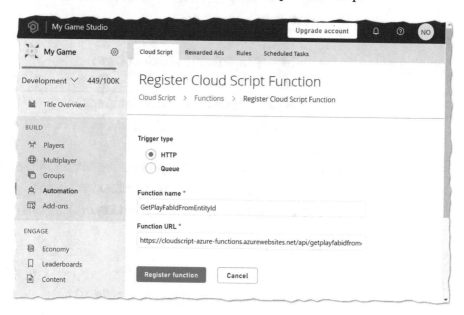

Figure 9-4. *Registering the CloudScript function*

Implement the Client

Finally, you have to implement the client code to access the Azure Function through the PlayFab API. Note that we use ExecuteFunction instead of ExecuteCloudScript, but it works really similarly.

Copy this code into the PlayFabCloudScript class in Unity and reuse all the client code you wrote for CloudScript:

```
public void ExecuteCloudScriptFunctions(string entityId)
{
            PlayFabCloudScriptAPI.ExecuteFunction(new
            PlayFab.CloudScriptModels.
            ExecuteFunctionRequest()
            {
                Entity = new PlayFab.CloudScriptModels.
                EntityKey()
                {
                    Id = PlayFab.PlayFabSettings.
                    staticPlayer.EntityId,
                    Type = PlayFab.PlayFabSettings.
                    staticPlayer.EntityType,
                },
                FunctionName = "GetPlayFabIdFromEntityId",
                FunctionParameter = new Dictionary<string,
                object>() { { "entityId", entityId } },
            },
            result =>
            {
                GetDisplayName(result.FunctionResult.
                ToString());
            },
            error =>
            {
                Debug.Log(error.GenerateErrorReport());
            });
    }
```

You can switch between the two methods (CloudScript and CloudScript with Azure Functions) by changing the UpdateDisplayNameCache method:

```
public void UpdateDisplayNameCache(string entityId)
{
    //ExecuteCloudScript(entityId); // with CloudScript
                                   (legacy)
    ExecuteCloudScriptFunctions(entityId);
    // with CloudScript Functions
}
```

Finally, if you start a chat using PlayFab Party, check if you can see the display name of the other players. There can be some delay before the entity ID changes to the display name, especially if you put your Azure Function in a non-US location. But following these steps, you can implement your own server-side logic. This gives you endless opportunities to integrate and use features that modern cloud services provide.

Summary

You'll need to use server-side code for several reasons. It can be due to security or the need to implement a custom feature that's not implemented by the actual game backend provider. The great thing is that, most times, you can make changes to the server-side code with no client redeployments.

PlayFab supports this through its CloudScript feature. Having the same serverless feature as Azure Functions became redundant. So it was a logical move by PlayFab to suggest developers use Azure Functions, which provide a much more powerful opportunity to implement server-side logic.

Still, the convenience of using PlayFab's API and ecosystem remained, providing game developers an easy way to implement custom features. However, this also means you have to learn about Azure and build some infrastructure, which can be a daunting task for a game developer.

Through the example in this chapter, you saw how to implement CloudScripts the old-fashioned way and by using Azure Functions. You also implemented the client side in Unity and extended the chat solution from the previous chapter. This way, you saw how it works end-to-end and how this feature can enrich your game.

Review Questions

1. What is serverless computing?

2. For what in your game can you use custom server-side logic?

3. How do you trigger a CloudScript in PlayFab?

4. Which language does CloudScript use?

5. What is the difference between CloudScript and CloudScript Functions?

6. What are the prerequisites to implementing CloudScript Functions?

7. How do you access CloudScript Functions from a client?

8. Give an example of what you receive in the function execution context.

9. How do you integrate PlayFab with Azure Functions?

10. How does the client differ when using PlayFab's legacy and the new CloudScript?

Index

A

Agones, 100
  fleet, 117
  fleet autoscaler, 118
  game server allocation, 119, 166
Animator, 10, 17
Ansible, 6
Apache Avro, 308
API Management Service, 144, 149,
    181, 183, 186, 187, 192, 210,
    212, 213, 225, 255, 258, 269,
    284, 296, 305, 327, 328,
    335–339, 346, 365
Authentication, 33–36, 39, 45–47,
    51, 56–61, 64, 65, 126, 133
Azure, 23
  Azure Portal, 23, 28
  Command-Line Interface, 23
  Cost Management + Billing, 23
  credit, 23
  free tier, 23
Azure Active Directory B2C, 45
  access token, 51
  application, 49
  redirect URI, 50
  register, 48
  switch, 49
  user flow, 56
Azure Blob Storage, 299
Azure Container Registry, 108, 109
Azure Data Explorer, 294, 308–310
Azure Database for
    PostgreSQL, 149
  firewall, 182
Azure Event Hubs, 300
Azure Functions
  Azure Core Tools, 218
  publish, 181
Azure Kubernetes Service (AKS),
    77, 104
Azure Resource Manager (ARM), 6
Azure Translator, 345
Azure Virtual Machine Scale
    Sets, 106
Azure Web PubSub, 326, 327,
    331–335, 339

B

BSON, 259
BuildId, 80, 95

© Balint Bors 2023
B. Bors, *Game Backend Development*, https://doi.org/10.1007/978-1-4842-8910-5

Printed in the United States
by Baker & Taylor Publisher Services